I0045419

Is Renewable Really Doable?

Exploring Clean Energy's Opportunities and Tough Realities

CRAIG SHIELDS

IS RENEWABLE REALLY DOABLE? — Exploring Clean Energy's Opportunities and Tough Realities copyright © 2012 by 2GreenEnergy. All rights reserved. Printed in the United States of America. No part of this book may be used or reproduced in any manner whatsoever without written permission except in cases of reprints in the context of reviews. For information, contact 2GreenEnergy at www.2GreenEnergy.com.

ISBN: 0615561829
ISBN-13: 9780615561820

Forward

We humans, as a species, have indeed changed a little bit over the millennia. We no longer regard monarchy as possessed of divine right, and we don't revel in or even tolerate the most obvious forms of physical cruelty to the extent we once did. Rightfully, we take great pride in the accomplishments we've made in human rights over the past few centuries. Though there have been some obvious and terrible setbacks, we can all feel good about the Age of Reason, the Enlightenment, the Bill of Rights, the emancipation of US slaves, women's suffrage, and civil rights, to name a few.

We have, however, changed in less wholesome ways as well. We once regarded the natural world with awe and reverence, and this is far less true today. Indeed, the importance of our relationship with the natural world is as profound as ever, but it is separated and hidden from us behind layer upon layer of mechanized commerce. All this has brought us to—and perhaps past—the edge of the collapse of the natural systems on which all of Earth's life forms depend.

Of course, hundreds of different books could have sprung from these premises, on topics from sustainable agricultural to energy conservation to the banning of nuclear weapons to the preservation of the Amazon rain forests. I chose simply to offer a follow-on to my last work, Renewable Energy – Facts and Fantasies (Clean Energy Press, 2010). In particular, I'd like to explore in a bit greater depth the "tough realities" that stand in the way of renewable energy.

As a civilization, and most certainly in my homeland of the United States, we seem quite stuck in our ways in terms of energy.

More than 80% of the energy we generate on this planet comes from burning hydrocarbons – a practice that is clearly unsustainable – yet we (especially Americans) are making dreadfully little progress in replacing these practices with solar, wind, geothermal, run-of-river hydrokinetics and biomass – all of which taken collectively represent less than 2% of our total energy consumption in the U.S.

Let's look for a moment at the phrase "a practice that is clearly unsustainable" in the paragraph above. Of course "sustainability" is a word that is enjoying a huge level of popularity right now, with all its modern connotations: green, eco-friendly, inclusive, life-affirming, etc. But in its purity, an "unsustainable" practice is one that literally cannot be continued. And, as I'll show in the pages that follow, this is the case with respect to our planet's current methods of generating and consuming energy. Whether your concern is financial, social, environmental, logistical, military, or whether you feel some level of sympathy for the people who suffer and die each year from respiratory ailments directly related to the aromatics caused by burning fossil fuels, the world will, at a certain point, be forced in another direction.

So why not now? Why, precisely, are we so slow to make a change here, when, for any number of reasons it's clear that our practices cannot continue? I've spoken with many hundreds of people on this topic over the past two years, and have amassed a considerable amount of information on the subject, of which I'd like to present a summary here.

But let me begin by asking a few questions that may stimulate your thinking as you read through the various short essays and interview transcripts that follow:

☐ Do you think it's likely that the wealthiest people on Earth, whose riches came from (and continue to derive) from the extraction of fossil fuels, will abandon trillions of dollars of infrastructure and future earnings – regardless of the findings of modern science?

☐ Do you think unregulated market economies do a good job at protecting the health and safety of mankind generally?

☐ Do you think that government regulation generally happens fairly and dispassionately, without undue influences from corruptive elements?

If you answered any of these questions in the affirmative, I'm afraid you're in for a rude, but much-needed shock as you read this book. Hope you enjoy the ride.

- —Craig Shields, Autumn 2011

FREE!
Subscribe to the
2GreenEnergy Alert
eNewsletter

Through an ever-expanding network of industry contacts, 2GreenEnergy reports on the renewable energy industry without the distortions of "Big Corporate Energy."

Subscribe to the free 2GreenEnergy Alert and get the latest on Clean Energy:

- News
- Interviews
- Technology Analysis
- Investment Tips

FIND OUT FOR YOURSELF
by visiting the following link:

http://2greenenergy.com/truth/

Table of Contents

Introduction

I hate to start this project in a way that could "un-sell" readers, but this is fundamentally a book for those who harbor a suspicion that they are not being told the truth. The credulous in our society – those who believe the information they receive is a pure and undistorted collection of facts about the actions and intentions of the actual underlying power structures in our world – may want to look elsewhere for reading material.

Yet who lives in such a fairytale world? Most of us realized long ago that we exist in a place and time in which the true causes and motivations for most of what we see around us on a global scale are seldom revealed for what they are.

For example, what type of person takes at face value the message that the media presented in the United States (echoed around the world in a matter of minutes) as the reason for the US invasion of Iraq in 2003: to "bring democracy to the Middle East?" That mantra: "a coalition of forces, led by the US, will bring democracy to the Middle East" was picked up, distributed in unison around the world, and repeated ceaselessly for days on end – to anyone gullible enough to believe it. Who on Earth believes that this media saturation occurred because of solid, honest journalism?

OK, if you're with me so far, if you haven't angrily returned this book to its vendor, I invite you to take a tour with me, in which I hope to shed some light on one of the most important issues of our time: energy. But again, if you think that there is nothing wrong with our energy policy, if you believe that there is nothing fundamentally unsustainable about the fact that 80% of the world's energy comes from burning hydrocarbons, you may want to reconsider the idea of continuing here.

But since you're still here, let's begin the tour. We'll start not with the current situation, but with a bit of history. Sadly, only a few people know enough about world history to understand how deeply tied the world's most powerful economic and political forces are tied to the energy scene. Let me do what I can to rectify that, by presenting the following short summary, which I co-wrote with my friend Cameron Atwood.

Oil and a Century of War

"All wars are fought for money."

– Socrates

"Give me the money that has been spent in war and I will clothe every man, woman, and child in an attire of which kings and queens will be proud. I will build a schoolhouse in every valley over the whole earth. I will crown every hillside with a place of worship consecrated to peace." – Charles Sumner, *the Republican Senator, and head of the abolitionist movement in Massachusetts.*

"The Iraq War is largely about oil."   *– Alan Greenspan*

A Few General Statements

Wars are sold by national leadership, and bought by the populations who pay for them with their tax dollars and sacrifice their loved ones to fight and die in them. They're sold as honorable pursuits with noble ends or, at worst, as unavoidable necessities.

This "promotional" aspect of war was perhaps never admitted more brazenly in recent memory than in the comment of Bush/Cheney chief of staff Andrew H. Card, Jr. on September of 2002, explaining why the Bush administration waited until September to press for public support of its Iraq policy... "From a marketing point of view, you don't introduce new products in August."

The economic stratagems that form the basis for war are now – and have long been – consistently hidden behind humanitarian facades, behind the accusations of actual and pretended crimes of allegedly cruel and dictatorial regimes, or behind supposed affronts to a carefully cultivated national pride. Often, combinations of these pretenses are used.

To cite a rare exception, in a single bold paragraph, a refreshingly candid military history of Britain from 1860 to 1902 called *Marching to the Drums* explains:

> With its opening in 1869, the Suez Canal became the principal waterway to Britain's most valuable overseas possession, India. It was therefore imperative for the British army to control all traffic through the Suez Canal, which meant first of all crushing the indigenous independence movements of Egypt and the Sudan.

This unabashed lack of hypocrisy and pretense in making plain the geopolitical realities of the time is rare enough in our contemporary media as to be nearly nonexistent.

However, an examination of the facts will demonstrate clearly that an unbroken line of policy has for decades determined our collective path of recurring conflict worldwide, and that this same line of policy is still in force straight through to the present day.

Oil and the Last 100 Years

The history presented to us in the books we read growing up, and those from which our children are now taught, gives the assassination of Archduke Ferdinand of Austria and his wife as the primary trigger of the First World War – this was "The War to End All Wars" – beginning with the declaration of war against Serbia by Austria-Hungary. This shallow assertion has long masked the motivations of the major powers involved.

The first military action of Britain in that war was the invasion of Basra, Iraq, to counter and prevent the completion of the German railway from Berlin to Baghdad (dimly remembered in popular culture as the Orient Express), which had already gone as far as Constantinople. Britain and the other European powers – France, Russia and others —vehemently opposed the construction of the last 900 kilometers to Baghdad.

Why was Germany so intent on the project? During the few years prior, the British Royal Navy had engineered its grand fleet – then the largest in the world – to burn oil rather than coal, and the German Navy (which had recently and rapidly grown to become the world's second largest fleet) had shortly thereafter done the same. Unlike Britain, however, Germany had no colonies that contained large reserves of oil. The fierce demand for that coveted energy resource was already driving geopolitical strategy between these two great navies and their respective monarchs.

In 1914, Britain sent 51 military divisions to Basra to join the second battalion of the Dorset Regiment which had already been deployed there. In the synopsis for his feature length documentary *Blood and Oil: The Middle East in World War I*, released in 2010, Marty Callaghan neatly summarizes what happened next:

Except for the Dardanelles/Gallipoli campaigns, the extensive combat operations in the Middle East during World War I have been largely overlooked in documentary programs. Given the historical significance of the Ottoman Empire's demise in 1918, and the ongoing importance of Middle Eastern oil reserves to Western economies, a close study of this conflict provides two important lessons:

1. The Treaty of Versailles, agreed to by the Western Powers in 1919, paved the way for military and political chaos in the Middle East, which continues to this very day.

2. Oil reserves in the Middle East became an important strategic concern for Western Powers, helping to justify their economic, diplomatic and military interference in the region.

After the end of World War I, most of the Ottoman Empire was carved up into "spheres of influence," controlled mostly by the British and French. The remaining territories became the modern state of Turkey in 1923 – after a five-year struggle by Turkish nationalists against Western domination.

With little regard for cultural, historical, religious and demographic considerations, the West sponsored the creation of several new nations: Iraq, Syria, Lebanon, Palestine, Jordan and Saudi Arabia. Thus, a "tinderbox" ignited into a multitude of wars, revolts, coups and military occupations that have made the defeat of the Ottoman Empire little more than a hollow victory.

A shrewd observer might suspect that the Western nations did in fact quite closely regard "cultural, historical, religious and demographic considerations," with an eye to the time-honored strategy of 'divide and conquer'—a strategy that has had precisely the designed effect, i.e., it produced a region of nations with populations that are divided against each other by internal conflict, and therefore crippled in their ability to effectively cast off foreign manipulation.

The US and UK have been heavily involved in the Middle East region ever since those resources were discovered there in Masjid-I-Sulaiman, in southwest Persia – later Iran – in 1908. Indeed, out of the ninety-five years from that fateful year to the US-led invasion of Iraq in 2003, the UK has been involved in military conflict and/or occupation inside Mesopotamia/Iraq in a total of forty-five of them.

Combined with the severe hardships brought on by the global economic collapse of the 1930's, the severe restrictions placed on Germany at the close of that war served as embers from which the inferno of WWII blazed forth to again envelop Europe in death and ruin. This conflagration spread again to Africa and the Middle East, because of the continued strategic value of the energy resources there.

A useful example of US/UK 'involvement' is in that nation formerly known as Persia – now called Iran. This is where that very first Middle East oil well was drilled. Iran had been a constitutional parliamentary democracy since 1906. Ten years later, Mohammad Mosaddegh was elected to the national assembly at the age of 24, and in 1919-1920 he went into voluntary exile to protest the treaty between the Iranian government and the British crown. He returned the following year, and unsuccessfully opposed legislation by the supporters of Reza Khan to crown him Reza Shah Pahlavi and replace the present monarch. He believed this legislation was a subversion of the original 1906 constitution. In 1941, the British finally forced Reza Shah Pahlavi to abdicate in favor of his son Mohammad Reza Pahlavi.

In 1944, Mohammad Mosaddegh was once again elected to parliament. This time he took the lead post of the National Front of Iran, which was an organization he had founded with the goals of re-establishing democratic rule and putting an end to foreign control of Iran's politics and economy. An integral part of the strategy of this group was nationalizing Iran's oil industry (which the British had controlled since 1913). One reason for the popularity of nationalization was that the Iranian people resented the refusal by the "Anglo-Iranian Oil Company" (later called British Petroleum) to share half of the profits from Iran's own resources – something that the Arabian American Oil Company (Aramco) had agreed to do in Saudi Arabia.

In 1951, Mohammad Mosaddegh was elected Prime Minister of Iran by an overwhelming majority, and straight away he began the nationalization of his nation's oil industry. Britain's Prime Minister Winston Churchill insisted that Mosaddegh was flirting with the USSR – playing adroitly on the anti-communist "Red Scare" in the US. This ploy was instrumental in influencing the Eisenhower administration against Iranian democracy, as were the views of Secretary of State John Foster Dulles and his brother Allen who headed the CIA at the time.

According to many reports —including that of James Risen of The New York Times in "Secrets of History: The C.I.A. in Iran" —our Central Intelligence Agency provided $1 million to fund Operation Ajax to bring Mosaddegh's people's government down. Kermit Roosevelt, Jr. (Teddy's grandson) later published his own account of his personal direction of the strategy for that overthrow. A complete publishing of the CIA's documentation of the planning and execution of this operation can be found at: http://web.payk. net/politics/cia-docs/published/one-main/main.html

The result of this coup was the autocratic and repressive rule of Britain's original selection for the ruler of Iran, Mohammad Reza Shah Pahlavi (known to American memory as the Shah of Iran), and the rise of his infamous secret police, the SAVAK.

Amnesty International in 1976 issued a report identifying the Shah's regime as having the worst record of human rights abuses in the world at that time. It was his decades of vicious repression that provoked the Iranian Revolution that ousted him in 1979 and established the theocracy that rules Iran today.

This example of our government's installation of and support for abusive regimes that respect our interests is not unique, either in that region or around the world. In addition to the Shah, a brief and incomplete list of dictators and authoritarian regimes installed and/or supported by US elected officials would include: Emperor Bao Dai of Vietnam, Chiang Kai-shek of China, Syngman Rhee of South Korea, Laurent Kabila of the Congo, Idi Amin of Uganda, Francisco Franco of Spain, Anastasio Somoza of Nicaragua, General Suharto of Indonesia, Hugo Banzer Suarez of Bolivia, Augusto Pinochet of Chile, Fulgencio Batista of Cuba, Saddam Hussein of Iraq, Muammar Qaddafi of Libya (for a short time), Manuel Noriega of Panama, Hosni Mubarak of Egypt, Francois "Papa Doc" Duvalier and Jean-Claude "Baby Doc" Duvalier of Haiti... One may also include the royal family of Saudi Arabia and the occupation governments of Israel.

With regard to Saudi Arabia, Saïd K. Aburish, in his 1997 book *A Brutal Friendship: The West and the Arab Elite*, observed, "Amnesty International, Middle East Watch, the Minnesota International Lawyers Association and other human rights organizations have documented endless cases of imprisonment, torture and elimination within the kingdom. Solitary confinement for years on end is a regular happening..., kidnappings and disappearances are common..., political executions without proper trial are frequent...

and even women are not spared torture and humiliation.... In February 1996 a ten-year-old child was left in the sun tied to a rope in front of a police station. In six hours he was dead, the victim of the merciless desert sun. The boy had criticized the House of Saud."

On the government of Israel, in his 2000 article "Continuing storm: The U.S. role in the Middle East," in the publication *Global Focus: U.S. Foreign Policy at the Turn of the Century*, Stephen Zunes wrote, "Israel represents only one one-thousandth of the world's population and has the 16th highest per capita income in the world, yet it receives 40 percent of all U.S. foreign aid. In terms of U.S. aid to the Middle East, Israel received 54 percent in 1999, Egypt 38 percent, and all other Middle East countries only about 8 percent. Direct aid to Israel in recent years has exceeded $3.5 billion annually and has been supported almost unanimously in Congress, even by liberal Democrats who normally insist on linking aid to human rights and international law."

Indeed, one can find captured occasional bald admissions of geopolitical motivations such as this account from Mark Curtis' 1998 book *The Great Deception: Anglo-American Power and World Order*:

> U.S. Senator and oil expert Henry Jackson noted in 1973 that Israel and Iran under the Shah were "reliable friends of the United States" who, along with Saudi Arabia, "have served to inhibit and contain those irresponsible and radical elements in certain Arab states...who, were they free to do so, would pose a grave threat indeed to our principal source of petroleum in the Persian Gulf."

It is little wonder that populations all over the globe find US pretenses of 'defending freedom' and 'spreading democracy' to be less than credible. The extent that our own people accept these charades as reality is a direct result of our collective ignorance of both our own history and that of the wider world.

It's quite clear that the very last thing that the most powerful interests in the world want to see is educated and enlightened populations standing up for their rights of self-governance and self-determination – in the Middle East or anywhere else in the world. In an interview in May of 2011, Noam Chomsky, dissident author and Professor Emeritus at Massachusetts Institute of Technology, laid the situation out in stark terms,

> "The U.S. and its allies will do anything they can to pre-
> vent authentic democracy in the Arab world. The reason is
> very simple. Across the region, an overwhelming majority
> of the population regards the United States as the main
> threat to their interests. In fact, opposition to U.S. policy is
> so high that a considerable majority think the region would
> be more secure if Iran had nuclear weapons. In Egypt, the
> most important country, that's 80 percent. Similar figures
> elsewhere. There are some in the region who regard Iran as
> a threat—about 10 percent. Well, plainly, the U.S. and its
> allies are not going to want governments which are respon-
> sive to the will of the people. If that happens, not only will
> the U.S. not control the region, but it will be thrown out.
> So that's obviously an intolerable result."

To illustrate the double standard with which international law operates, the crime for which defendants at the Nuremburg Trials were hanged was "planning and waging an aggressive war." ... Not genocide, not slaughter of one's own people, not possession of weapons of mass destruction, not refusal to disarm – simply for "planning and waging an aggressive war." If those standards were applied to more recent history, wouldn't some of our modern presidents (and their cohorts, e.g., Tony Blair) find themselves fitted with brand new neckties of a type and function not at all to their liking?

The Times of London may have forgotten itself when it headlined an article in its July 11th 2002 issue, "West Sees Glittering Prizes Ahead in Giant Oilfields" which said, in part:

> President Bush has used the War on Terror to press his case for drilling in a protected Arctic refuge, but predicted reserves in Alaska are dwarfed by the oil wells of the Gulf.

> Anthony Cordesman, of the Center for Strategic and International Studies in Washington, said that the issue for the US was as much the security of the Gulf as access to particular oilfields. "You are looking down the line to a world in 2020 when reliance on Gulf oil will have more than doubled. The security of the Gulf is an absolutely critical issue."

> Gerald Butt, Gulf editor of the *Middle East Economic Survey*, said: "The removal of Saddam is, in effect, the removal of the last threat to the free flow of oil from the Gulf as a whole."

> Iraq has oil reserves of 112 billion barrels, second only to Saudi Arabia, which has some 265 billion barrels. Iraqi reserves are seven times those of the combined UK and Norwegian sectors of the North Sea. But the prize for oil companies could be even greater. Iraq estimates that its eventual reserves could be as high as 220 billion barrels.

> Three giant southern fields —Majnoon, West Qurna and Nahr Umar have the capacity to produce as much as Kuwait. The first two could each equal Qatar's production

of 700,000 barrels a day. "There is nothing like it anywhere else in the world. It's the big prize," Mr. Butt said.

Extraction costs in these giant onshore fields, where development has been held up by more than two decades of war and sanctions, would also be among the lowest in the world. Provided that the US can ensure stability in a post-Saddam Iraq, it would take five years, at most, to develop the oilfields and Iraq's prewar capacity of three million barrels a day could reach seven or eight million, industry experts said.

However, regime change in Baghdad will be of little value to international oil companies unless it is followed by a stable Iraq with a strong central government. Companies can't go in unless there is peace. To develop Majnoon, you need two to three billion dollars and you don't invest that kind of money without stability, one industry analyst said.

The Currency Used to Buy Oil -- US Dollars

On the subject of money and oil, let's return to historical matters briefly for some useful background. In a 1971 meeting of the Organization of the Petroleum Exporting Countries (OPEC) it was agreed that – regardless of the national origin or destination of the transactions – the entirety of all world trade in oil, and oil futures, was to be conducted only in US dollars.

This means that every entity wishing to engage such transactions had to buy US dollars for the purpose, and the demand for the currency skyrocketed. This condition has allowed our nation to transform itself from the largest creditor nation to the largest debtor nation with relative impunity – as long as this massive trade is required to be transacted solely in US currency. Any major deviation from that oil/dollar trade protocol – for example from dollars to euros – would result in a glut of US dollars on the currency market, as traders exchanged them for euros, and the hollow house of greenbacks would collapse. And until recently, the prospect of that deviation was thought to be impossible.

However, on October 30th 2000, in the New York office of French Bank BNP Paribas – the UN administered account through which Saddam's regime was selling over two million barrels a day in the "Oil for Food" program – the request was received from the Iraqi government to change the denomination of the account from US dollars to euros. At the time, the euro was trading at eighty cents on the dollar, and the Iraqi officials were warned that, while they were not prohibited from changing the denomination, they were certain to lose 20% on every transaction. Yet these officials chose to proceed in the face of these losses.

During the very next year, the euro rose 25% against the dollar. At that point the government of Iran chose to change the denomination of their central bank reserves to euros from dollars. Soon after (December 7th 2002), the government of North Korea announced that they would transact all foreign trade in euros.

Perhaps it should not strike anyone as purely blind coincidence that these three nations, Iraq, Iran, and North Korea should be the very three nations George Bush proclaimed as constuting his "Axis of Evil" in his January 29th 2002 State of the Union speech – where he stated, "America will do what is necessary to ensure our nation's security... I will not wait on events while dangers gather."

Likewise, the hostility of oil-interested political figures in the US toward Hugo Chavez, the three-time democratically elected president of Venezuela (the world's sixth largest in crude oil reserves and fourth largest US supplier of foreign oil), could be partly explained not only by his nationalization of his country's oil industry and reserves, but also by the proposal he floated in Spain before leaving the chair of OPEC in November of 2007, that every OPEC nation should move their trading from US dollars to euros.

In addition to our financial dependence on trading oil in dollars, it would be hard to overstate our nation's addiction to foreign oil itself, and there apparently isn't much our leadership hasn't been prepared to do to get it.

United States domestic oil production peaked in 1970. By 2005, our imports were twice our production. On August 21st 1975 the Committee on International Relations, Special Subcommittee on Investigations of the US Congress issued a report prepared by the Congressional Research Service called *Oil Fields as Military Objectives: A Feasibility Study.*

A digital copy of this report is available at: http://www.mtholyoke.edu/ acad/intrel/Petroleum/fields.htm

The purpose of this paper was stated as follows…

> …to provide perspective, so that Congress could participate most meaningfully in deliberations to determine:
>
> - Whether we should go to war to excise the effects of any given oil embargo against the United States and/or its allies
> - What strategic and tactical objectives would best serve U.S. purposes if the answer were affirmative
> - What forces would be essential
> - What special expenditures could be expected
> - What risks would be entailed
> - What benefits could accrue

The question of drilling more wells in the US is moot – of the nations with the top 16 oil reserves, the US has little more than

2%, and without imported oil that domestic reserve would be exhausted by present consumption in a little less than three years.

Who make up that "sweet sixteen?" Saudi Arabia, Iraq, Kuwait, United Arab Emirates, Iran, Venezuela, Russia, Nigeria, Libya, China, USA, Qatar, Algeria, Mexico, Norway, and Brazil. That list reads like a *Who's Who* of modern American political/economic/military intervention, doesn't it? Now, who's the largest single consumer of petroleum fuels in the US? ...The Unites States military.

China has 1.3 billion people and has a military 200 million strong – that's less than 20% of their population and equal to two-thirds of ours. India has over a billion people. Both these countries are advancing technologically with growing economies, and both possess nuclear weapons. Their growing infrastructures are getting more energy thirsty by the second, and in many respects they're coming up using our oily technological model. China has been very forward-thinking in its active and well-considered pursuit of renewables, but its consumption of oil is still growing rapidly. Consumption outstripped its domestic production in 1992 and since then has quadrupled from just over 2 million barrels a day in that year to over 8 million in 2009. Following that curve it will double again by 2016 and again by 2025.

Uses of Oil

Of course, we modern humans don't just burn oil for personal transportation and the military, we also use it to feed ourselves, and in a big way. Modern petroleum-intensive farming, storage, preservation and distribution techniques have increased agricultural delivered yields exponentially as world population has steadily climbed from 2.5 billion in 1950 to 7 billion today.

In Willits, California, the Ecology Institute has calculated that the minimum area of agricultural land needed to feed one person *without using oil* is 2,800 square feet – provided that person keeps to a vegetarian menu, and uses bio-intensive farming and the composting of all waste from plant production and human consumption – to include the bodies of the dead… nothing can be wasted.

All that calculation is generously assuming that we don't turn to violence, which – as we've seen – does not appear a reasonable assumption. Naturally, a robust web of life and a reasonable climate will also be necessary. Of course, the global estimate of total arable land is about 12 million square miles, which equates to about 47,000 square feet per person at our present population, but that's evenly dispersed, while we instead live in a world of massive cities.

The real question is this: What is the energy necessary to produce, preserve and distribute the required nutrients (not just empty calories), and what is the true and complete cost and availability of that energy? In terms of the calorie tradeoff, the most well-known estimate probably comes from Michael Pollan's open letter to the presidential candidates, published in the New York Times October 2008 under the title Farmer in Chief:

> The 20th-century industrialization of agriculture has increased the amount of greenhouse gases emitted by the food system by an order of magnitude; chemical fertilizers (made from natural gas), pesticides (made from petroleum), farm machinery, modern food processing and packaging and transportation have together transformed a system that in 1940 produced 2.3 calories of food energy for every calorie of fossil-fuel energy it used into one that now takes 10 calories of fossil-fuel energy to produce a single calorie of modern supermarket food.

Estimates of the portion of our energy consumption devoted to our food system in America vary between 9% and 19%, but it is surely significant. We won't ever actually "run out" of oil, but we will soon reach the point where oil – and all other fossil fuel – simply becomes too expensive and too energy-intensive to use. It will cost more money and more energy to pull from the ground and to refine and transport it than the margin and the economy can support.

Where This Is Going

So, what are we to do if we want to avoid suffering the complete collapse of our modern societies into a feverish strangled clutching at each other's throats? We'd best realize that the answer is us, you, me, here, now, standing up and doing something – not just talking, but actually doing something, too – to use those last dwindling trickles of cheap fossil fuel and global capital to build ourselves a clean, sustainable replacement economy that uses renewable energy from the modern sun. Our historically recent but astonishingly persistent philosophy of wasteful competition, and our animal tendency to resort to brutality in desperate times, must both be thoroughly conquered.

What we cannot do is wait any longer on our pocketed leadership, and claw at each other over the scraps.

Craig's Interview with Robert Pollin, Ph.D.

If you want to see a resumé that's "as long as your arm," you may want to lay this book aside for a moment and check out: http://www.peri.umass.edu/219/. If you do, you'll understand why I was so happy that Dr. Pollin agreed to speak with me and convey his sense of the economics that underlies the migration to clean energy.

Among other things, Dr. Pollin serves as Professor of Economics and Co-Director of the Political Economy Research Institute, University of Massachusetts-Amherst. He also functions as a consultant to the Energy Department on implementing the Obama Administration's stimulus program.

RP: Thank you for sending me your book.

CS: Oh, I was going to ask if you had received it. You must have gotten it just yesterday.

RP: Yep, I did. I appreciate it. It looks really interesting.

CS: Well, I appreciate your saying that. This project is a bit actually fairly different. I'm not an economist, but through the process of doing the first book, I've come to realize that the real gating factors on these things are pretty much exclusively political and economic. I'm interested in getting at the truth here, and I'm glad you're willing to speak with me.

Let's start with jobs generally, before we get to "green jobs" vs. "other jobs." When we talk about job creation we're talking about the net increase in the number of full-time jobs for the people living within U.S. borders. Is that correct?

RP: Yes, when I do a report and I say green investment will create 1.7 million jobs, I mean full-time jobs within U.S. borders.

CS: So, again, before we get into the green jobs, I want to know what is the prognosis for job growth generally—jobs in the U.S. economy.

RP: It's pretty grim right now, isn't it?

CS: It seems that way to me, but I would certainly be interested in what you see.

RP: Well, I wrote an article in *The Nation* last March on jobs, and I made an argument that we could create 18 million jobs by the time that Obama runs for re-election. I laid out what I thought was a pretty practical plan for achieving that. Also, it sounds like a ridiculously ambitious goal, but what I also said in the article was that if you look back to previous recoveries from recessions, in 1976 to 1979, we achieved the rate of growth—not the *number* of jobs—but the *rate of growth* in job creation equal to what would be the equivalent to creating 18 million jobs between now and November 2012. So it's not like it's never been done before; it was done 35 years ago.

Now, obviously the world is different and the U.S. economy is different, but the main thing is that people say we just blew all this money on the stimulus that didn't do anything. The stimulus actually, in my opinion, did a lot; it's just that the crisis has been so severe. And so they had a lot of ground to make up.

So yes, we need to continue with stimulus, but the problem in my view if I had to point to one thing that is holding us back is that the credit system is still locked up, and especially for smaller businesses. We need policies that will target that, because if the government spends money, but if it's not leading to the private sector spending, then it's not going to succeed. So it's the right combination of policies which is going to determine just how bleak our job picture is over the next couple of years. If we keep limping along at the rate we're going, it's going to be a bad scene for at least three or four years. But it doesn't have to be that way.

CS: Well, could you give me an example of a policy that you feel would unlock that credit system?

RP: I laid it out in the article in *The Nation,* and I've also laid it out in a couple of other more recent things. I was asked by the staff of Senator Bernie Sanders to come up with a jobs plan, and this was April 2010. And I did, but he unfortunately did absolutely nothing with what I gave him.

The New America Foundation had a "Plan B for Obama" symposium. I can send you that, but the basic ideas in it are extremely simple. There are essentially two ideas. One is we already have a very extensive set of loan guarantees, including those for small businesses, that can be quite effective in reducing the perception of risk, and that's the main thing holding back the financial markets now: risk perception—on both sides of the credit market, borrowers and lenders.

The loan guarantee level is about $300 billion a year when you add up all the existing programs. So I say double the level and basically put it into small businesses, and by small businesses I don't really just mean tiny; I'd say the smaller half of the entire universe of businesses in the country. That's number one.

And then number two is to make the banks think seriously about picking up their lending by charging a tax on their excess cash reserves that they're holding. Right now the banks are holding about $1.1 trillion in cash reserves, which, by contrast, in 2007 they held $20 billion. So that's a $1.08 trillion turnaround. Now, it's true that the level of cash reserve holdings in 2007 was too low, and that this was one—not the major—but one of the contributors to the financial crisis. But to go from $20 billion for the whole economy to $1.1 trillion is absurd. It's only happening because the banks can borrow at zero percent. So they're just loading up with cash and they're sitting on it. The whole point of having a zero interest rate for the federal funds rate is not so that banks can sit on cash, but that they start making loans for productive activity.

CS: Well, that's very interesting. Before we get into this stuff about clean energy, and I have a whole raft of questions for you about that, but I'm just interested in rounding out my and my readers' understanding of macroeconomics in general as they might apply here. When I was a kid we learned about the Phillips Curve, relating unemployment to inflation and suggesting that full employment implies or creates some level of inflation. Now, so what's going on here? Is what we have now consistent with that?

RP: Yes, I think the general picture today is pretty consistent with the Phillips Curve because we do have a positive inflation, but it's almost nothing. We could go to deflation in five minutes if the government stops spending money, because nobody else is spending money. Deflation is more dangerous than inflation—and the Fed knows this. The reason it's more dangerous is because deflation makes the value of outstanding debt more burdensome; it's more difficult to payoff $100 when your wages have gone down. The $100 debt is a fixed value over time, but with deflation people's wages and purchasing power goes down. So you could invite another financial crisis through deflation. So the Phillips Curve I think is kind of more or less working.

Of course it's not the burning issue at the moment because we're nowhere near a full-employment economy where you might start to see upward pressure on wages and that gets passed on into prices, but the Phillips Curve works within a given institutional environment. Let's say you were concerned in full-employment with inflation. You could dampen the inflationary pressures through policies, for example, if we are really convinced that full-employment workers drive up prices by driving up wages. So maybe you have some kind of pact with labor where you say: If we can get the economy to full-employment, then you need to keep wage increases no greater than the rate of productivity growth. In which case, wage increases would not be inflationary.

So the fact that we don't have that is what makes the Phillips Curve still viable. It's interesting, in the 1960s when we *did* approach full-employment, and we *did* have accelerating inflation—though only like four and a half percent—there were discussions at the highest levels about creating some institutional bargaining setting so that you would have to retreat from full-employment; you could maintain a full-employment economy while also being a low inflation economy.

CS: Okay. Well, let me ask you this. Isn't our money supply going through the roof? I mean, it's common wisdom that we print money to do programs that we can't afford. Is that true? And if it is true, why isn't that in and of itself causing inflation?

RP: Well, I've never been a proponent of the view that the growth of the money supply causes inflation, except in extremes. Sure, if you take the case that Milton Friedman used to describe: if the government doubles the amount of cash available, drops it from a helicopter, everyone picks some up and so everyone is walking around with twice as much money as they had last week, then sure, that will drive up prices. So that's fair enough, but that's really not the realm of interesting situations, because that's not going to happen. I mean, it did happen. It happened in Germany under the Weimar Republic; it's happened a couple of times.

In my view, the money supply issue has always been a red herring. It's very hard to even measure and observe the money supply; nobody really truly knows what it is—and that's why the Fed has three different definitions of money supply and measures of the money supply. The extent to which they lubricate economic activity depends on the velocity in which they can be transferred around the economy. And the velocity of money is often institutionally dependent. The more you have financial innovations, the easier it is to transfer multiple times a given amount of liquid assets or money. There really isn't any evidence, other than in hyper-inflations, that something we call the money supply is causing inflation.

The question is okay, well why not? Why isn't there? And the answer is that the thing that causes inflation within the normal Phillips Curve setting is what Phillips identified.

It's when workers can bargain up wages; they have the power, under full-employment, they are more self-confident; they have more bargaining power and they push up wages faster than the rate of productivity growth. So wages are going up faster than the rate in which we are producing new things. That's when you have demand outstripping supply.

Now, just as an historical fact, for the last generation wages have been way below the growth of productivity. Wages have basically been stagnant since 1973 and productivity growth has doubled. So we're very, very far from a situation in which you can blame whatever inflation exists in the economy on workers' bargaining.

The other big factor in inflation is of course what we in the profession call "shocks," like the oil price increases that were very rapid. Of course, that will cause inflation. If you quadruple the price of oil tomorrow, we'll have more inflation. But that also is something that is not determined by the money supply, but by institutional considerations.

CS: Well okay, let's move to the subject of renewables and how this whole thing plays there. I don't have any more overall questions about macroeconomics, but obviously please don't hesitate to throw stuff like that in; this is very interesting.

When we talk about job creation and renewables, people talk about 275,000 new jobs, for instance. Let's start with the actual number itself. It seems to me that that number must be tied to a certain penetration rate of renewables. In other words, if we say we're going to 10% renewables by 2020, it would seem that that means something completely different than if we're going to 25%. Where do people come up with the numbers?

RP: Okay. Well, I'm one of the main people that comes up with those numbers, so I guess I can answer that.

CS: Good! [chuckle]

RP: First of all, we think about two different sources of job creation within the clean energy agenda. Renewables is one and the other one is investments in efficiency. They are quite distinct. The real big source of job creation, certainly for the next five years or so, is not in renewables; it's in energy efficiency.

For example, think about retrofitting the existing stock of buildings; that is a massive project. That's roughly a trillion-dollar project economy-wide and you get big, big savings. You get high rates of return. You have very low risk. Talking about low risk, we *know* it works. There are no fancy technologies; they are straightforward well-known technologies. So in our estimates, the retrofit project, which is really an imperative, is the single biggest job driver in all the clean energy discussions.

CS: Well, it is true that something like half of our energy consumption is in buildings.

RP: It's 40 percent, but 40 is a lot. And also most of the consumption in buildings is electricity, and electricity is only generated with a huge amount of waste. So for every energy unit of electricity that we generate, we lose two. Every time you raise efficiency in building, you not only save that one unit of energy that isn't needed in the building, you actually save three units. So that's a big deal.

CS: Okay. So you're describing a $1 trillion enterprise over how many years? And what's the job trajectory associated with that?

RP: Well, of course I don't know if it's exactly one trillion. My own estimates are in the range of $800 billion worth of work if you retrofitted basically the entire existing building stock to the level necessary, which of course is not going to happen, but at least analytically, there's no reason for it not to happen because it *does* save people money. So that is a big project, and think about it, there's no way this is importing competition; it has to be done in local communities.

And it's relatively labor intensive; it offers opportunities for people with relatively low credentials. To retrofit an average project if you spend $1 million, you'll get about eight jobs directly, and another eight jobs either indirectly—meaning jobs for the suppliers—or jobs created through a multiplier effect, through people having more money because they have jobs and then they're spending the money. So you'll get between 16 to 17 jobs per million-dollar expenditure in retrofit projects.

Which is good. It's not the best, but it's certainly the best in the area of energy.

CS: Well, let me understand this. So first of all, 800,000 times 17 is a huge number.

RP: 800,000... you mean... oh, 800,000 billion?

CS: Well, I'm just dividing a million into 800 billion. That's 800,000, times 17 is over 10 million.

RP: Yeah, okay. Of course, it's a huge number. Now, so this is a project that could go on for 20 years and could make everybody save money – and I mean *everybody*. There are subsidies out there, but the market really hasn't taken off yet.

CS: You bring up a good point about this thing with the low-end jobs. I mean, all jobs aren't created equal and I'm sure the analysis that you've done here is included in the stuff you write. But briefly, do we *want* a huge volume of jobs at the $30,000 a year level?

RP: Well, we've lost two million of those jobs. So my answer is yes. It's not like those are the only jobs that are going to get created. Let's compare spending money on green energy versus fossil fuels. You're going to get about three times more jobs per dollar of expenditure through clean energy, and here I'm referring both to efficiency and renewable investments. Three to one.

Now yes, part of that is because the pay level and the skill requirements for the clean energy jobs tend to be lower. I don't see that as necessarily so bad because it creates more entry-level jobs. Some of them have decent job ladders, and the other thing is because you're creating three times more jobs overall, in absolute terms you're going to have more jobs of all types, of all quality levels, of all pay levels. That's something else that I've shown.

So yes, proportionately, dollar for dollar you get higher quality, more skill and education requirements through spending in the fossil fuel economy, but that does not compensate for the fact that dollar for dollar you get three times more jobs overall in clean energy; you get more jobs at all levels through the clean energy economy.

CS: So, if you were king of the world, you would create subsidies to unlock the credit markets, and to move enterprises at all levels: small, medium, and large associated with this efficiency—and then later renewables?

RP: I'm very positive on renewables, but there are a couple of things about renewables that don't make them quite as attractive right now as a *jobs* program; they are very attractive as a long-term source of energy. In fact, in 30 years I think the entire globe should be run on renewable energy. People have done research showing that this is technically feasible; the challenge is making it economically feasible.

CS: Right. Talk to that please.

RP: Okay, right now wind power is approaching parity with coal in terms of energy units generated per dollar unit.

PV is four to five times more expensive than coal. So that's not close. Geothermal is close. Hydroelectric of course can be very cheap, where you have the water power. But the two big ones are wind and solar. If we're going to really transition to an economy run by renewable energy, we need to really load up on wind and solar. Wind is coming along nicely, and solar is still way behind, though there is a lot to like about thin film, so that you don't have to put these gigantic panels on peoples' buildings and so forth. But the technologies are just not quite there.

It doesn't mean they can't *get* there; it means that as part of a U.S. industrial policy, we have to be committed to supporting this. Part of the Obama stimulus program certainly *did* support it, but that is running out. What we need is a recommitment to support this.

Then the other factor which distinguishes renewable from efficiency investments is that you have import competition. We can buy solar panels and windmills from Denmark or China, and they're churning them out. There will still be job creation in the United States if for no other reason than assembly; at least you have to assemble. You can have a wind farm in the United States, and you can manufacture the wind turbines in China, but then at least you have to assemble them in the U.S. But we don't just want to do assembly; we want to do the whole thing. This could be a gigantic world market in the next generation, and therefore, the U.S. doesn't have to *dominate*; I'm not saying we have to have the whole market ourselves, but I think we need our fair share.

And the only way we're going to get there is by having an industrial policy similar to the industrial policies the Pentagon has conducted on behalf of things like the Internet, computers, and jet aviation that were very successful. You probably heard about the U.S. steelworkers complaining to the WTO (World Trade Organization) that the Chinese were violating the WTO by putting too *much* money into renewable energy.

CS: Yes.

RP: Well, do we care about global warming or not? We should be celebrating that. We should say, "Well, we'll go double up on them because we don't want them to take the whole market."

It's not exactly a constructive contribution to say they're spending too much money; that's unfair.

CS: Well, what should happen and why is it not happening?

RP: Well, some of it *did* happen. Again, the stimulus program—and I should declare that I am a consultant to the Energy Department on implementing the stimulus program; I am obviously favorable toward it, but I'm not a member of the administration. I'm just a consultant so there are no limits on what I can say or not say.

But the notion of something like $100 billion getting committed to promoting clean energy was a major breakthrough, a major achievement. Of course, now everyone is saying the stimulus didn't work, but let's just say for starters that at the very least it captured a new idea—that investing in a green economy can be good for jobs and good for growth. Before that, the prevailing view was that you could have environmental protection, but to get there you're going to have a tradeoff with jobs and growth because you're going to have to slow down growth with all these regulations. So *now* we're saying it can actually be an engine of growth and job creation, and that's my view; I support that view. That's why the administration hired me.

So there *is* progress. Now, whether that is going to get defeated in the next couple years; people just say, "Well, it was just garbage. It never worked." I can't predict that. Certainly, that sentiment is floating around.

CS: Yes. You'd have to really be not paying attention not to see the backlash.

RP: Oh yeah, the backlash is real, and I understand it, because there's officially 9.6 percent unemployment. I'd say a better measure is 20 percent unemployment. So of course people are angry, and they've heard correctly that we have this gigantic stimulus program, we have a fiscal deficit of ten percent of GDP, that's true. Historically unprecedented since World War II, that's true. And we still have ten percent unemployment. Well, the reason we have ten percent unemployment is not because the stimulus failed, but because, as I said at the beginning, the magnitude of the crisis was so severe. So people, including myself, were not ready to have to confront a crisis of this size; it's new territory. So the stimulus works. When they spend the money the stimulus works. All the things that I've observed with the Energy Department—the big problem is getting the money out the door.

CS: Right. I was going to ask you about that. We're talking largely about the money under ARPA-E?

RP: Yeah.

CS: Okay. I may have mentioned that I have a website having to do with renewable energy: www.2greenenergy.com, and that I have ten thousand subscribers who are constantly blogging, talking to one another about their viewpoints on this. And I see a great deal of concern that the money that came through the DoE under ARPA-E was not *fairly* allocated – that 31 out of 32 projects went to billion-dollar-plus organizations. Where is the support of true innovation, they ask, of people who have great ideas who could carry them forward quickly? Is this true, or is this just misguided chatter?

RP: I think that having been involved in the mechanics of getting this underway and implemented, it *is* difficult. Obama said in the *New York Times*, "One thing I've learned is that there's no such thing as a shovel-ready project." I saw that myself; obviously at a lower level, in implementing the stimulus program. So things are slower than we would like. They're more bureaucratic, and you don't have the infrastructure in place in either the public or private sector, as yet, to make it an efficient process, much less a fair process. Given that it is not an efficient process, of course people who can afford fancy lawyers and lobbyists are going to have a big advantage; that's the reality. It's not a pretty picture, but I think if we keep pushing on it over time, opportunities are going to open up for smaller business as well.

CS: Okay. Well, I guess that's where I'm going with this, or at least, that's where the people who blog on my site are going. In other words, especially with the Supreme Court decision granting personhood to corporations and now they can spend whatever they want to influence our democratic process in whatever way they please, you have a level of corruption that just makes the whole thing ridiculous. What's your viewpoint on that?

RP: Well, there is a counter-force which I would say is organized around the Internet. What are big businesses really buying when they buy politicians? You can't just put money in their pockets. I'm sure somebody does do a bit of that, but the real thing they buy is the ability to mount effective campaigns to win elections. The single most supportive thing is buying television advertising.

With the Internet over time, I think that is going to be a diminishing force because you can put anything out on the Internet. I mean, just look at the example of George Allen from Virginia. He was a shoe-in for senate and was considered a serious Republican candidate for president in 2008. He was running for re-election in 2006 and he made this really outrageous racist statement that got caught on the Internet—and he just lost. His whole political career was over.

So over time, people who actually believe in democracy and some semblance of a fair society can use the Internet as a resource. Sure there are major advantages to having money, but I think those could be diminished over time through effective use of the Internet.

CS: I hope you're right.

I've been asking a lot of folks about subsidies for fossil fuels vs. renewables. Have you studied this?

RP: It's actually pretty hard to pin down the level of subsidies going to fossil fuels. And I don't think that the subsidy issue per se is the main advantage of fossil fuels. The main advantage, at this point, is that it's still cheaper, and in front of us we have a whole infrastructure in place and we have all of our transportation system designed around fossil fuel. So it's going to take a long time to get off of that because it is so integrated into the economy.

But the main thing for me with efficiency is that you shouldn't need subsidies. If it's true what everybody says that you can get a 30 percent rate of return through an average efficiencies investment, that would mean that everybody should be doing it. Effectively, it would mean that their energy bill goes down from $1,000 to $700, so everybody should be doing it—even without a subsidy. Now, that's not happening, and the reason it's not happening is because people don't want to pay the up-front money; it's a big hassle and so okay, they just keep paying more. But over time it will happen, with more innovation—and here I'm not talking about subsidies—I'm talking about innovative, creative business plans to capture that opportunity sitting there.

CS: Looking at this from the standpoint of microeconomics, if you're an individual homeowner let's say, you may not want to shell out whatever it costs to put insulation in your walls, etc. But if you're a CFO, you pretty much have to make investments that pay off, don't you? In other words, if you get a 30 percent return on an investment, you do it regardless of *what* it is, don't you?

RP: Well, so this is something I've been pretty interested in. Often people say yeah, why isn't everybody doing it? And I think it's that the market is undeveloped. The hassle factor is huge. If you're talking about a CFO for a company, they're probably in a big office building. So it gets more complicated in terms of who has legal authority. So it's all these institutional things that are blocking what seems to be the inevitable way forward.

CS: Okay, that's interesting.

What I'm really about here is trying to pull apart the migration from fossil fuels to renewables and wondering *when* it's going to happen, *why* it's going to happen, and *why* it hasn't happened already. You talk about the existing infrastructure; it's in front of us, and fossil fuels are cheap. All of these things are true. The last of which, i.e., that it's cheap, I think is the most interesting and important. Why is it cheap? Isn't it artificially cheap?

RP: Definitely. The price of fossil fuels does not reflect the social cost that we're bearing.

CS: Well, the social cost, do you mean the externalities? It does seem that we're starting to have conversations about this. Ten years ago you'd get a blank stare telling somebody that you wanted to talk about quantifying the comprehensive cost of fossil fuels. People are starting to talk about that now, but what do you see as the trajectory for internalizing those externalities?

RP: Well, in Europe they do. If you buy a gallon of gas, it's somewhere in the range of $10; they have massive taxes on it. Maybe it should be a cap system, maybe a tax system, but at the very least we have to raise the price of buying retail gasoline to reflect the social costs. That is what the cap and trade bill was supposed to accomplish. That is certainly not passing this go-around, which is a big disappointment, but that's what's needed. Basically there are three gigantic projects. One is to put a price on carbon, two is to squeeze every penny of efficiency out of the energy system, and three is to build an effective set of renewable energy sources.

Now, we haven't mentioned nuclear power and carbon capture technology, which a lot of people are counting on as the real path of the future. I'm not favorable on either one of them, but that's my view.

CS: Okay. To facilitate the conversation, I just emailed you a piece outlining certain kinds of subsidies that I've been compiling. I don't know much about any of them, but it seems to me that there are two elements of this thing. One set deals with the externalities, even though they are difficult to quantify. For example, global climate change is an important thing for most of us, but how important? Establishing the actual cost in terms of long-term environmental damage, I would grant is a difficult thing. But the rest of these things aren't at *all* difficult. In other words, we pay $4 a gallon for gasoline, simply because we got extremely favorable treatment of oil and gas.

RP: Well yes, it's definitely been supportive and not only directly, but through favoring internal combustion engines and the highway system, as opposed to having light rail and rail. So all of these things are either direct or indirect subsidies and support for the fossil fuel economy. We basically have to go in reverse. I am not a climate scientist, so I cannot tell you what the definitive arguments are. But I do know this: if you have something like 75 percent of serious climate scientists saying that we face a non-trivial possibility of an ecological catastrophe in 20 or 30 years if we don't do something, then you have to take that seriously even if they turn out to be wrong. If these people are saying there is a serious chance of this, you have to go with it.

And not on the basis that we know for sure that it's going to happen; it's on the basis that there's a non-trivial probability. It's just like the reason we take out insurance policies.

CS: OK, thanks, Bob. I know you have to run; let's pick this up next week.

Part Two

CS: Thanks again for your help.

Of course you hear a lot about the tea party, which seems to have convinced a lot of people that the Obama administration is over-spending, and taking us to socialism. A faint voice on the other side is saying that federal spending isn't high enough to stimulate the economy and historically we've had much higher spending as a percentage of GDP to drive recoveries. What's your take on this?

RP: Well, first of all in terms of just on the data, I don't think there's really any dispute that the level of deficit spending in the economy right now is historically the highest it's been, other than World War II. Federal deficit spending right now is about ten percent of GDP. During World War II we got up to about as high as I think 26 percent GDP. For those years of World War II I think it ranged about 19 or 20 percent. Other than that, during peacetime the closest we've gotten was in 1983 under Ronald Reagan when it was six percent of GDP. So there's no question that the level of deficit spending is very high.

Most of the drivers for the rise in deficit spending were the severity of the recession itself, because when you go into recession, of course, tax revenues go down because people's incomes are going down, and their property values have collapsed. So you have a reduction in property tax revenue and income tax revenue; at the same time you have a dramatic increase in the so called automatic stabilizers: unemployment insurance, and healthcare for people that fall below a certain income level. So all of that happened without the formal stimulus program that the Obama administration got passed in February '09—that was $400 billion a year for two years in new spending and tax cuts. Add it all up and you have a very traumatic increase in the fiscal deficit as a share of GDP.

One of the ironies of the current situation is the interest rate on U.S. Treasury bonds and bills—short-term and long term—is very low. The theory would tell us it should be high, meaning if your government is running a very big deficit, it's more difficult to attract people to lend us money, all things being equal. In fact, it's turned out to be just the opposite. Everyone wants to lend money to the U.S. government because it's probably the world's safest asset.

The interest rate on, say, six-month Treasuries is less than two percent. Even though we have a very high fiscal deficit, the borrowing costs on that deficit are disproportionately low. So that under Ronald Reagan, when we ran a six percent GDP fiscal deficit, the average interest rate on say a five year Treasury was more like 13 percent; now it's more like three percent. So the burden, we talk about burdening our children and future generations, what that really boils down to is the interest payments. So those interest payments are far less burdensome than they would have been if the interest rates had been high. So yes, the deficit is very high, but the interest payments are not so severe as they might be.

But your question was: What's going on with this? Is this leading us to socialism or financial ruin?

In my own view, no. I've written some stuff I can send you if you want. The problem was if anything brought us to the brink of ruin, it was the financial crisis brought on by Wall Street hyper speculation and the deregulation that proceeded that, which enabled hyper speculation. Warren Buffet even has an article in the *New York Times* in which he thanks Uncle Sam for bailing out the world economy from this crisis brought on by hyper speculation and over leveraging. We needed a counter for this because the world's biggest financial institutions and non-financial institutions like General Motors were on the verge of total collapse. Who knows where that would have led us?

That's what really explains the magnitude of the fiscal burden. In my view it's very unfortunate that the debate has shifted so quickly away from understanding the causes of the crisis and saying government actions, however inadequate or poorly done, seem basically correct as a response to a crisis that Wall Street created. The idea now is that the government's fiscal deficit itself is a crisis. It's not.

CS: All right. Let's move onto clean energy specifically and it seems to me, and I don't think I'm unique in this position, that capital formation in clean energy has been horribly feeble of late. Why is that?

RP: Well, the first answer I think is the recession. People don't want to invest in clean energy because they don't want to invest in anything other than U.S. Treasury Bonds. So the level of risk aversion now is so high. The banks are sitting on a trillion dollars of cash reserves—unprecedented. Non-financial businesses are sitting on I think around $2 trillion in cash reserves. So it's not like there's no money around; it's just that there's no appetite to gain investments in productive activities. So that applies across the board, not just to clean energy.

On top of that, clean energy is obviously, for the most part, a new venture or a risky kind of venture; it's moving into uncertain territories. That's really why nothing is happening. Well, countering that, you did have in the stimulus program $100 billion in it to support clean energy activities and of that, $75 billion was various kinds of incentives for state and local governments, but primarily for private businesses to get into clean energy with government support.

But you can lead the horse to water, but you can't make it drink. So a lot of those incentives have not been taken up because you don't have businesses prepared to start undertaking these kinds of risky activities.

CS: I was going to come at this later, but as long as it's come up, do you know who Peter Morici is?

RP: Oh yes, I've seen his name.

CS: From the University of Maryland he says much of the green stimulus funding was squandered. What is he talking about and is he correct?

RP: Well, okay. I actually have seen, and I think I told you I've been consulting with the Energy Department on implementing this, and I don't agree with that. I think that it's fair to say that a lot of the money was *unused* because of difficulties of getting private businesses to get into this whole endeavor.

That's different than saying money was squandered. I don't think money was squandered. The projects that I tracked which are essentially all of the projects that have been undertaken thus far, the job creation numbers that have come in are almost exactly the numbers that I predicted. It turns out that the things that my colleagues and I have said in terms of the opportunities for job creation pretty much got through on a dollar for dollar basis. The problem is bringing these projects up to scale. So the last time I checked maybe 20 percent of the overall money that was intended for clean energy investments had actually been spent. Now we're kind of at the end of the formal stimulus period. They had always projected that the clean energy investments were going to spill well past the two-year period of the formal stimulus and would go at least for another three years.

I'm not an expert on inside Washington stuff, but to my knowledge what's happened is, given this new shift in perspective towards deficit reduction, they're taking the money out of the clean energy projects and putting it back into general funds to cover the deficit.

I don't think it's fair to say that it was squandered, but rather that the project hasn't been as successful as I certainly would have liked. That's because it hasn't been used—and part of the reason it wasn't used so quickly was that they didn't want it to be squandered. They didn't want people like Peter Morici to say, "Look what you did with the money." They were pretty careful for setting up guidelines for getting money out and giving subsidies.

CS: Here's another viewpoint on this spending on renewables from Samuel Sherraden, economic analyst at the New America Foundation (progressive think tank), who says, "Spending on renewables is slow to get out the door. Leaks to foreign companies are an inadequate driver of jobs and growth may not create a strong exporting industry."

RP: Well, I think there's a lot of truth in that. I think you can divide up the overall clean energy project broadly into two categories. One is energy efficiency investments, and the other one is renewables. In the area of energy efficiency, it's much easier going because, for example, if you're retrofitting the existing building stock, you don't need any new technologies to do it; the technologies are there. The rates of return are pretty well known and everything takes place on site, in the United States, in specific neighborhoods. So all of these things are major positives. On top of that, you have a construction industry that is very slack, so there are a lot of underutilized resources that could be quickly brought on board to do these things. That's one thing.

You can say similar things about investments in public transportation—if you just expand existing public transportation systems as a source of energy efficiency. You can say more or less the same thing about investing in upgrading the grid.

Now, then you shift into renewable energy, which is at the level where a lot of the activity is around research and development, and the commercialization to drive down the price of, in particular, renewable electricity, to compete with fossil fuel electricity—and it's not there yet. Wind is getting close to coal, but wind has the problem of intermittency.

It also has a problem that arose at a debate at Stanford Thursday night: not in my backyard. Everybody thinks wind is a great idea except they don't want to see any windmills. I don't know how serious that one is, but I've heard it raised. Solar is not cost-competitive; it will probably take a decade to get there with a lot of investment. Geothermal can be cost competitive. It's more limited in terms of what it can deliver. With hydro you need rushing water; it does pretty well, but it's limited. Really the main show is around wind and solar, and there are issues of getting to commercial level of delivery.

Of course, a lot of the activity is around manufacturing. So what's to say that if they're doing them cheaper in China, maybe we should just buy them from China. That is a question. I don't think that's what we should do. This debate at Stanford on Thursday was on the merits of green jobs and all that stuff. But nobody was really arguing the point that over the next generation we have to convert to a clean energy economy. It's a question of how you do it. So if we all agree on that, broadly speaking, then I would say it would sure be a shame to have zero manufacturing of the most important products in the economy. I mean after all, energy is what drives every economy whether it's fossil fuel or renewable energy.

To relinquish that altogether as an area of growth for the U.S. economy seems to me pretty foolish. If China and Denmark and Germany are ahead of us now in renewables, I think it should certainly be a matter of policy priority to bring us to the point where we are competitive. I'm not a protectionist; I'm not saying we should never buy things from other countries, but we should have competitive industries. The way you get competitive industries from nothing is they have to be subsidized, just like the Internet was subsidized by the defense department.

CS: Right. Well, you bring up an excellent point and that is: nobody doubts that we're going there. Nobody looks at a Hummer on the street and thinks we're going to be driving cars like that in 100 years. We're clearly becoming more aware of the impact we're having on the planet. I guess we all hope we get there soon enough before we have truly ruined the place. So I don't think that's a real debate; I think it's how we get there.

Could we go back and talk about your viewpoint on subsidies, please?

RP: Well, as a matter of principle on all subsidies for all purposes, I think that this is part of what public policy is supposed to do. It's supposed to reward the things that we need that the market is not good at establishing as a need, and promoting them. Now, of course that's at a very high level of principle and abstraction. But then what really happens is that people who have the most money hire the most lobbyists. That actual real-life behavior might lead us in the direction of saying it's better to have no subsidies whatsoever, but I really don't think we should surrender to that point of view.

I think that in terms of public policy, because there are things that the market clearly does not do well—and taking care of the environment is probably the best example—that we need government interventions to achieve those things that cannot be achieved by any other means. Certain important things cannot be achieved through free market operations; even Adam Smith recognized that back in 1776. It's just not logical to say that because subsidies could lead to corruption that there should be no subsidies. I think that we have to fight for logical subsidies, efficient subsidies.

There's a lot of room to debate around exactly how you deliver subsidies—how you promote things that have social benefits that exceed what the market can capture. That's really what it's about. Sure we can debate exactly how you do that. In fact, I was surprised; when I was at this debate at Stanford my opponent was not really against promoting the green economy; the only thing he was saying was that government is going to screw it up. He didn't even say then there should be no subsidies; he just said we should design programs that create incentives for private actors as efficiently as we can, with maximum protection against corruption.

Now, I completely agree with that; I don't have any problem with that at all. And in any case, I completely agree with the proposition that if we're going to build a clean energy economy in 25 years it's *not* going to happen primarily through the government, because the government doesn't have the resources or the capacity. So most of it *will* be done in the private sector, but the private sector *does* need the proper signals, incentives, subsidies, whatever you want to call it. That's really the real challenge right now.

CS: But according to what I've read, and discussed elsewhere in this book, we *have* subsidies. We have several dollars in subsidies for oil and coal and gas, largely oil, for every $1 we have in renewables. So the problem isn't that we don't have subsidies; the problem is that we're rewarding the precise thing we're trying to get away from.

RP: Yeah. I don't have a precise number. I've looked into that somewhat myself. It's hard to pin it down, which is part of the problem in itself. At the very least it shouldn't be hard to pin down, but it is. Here we've said we want cheap oil; cheap oil is the foundation of our economy. So let's really encourage it, get it really super-cheap and then we can build businesses on the foundation of that cheap energy.

CS: Yes, and we've done that; we did that in the 1930s. I wasn't around in the 1930s, but had I been, I don't think I would have objected to it. But now, what you have is artificially cheap oil that makes it impossible for capital formation for competitive goods.

RP: Right. So number one, the real issue for me is not to eliminate the idea of subsidies, but to throw them into reverse, and to make them consistent with our ecological and social requirements for our generation, which is to build a clean energy economy. So we have to fight for those things.

I was at a conference once and there were people from the American Petroleum Institute. They came up to me afterwards and they said, "You know, in order to make this whole clean energy thing work, we're the ones that are going to have to take the subsidies and we're the ones that are going to make this happen." I said, "More power to you." If they are going to do it, then let's see you do it.

CS: Well, that was a very polite response. There are some people who would have said, "Bullcrap! How gullible do you think I am?" [chuckle]

RP: Well, of course whether they were sincere or not is another matter, but I guess they thought they had to kind of at least show me that that's the way they were thinking.

CS: Well, that's brazen, in my opinion.

In any case, let me ask you more about dealing with the externalities of fossil fuels. This of course is the idea that the consumers and producers of energy need to pay immediately—not pass the costs to their grandchildren—but pay the true and comprehensive costs of what it is they're producing and consuming. What do you think of this argument? Does it have any legs? Does it have any merit?

RP: At a fundamental level of principle, that's what it's all about. It's why we must build a clean energy economy and more generally a green economy. It's not just about CO_2 emissions, although that's certainly the most dire problem. But yes, this is what I'm saying about going all the way back to Adam Smith, who clearly recognized that markets do not accurately price everything.

He was clear on that, and this is why we need these so-called public goods. We need to do things as a polity that are not going to get captured through simply bartering. Adam Smith was the one who extolled and explained it so beautifully. That means there is really no option to having people through public policy and voters make these hard decisions about government involvement and government creating laws, subsidies, regulations, and what's the right combination. It would be very nice to say that we'll let the free market handle it so we don't have to bother, but we know we can't.

To internalize the externalities, it's all a matter of how you do it. The guiding principle is the recognition that markets are not going to do it by themselves. The second principle is where we started in this, and that is yes, governments are going to screw up. There is no question that governments will be corrupt some of the time, but since we don't have any choice but to use government to internalize externalities, then let's think about ways in which we can have public policy work most efficiently and with the least amount of corruption.

CS: Right. But all this comes at the expense of a short-term cost. In other words, all this long-term public good comes at the expense of short-term pain. It doesn't sound like we have a terrific appetite for pain, now or anytime, and *especially* now. In particular, it sounds like you're asking elected leaders to make unpopular decisions, which sounds impossible, and perhaps explains why we really don't appear to be making any real headway here. These are people whose jobs come up for renewal every two years, and an unpopular decision... in other words, a decision whose merits aren't felt in that election cycle might be career suicide.

RP: Well, my background is not as an environmental economist. When I got into this, the real question I was trying to ask was exactly your question. i.e., this tradeoff between pain and gain. How much pain do we have to experience in order to get the gain of environmental protection? The big question I was trying to ask is: what if we thought of this as a new growth engine—a new source of job creation, just like if you think about the development of the railroads, or the development of the auto culture, or the suburbs in the 1950s. Whether we like them or not, it was a massive source of new opportunity, a new way of rebuilding the economy, a new fundamental infrastructure—by the way, fueled by fossil fuel energy. So if you think of it in that way, then at least conceptually you could see it as not necessarily a pain-versus-gain tradeoff, but as a big gain because it's a whole new way of restructuring the economy. It's massive new opportunities for innovation, for investment, for job creation, all in the long-term epic project of creating a clean energy economy, moving away from the fossil fuel economy. Now, if you do it that way then in my opinion, and this is basically what I've been writing about on this question for a few years, it's not pain versus gain; it's net gain all around.

You get big job creation. You get great new opportunities for innovation, wonderful things for creative people to work on, a whole lot more interesting and important than Facebook or whatever happens to be the latest new toy on the Internet. You create a whole new way of powering the global economy on the basis of renewable energy, and then you *do* it; it's a massive project. It's going to create a lot of jobs of all kinds for all kinds of people. Of course, we're going to move out of the fossil fuel economy and we have to manage that transition, but we are also going to create a lot of new jobs—a lot of opportunities for innovation, and it can happen in every community in the U.S. and throughout the world.

For example, think about the developing world. If I were working on sub-Saharan Africa on macroeconomic policy, the question in most of the world in terms of macro policy, at least before the financial crisis, was inflation control. Their whole framework for growth and job creation was about inflation targeting. You've got to keep the inflation rate down to three, four, five percent. Now, the major source of inflation in most developing economies, if not most economies all over the world, is the price of oil, which is very volatile. If you could transition in a poor country to running the economy on renewable energy instead of fossil fuels, you've just lifted the biggest single constraint on economic growth in the whole economy.

CS: Wow! That's fascinating.

RP: Yeah. So again, it's not just the U.S. I think we should think of this as a great new opportunity for all kinds of things to happen.

CS: Yes. Well, there's no doubt that it is. I guess the question is really breaking this down so that people see it. Here's a question for you based on that. You don't live in California so there's no reason you should be tuned into this debate that went down in our November mid-terms, but we had a thing called Proposition 23 that would have essentially eliminated our commitment to clean air. And it came frighteningly close to passing, based on its proponents talking about how we would lose jobs in terms of diesel trucking and so forth. If you clamp down on these emissions you're going to lose two jobs for every green job you create. Now, personally I know that there are lies, damn lies, and statistics—and I certainly don't trust whomever came up with that idea, but I guess my question is how do you substantiate what you're saying?

Take what you just said, Bob, as an example. How do you say that okay, yes we have a problem with brown jobs going away and yes, we've got various problems, but the net gain is going to be overwhelmingly positive. Can you substantiate that in some way?

RP: Yeah, that's been a major focus of my research, and nobody really disputes it. I used data from the U.S. industrial surveys, which are organized by the U.S. Department of Commerce and the so-called input/output tables. Input/output simply means they organized all the data that they get from businesses; it shows what every business does, and what they buy to do the things they do to produce. So labor, materials, energy, land, how they combine, and then the outputs are what they produce. Using that statistical tool, the basic finding is that activities around building the green economy create three times more jobs per million dollar expenditure as maintaining a fossil fuel economy.

Nobody disputes that. I'm telling you *nobody*. I've been attacked by all kinds of think tanks and researchers, but they can't really dislodge that basic point. The reason you get that is actually fairly straightforward. What we're doing is comparing the creation of a new economy and new sectors, that is, a green economy versus maintaining the existing brown energy economy. So anytime you're going to be investing in something new versus maintaining something in place, it's going to create a lot of new job opportunities. So that's really what the basis for my finding is, and, as I said, it's held up under pretty intense scrutiny. My model has been adopted by the U.S. Energy Department and everybody knows that the numbers are basically right.

The only question is, again, what does this mean in terms of policy? What does it mean in terms of government? We can debate that a lot, but you cannot really debate the fact that investing in the clean energy economy will create more jobs for a given dollar.

CS: Okay, that's great.

Let me ask you to react to this: I heard somebody say that most of the people who talk at high levels like this don't understand decision-making of an organization that just invested a few billion dollars in a new pipeline across Asia or wherever. He said, "Who's realistically expecting these people to just write this off as a loss?"

RP: No, I don't think they need to write it off as a loss because if we're going to have a clean energy economy in 25 years, they could be making money for 25 years. Now,

I think it's only right for them to expect that they need to start absorbing ... in other words, internalizing the externalities. They've been hearing about it for years and they need to recognize that burning fossil fuels is bad for the environment, and the people in the industry are going to have to start paying the price for that, instead of getting subsidized. That's fair enough. And then they can decide what they're going to do. Right now, fossil fuel energy investment and consumption remains a highly profitable business, and the transition is going to take place only little by little, but it must take place and it must move forward.

CS: Right, it must, but I think the reason why I'm cynical about this is that it goes back to this pain-versus-gain thing. I'd like to think someone could run and win on this platform, but I'm not sure how realistic it is. I'm not a political strategist, but I don't know. I hate to impugn the integrity of elected leaders, and I know there are elected leaders who do the right thing even though it's unpopular, they're called "former elected leaders."

RP: [chuckle] Well, like I'm saying, the stimulus program was, in my view, a major and positive breakthrough. It recognized that investing in the environment could be good for jobs. That is an idea that had not been around much. The idea, maybe still a prevailing idea, that you can protect the environment, fine, yes, but it's bad for jobs; it's bad for economic growth. I think the stimulus program was a gigantic investment on behalf of the view that investing in the environment could be good for jobs. So this pain-versus-gain thing, of course, on a micro level there will be many, many cases—and there have to be adjustments to and acknowledgement of that, but in the macro view, it's not true. You get more gain for investing, if by "gain" we mean opportunities for people, opportunities for communities, opportunities for innovators, opportunities for investors.

You're going to get more gain by investing in the green economy. It's going to take awhile for that to fully sink in, but I think it is slowly sinking in, and I think the stimulus program was one important step in behalf of that idea.

CS: I don't doubt that.

When you say "macro perspective," I think what you're doing is contrasting that to what we have here in California as an example. We have very strict emission standards; we can't burn coal here. But we can sure as hell buy coal-fired energy from Arizona or Nevada where it's perfectly fine to burn coal. So all of a sudden you have created an artificial imbalance – like where Mexicans want to come across the border to the United States to work.

RP: Yeah, I haven't noticed that the Arizona economy is in a whole lot better shape than the California economy. The environmental controls are less, but I don't think there's a lot of evidence that tells us that having environmental standards in California has led to California's being a mess; of course, the whole U.S. economy, and for that matter, the global economy is in a mess. It's not because of environmental standards; it's because of deregulation on Wall Street. That's what created the global mess. We can have very healthy economic growth with lots of job opportunities—in fact, we already have, through creating a clean energy economy.

If we're going to put a tax or we're going to have a cap on fossil fuels, of course it's going to hurt the fossil fuel industry; it can't help but do otherwise. But it's also going to help the renewable energy industry. When you transition from fossil to clean energy, you will create more jobs, more opportunities, and more innovation. I mean, just as a simple example, if you say $1,000 instead of going to an Arab oil sheik is going to Cleveland, Ohio to retrofit buildings, well that's a huge opportunity right there.

CS: But I want to try to understand the viewpoint that says, "You're talking about taxing trucking companies and dry cleaners and all the people that are only tangentially involved with a consumption of energy..."

RP: And the effects on them will be tangential. If we talk about the overall macro effects, if you have an economy where there's a higher level of job creation, that will help the truckers. There will be plenty of need for truckers to deliver wind turbines and solar panels. So even if they're not delivering pipes for oil pipelines, they're going to be delivering solar panels and there will be more of them to deliver solar panels.

CS: OK. Let me ask you: I have a friend who's a financial analyst in renewables, and he spends most of his time looking at stuff happening outside of the United States, because he's so frustrated with the uncertainty, the bickering, the bureaucracy. Of course, you could argue a lot of things about that. But he says if you want to know what's happening in the world on this thing, look to markets in Europe and Asia and elsewhere, but also note that the companies like GE don't care if they can't create jobs in the United States. They want profitability. They don't care where their jobs are – or either where their customers are, for that matter. They'll find people who get it, and be profitable wherever that may be. In other words, it's our loss. Is there any truth to that in your estimation?

RP: Yes, total truth. Yeah, why should they care? The point is our public policy is supposed to be where we have the interest of the United States citizen at the heart of things. We should be creating opportunities for people in the United States. Again, I'm not a total protectionist, and so it's fine if there's innovation in other countries, but there also should be innovation in this country. We should have a decent manufacturing base.

CS: Well, this has been everything I hoped it would be, Bob. I really do appreciate it.

RP: Okay. Great talking to you. Best of luck with the project, and please keep me informed.

Craig's Interview with Wally Rippel

Wally's list of accomplishments in science and technology spans half a century; in fact, he is best known for two achievements separated by almost 40 years: In 1968, he built the Caltech electric car and won the Great Transcontinental Electric Car Race against MIT, only to re-appear in the 2006 documentary movie *"Who Killed the Electric Car?"*

I've known Wally for several years, and every time we talk, I feel I'm a better person for having had the opportunity. Primarily a scientist, Wally brings a profound understanding of the impact that technology has on our world in a great number of ways, including ecologically and sociologically.

The focus of the interview here is cold fusion, along with an exploration of the sad and ironic ways in which politics has invaded the realm of science.

CS: Wally, thanks for taking time for me, and good to see you again.

As I mentioned on the phone, this book is an exploration as to why we don't have renewables in any great amount. And obviously, this is a blend; there are many reasons I'm sure, but I'd like to get as many of them documented as possible.

WR: Well, yes it's a blend, and it's a matter of how much of each: technological, political, economic, and criminal.

CS: Ha! Well, that's what I'd like you to talk about, starting with the experiences you had at Caltech, and I'm sure since.

WR: Of course…, On the plus side, let's be really honest here. Wind has been growing and it's been growing obviously faster than coal on a percent basis. So that's good. The next thing is, if we look at a technology like natural gas, it wasn't ten years ago people said we were going to have to import large quantities of natural gas. We've developed new technology for getting to reserves that we didn't know existed, or if we did know about them, we couldn't get to them.

CS: Fracking, in other words.

WR: Fracking, exactly. So everything is a moving target. Not just the renewables are getting better, but there's other things happening.

CS: Absolutely, and I'm sure you can say the same thing about oil exploration as well. There are constant rumors or whatever that there's enough oil under South Dakota…

WR: Well, there's a little deception here of course. When they say that, they're not talking about conventional oil. There are large quantities of hydrocarbons. Unfortunately, they do come at a higher environmental cost. It's not lower, it's worse. It's offset a little bit by improved technology, but we're led to believe that there are no problems in all these things—until there's a problem.

CS: Right. Like somebody's drinking water catches on fire.

WR: Exactly. We saw that. I guess *60 Minutes* did a thing on that. And of course there are negative environmental effects even with the best of renewables.

CS: Absolutely. Well, let's explore all of this. Perhaps we can start with the fundamentals of clean energy technologies, and note that the price per watt is coming down. Where will this take us? To what degree does Moore's Law apply here, which would suggest that we'll see continued exponential improvement, where most people would say we're running out of growth potential with respect to things like PV.

WR: Yes. Growth potential is there, but it's not there in the same way that it would be with computer technology; they are two different things. One has to really look at this and say okay, how much can this drop? Let's look at the cost of the raw silicon and processing. How sensitive is that to volume? So from the little I know, and I'm not by any means educated in here, but a dollar a watt seems like a very realistic thing, where a penny a watt does not. If it were computer technology, you would say a penny a watt will be here in some years and it will continue falling after that.

One of the elements with PV that I think is needed is not even the conventional technical discussion; I think we need some artists and architects to be involved. You look at a lot of PV installations, and it doesn't add to the architecture. But I think if it's done right, people would want the PV look for their house even if it wasn't operative – and clearly that's not the case. But if you look at the best technologies, the Dutch had these windmills as they called them, and they're wonderful tourist attractions even though they're all dead; they don't generate energy, but they look nice.

There's an interesting thing about technology, when it's done right it has its own beauty. I don't know about you, but I love looking at a jet plane. They're not styled, but they look beautiful. They're designed to meet the requirements of aerodynamics, but they have a beauty. That's not true for everything; utility poles don't look attractive, but a lot of things do.

So the interesting thing about PV is that it does not have to get down to the cost of wind in order to be very competitive, because it's competing at the residential level, not at the wholesale level.

CS: True. And it's essentially daytime stuff, contrasting to wind. It has a completely different set of characteristics in terms of a grid mix.

WR: It's very synergistic with electric vehicles, especially when electric vehicles become V2G vehicles.

CS: Why would that be, given that most electric vehicle charging will be done at night?

WR: Well, if you have a vehicle-to-grid car, and you drive it to work every day, you only need to recoup the energy that you used getting to work; if it's a high to moderate rate charging, it's typically less than an hour. So now you have the battery able to do something; it's providing this regulation function that's putting in a kilowatt-hour to the utility, taking one out, and moving it back and forth during the day which allows you to have more PV than you would otherwise. It's a regulation function.

And people point out that one of the limiting factors with both PV and wind is the variability. But here's a load that can complement that short-term, such as a battery-electric vehicle. I've done some crude calculations on this showing that if I add one electric vehicle, I can add more PV or wind than that electric vehicle uses in terms of energy. So I have a growth scenario.

Now, getting back to your fundamental question. I watch the news on CNN and there's a great deal of advertising that the hydrocarbon people are doing, as they try to convince me that what's underground is good for the economy—that oil, natural gas, and coal are good things for us. I do not see anything approaching that level of advertising from the renewables. They don't have the money.

I suspect that what is being done here is not just advertising, it's advertising with a little different bent than usual advertising. I believe the energy companies are not worried about selling more of our product; that's not why we're advertising. What we're going to do is to addict the user, the network, or whatever – to our money. Every month the check comes in. But if CNN wants to run a program that is counter to the sponsor's interests—and there's no law against this—we tell them we can't be a sponsor for a program that is going to hurt our interests. If you do that, we're going to have to withdraw our funding. Now, if that came to the public eye, it's no problem. People would say, "Well of course. Who says that ExxonMobil has to fund something that is counter to their interest?" However, the effect is the same as paying CNN to not run that particular thing.

CS: Absolutely. I agree with you, even though every time I write something like this, I get my head handed to me.

WR: In 1968, I drove an electric car across the country and in 1969 a group in Pasadena set up a thing they called the Autobiography of Pasadena. It was a bunch of old cars that were in a parade and I was asked to be the grand marshal, because of the electric car race which had been won by Caltech just months earlier, and I accepted. While I was here in California, I had been a grad student for awhile. I visited Dr. Lee DuBridge whom I knew a little bit, the president of Caltech. We had good conversations, but one of the things I noticed was the fact that he always referred to the electric car race under my name. Everyone else called it the Great Electric Car Race—Caltech and MIT; the names were always prominent. He never did that; he always used my name.

CS: The Wally Rippel car races? It was Wally Rippel versus the world?

WR: That's right. Wally Rippel versus MIT. So I said, "In a way I'm flattered, but why do you do this? And he paused and he said, "As president of Caltech, my number one responsibility is funds coming into Caltech." And then he looked at me and he said, "You understand the rest." End of conversation.

CS: But at one point, didn't you say specifically that Union Oil had aggressively threatened to cut its funding to Caltech if certain steps weren't taken?

WR: Yes. Fred Hartley was then on the board of directors at Caltech who was also, I guess, CEO of Union Oil. It was explained that all of this was a problem for Caltech. The vice provost who had been provost at Caltech 12 or 15 years ago, very capable physicist, left Caltech to work for British Petroleum. And then he left British Petroleum to become the head of the Department of Energy Science. This was the person who convinced the world that cold fusion was junk science. He directly stated that Fleishman and Pons were fraudulent—and he had the credibility to make that statement. I've been very troubled by that, because just seeing the scientific data, it doesn't correspond to that. I see a reality there.

I felt a great deal of unfairness was done. I did not see a professionalism. I spoke to some of the Caltech faculty who were part of the debunking process and I did not feel it was a professional response; there was something else involved.

More recently, I was able to do this: I offered to make a significant donation to Caltech for their doing research in the cold fusion area even if that research would continue to debunk it. The offer was over $100,000.

CS: Generous.

WR: Yeah, I'm lucky that I could do that. And the development association of Caltech went to the physics department—I wanted it to be through the physics department—and the physics department said, "We will not do this. We will never do it. It will not be done here at Caltech." And the development person said, "Well, do you believe cold fusion to be fraudulent? Invalid?" And the person said, "That is not the issue. The issue is: the fact that we debunked it means we can't go back and revisit it. It will not be done here."

I asked, "But what about if this is scientifically valid?" The person said, "It doesn't matter. We will not do it. Period."

CS: That's interesting, that's sad. But you seldom have an umpire reverse his call at a baseball game even though he goes, "I can't believe I just did that."

WR: But in science this has to happen.

CS: That's true. That's not a great analogy is it?

WR: No. When I started at Caltech in 1963, just for the heck of it I asked some of my professors whether they believed the general theory of relativity to be true. About half of them did; half of them said it was probably not true. When I graduated it had changed. Almost everyone had accepted it then, but we're reminded that Albert Einstein got the Nobel Prize not for the theory of relativity, but for something relatively minor—the photoelectric effect.

CS: In 1924 if I'm not mistaken.

WR: Right. There are surprises that happen in science. As a matter of fact, the best things that occur in science are, of course, surprises. The things happening that are what you simply thought were going to happen anyway are very dull.

In 1900, people said the idea of a flying machine is going to take 1,000 years to develop. It's very complex because they had already made these complex things with flapping wings and they didn't work. There was the common belief that if it's that complex and *doesn't* work, it's going to have to be very much *more* complex—and most people didn't realize that the idea of an airplane was actually very simple.

CS: With a fixed wing, in other words.

WR: Yes. Even the Wright brothers had it more complicated than it needed to be with the Wright Flyer. The key to the airplane was just understanding the lift surface.

CS: The Bernoulli principle.

WR: Exactly. Once you understood that any object has lift and drag, you can optimize it. Then going a step further and control the surface; you can create forces that will control roll and yawl and so on. And you can even apply these principles to the propeller to make a good propeller; all of them were bad propellers that people had beforehand. You realize: Wow, this is not so hard.

CS: All right. Well, this brings up a point I wanted to ask you. What a coincidence this was. On the way out to see you today, I had my weekly call with (EVWorld editor) Bill Moore. Guess whom Bill interviewed earlier today. Rossi.

WR: Oh, wow! Well, this is quite a topic here, because I'm involved now in it. Does Rossi speak English?

CS: I believe so; I didn't hear the interview, but Bill didn't mention an interpreter. Rossi moved from Italy; he lives in Miami.

I'll tell you, when I heard this I almost had to pull the car over. I was so shocked, I wanted to know: What's the essence of it? What does it say? He goes, "Well, he's got these things that use nickel."

WR: The reaction is nickel which is 28 protons in the nucleus. One proton is added which is the hydrogen, and that becomes copper. And the energy release is about five or five and a half MeV. You're familiar with...

CS: Million electron volts, yeah.

WR: A chemical reaction is on the order of two eV, and that's a high-energy chemical reaction. So you're talking about millions of times the energy. These experiments—assuming they're not cheating—prove that it *has* to be nuclear. You can't account for that energy otherwise. The Rossi experiments are a decedent of things done by others, Focardi in particular.

There's been a lot of information given in Europe. It's been blacked out here in this country; there is no talk at all about it.

The Focardi experiment is very simple. You start out with nickel rods that are in a chamber. The air is all removed, and hydrogen is put in—a little less than an atmosphere of hydrogen, and you raise the temperature to about 500 or 600 degrees C. Then you need to trigger the reaction and he's done that in different ways. Focardi has done it by fluctuations in the hydrogen pressure and so on, and you trigger a reaction in which four nickel rods that are the size of a drinking straw produce on the order of 20 or 30 watts of excess heat over a period of months.

CS: 20 watts of excess heat? Well does that square with... you have $E=MC^2$; C^2 is a big number.

WR: Well, this is using a tiny amount of the nickel and a tiny amount of the hydrogen in it, but the reaction rate is obviously limited by the fundamentals of the cold fusion process, is which is not understood.

CS: But essentially there's enough ambient kinetic energy in the heat; in other words molecular motion, to cause an occasional absorption of the proton, right?

WR: Well, the hydrogen is absorbed by the nickel just like platinum absorbs hydrogen. Nickel not quite as efficiently, but hydrogen is taken into the lattice spaces.

CS: Which produces an enormous amount of energy, that's where you get your 5 MeV.

WR: Yes, there's a nuclear reaction that's a proton absorption reaction where the nickel nucleus gains a proton, the number of neutrons remains the same, and that corresponds when you add one proton to a nickel nucleus you have copper.

CS: Right. So it's an isotope of copper.

WR: It is a common isotope.

CS: Okay. But my point is, even if that happens occasionally, you would think it would produce more than 20 watts.

WR: In order for the full amount of hydrogen and nickel to be consumed, that reaction would have to run for several hundred years. The rate at which it's operating… it's perking along at a low level.

CS: Well I mean, I'm not trying to say that this isn't exciting. I'm just surprised that it's only 20 watts considering it's a nuclear reaction, which you think of as being quite large.

WR: Remember, the stuff that Fleishman and Pons did was on the order of ten watts. Now, Rossi comes in and he claims to have a catalyst and he's working with a powder where there are much higher surface areas, and he is achieving kilowatts of excess heat—more than ten kilowatts in some cases. And the thing with his experiment is that his catalyst is secret. He's not going to tell anyone.

CS: Until October.

WR: Yes. In October he is selling a million watts worth of reactors to an entity in Greece.

CS: Right. So you were saying that there is some reason for suspicion here considering that either he or one of his collaborators was indicted on fraud charges.

WR: Well, the first thing is—and I want to be very clear on this—I believe in the reality of cold fusion. If anybody doing any experiment with cold fusion is claiming to have positive results, I'm open to it, but I will put the bar very high and it should be.

And I said repeatedly that the bar should be high, but don't throw the bar away. If a doctor came to you and said he's able to reduce a certain type of skin rash. And you say okay, that's one thing. If the doctor says, "Oh, and by the way I forgot to tell you that I can take people who are dead and bring them back to life." Well, the bar is going to be a lot higher for that second claim.

CS: Yes. And I would suggest raising the bar for the first claim now that he's made the second claim.

WR: [chuckle] Yep, I'll go back and look at that too; good point. With Rossi, he had supposedly, in an earlier venture, I don't know what device it was—some type of thermocouple or thermionic device. He claimed to have achieved a much higher figure of merit than anyone else could, and based on that he entered into a business venture which was profitable. After the fact, it was shown that what he had was nothing better than what the prevailing technology was. I know none of the details.

Rossi got his start mainly from Focardi. Focardi is a physicist and he's published, and I've read the papers, and he's a little bit incomplete and a little bit sloppy I think, but he's definitely not a fraud and the stuff that he's doing, from everything I can see, is 99% likely real. So my guess is that Rossi thought that this was an interesting opportunity, because most people don't believe this, so I'll start it with this. My guess is that in some way he is able to exaggerate the results. Now, it's possible that he discovered something, but my guess is probably not.

And my guess—and I'm just guessing here—is that if you stripped away all the stuff that Rossi has, what you'd find is that he's not really doing anything better than other people could do. I'm guessing that because people usually sign their name twice with the same signature.

CS: Well said. Good analogy. The more obvious thing that makes this interesting is that if any version of this is true, this will eventually crack the code. We won't have an energy issue very long if we can figure out how to take advantage of low energy nuclear reactions.

WR: The important thing to think of is if this is true, what are the implications? The United States has been in denial about this—not so much in Italy. The attitudes there are quite different, in Europe in general. So I can see the United States being the odd man out.

CS: I'm reminded that somebody told me recently: Think of the infrastructure that's invested in fossil fuels. Do you expect these people to write down trillions of dollars of losses, just because someone comes along and says we want clean energy?

WR: That's right. Well, that's why I wonder about someone like Steve Koonin who left Caltech to work for British Petroleum and then he left British Petroleum to head up the Department of Energy. He was the one who made the statement about Fleishman and Pons being fraudulent, and at the Department of Energy he has refused to look at anything that has any connection whatsoever with cold fusion. As you know, I wrote Steven Chu, the head of DoE a letter, and I took a very non-committal attitude. I wrote, "I read papers and it seems that there's something here. Yet, most mainstream science and especially DoE says that this is not real. Where do you stand? And do you plan to look at this again?"

After the second similar letter, I got a reply back from one of the people in the nuclear area that was very interesting. I'll give you a copy of that if you want, but the letter basically said that in 1989 they looked at it, and then some years later they looked at it again, and both times they concluded that cold fusion would not be a significant source of energy in the near-term. Well, I knew that was not what happened in 1989. In 1989, the conclusion they had was that it didn't exist. It was either fraudulent or that it's just a gross error.

So they changed. They changed what their reason was, pretending that they hadn't changed—and that is always a red flag that something is wrong. So I think there's a possibility that really you have to look at the details—and it's hard to get these details. Is the Department of Energy part of a conspiracy? Clearly, you can see that the scientists have a vested interest, because they were working on high temperature fusion and at the peak there was a lot of money being spent. Since 1950 there has been over $30 billion spent on conventional high-temperature fusion. For many scientists, this was their lives, and it was how they paid their mortgages. So something like cold fusion would be, for anyone in that position, a legitimate problem, because something comes along and it may change everything, and you may be on the outside rather than the inside when it comes to the next round of funding.

Also, there's just a personal thing. I have a belief system, and even though I'm a scientist, yes, there are things that I believe. If someone comes along with something that seems to threaten that belief system, I'm threatened personally; and so there's that element. You saw the physicists responding in an almost adolescent fashion in 1989 with a meeting in Baltimore, where they cheered when Nate Lewis spoke with his results. It was like a Super Bowl thing.

CS: How strange. I don't know how I would have reacted to seeing that. I guess I would have been a bit shocked to see scientists acting like school kids.

WR: I understand a little bit of it because most of the things in the category of cold fusion—and there's a lot of these cuckoo ideas that come up—people do not understand physics 101. Here is something that, yes, it seemed to be a level above that because this was done by a Ph.D.— and a well-respected Ph.D., Martin Fleishman—but he wasn't a physicist. So there was a little bit of that element. This is an outsider and he doesn't understand nuclear physics; he understands chemistry, not physics. And how dare he meddle in something outside of his area, which we understand. What he's saying is we're all wrong, or at least he's implying that we've missed something and he's found it.

So I can see there being that emotional reaction and I think the reaction in 1989 can definitely be excused, but what didn't make sense is if you look over these intervening years, you have these conferences; you have a lot of positive results. The issues of repeatability get dealt with pretty well; you have much higher repeatability. You've got a wide variety of people doing things in different countries. And for the Department of Energy to continue with their approach that this doesn't make sense; the U.S. Patent Office will not patent anything connected with cold fusion. The major publications, especially in physics, e.g., *Physics Review,* will not publish anything. As I say, raising the bar is okay, but throwing the bar away doesn't make sense.

CS: Right, yep. Now, aren't you working on this yourself in some way?

WR: Yes, let me tell you what I'm doing extracurricularly. I'm working with referring corporations as a matter of fact to repeat some of the Focardi experiments that were done ten years ago, which is just what I told you about with the nickel rods in the hydrogen atmosphere. I have access to some things that probably Focardi didn't. Nickel is a ferromagnetic material and it has a relative permeability of about 600. It's in a class similar to iron.

That means it's 600 times that of a vacuum; magnetism flows through nickel 600 times easier than it does through empty space or air or a non-ferromagnetic material like copper or aluminum. When you put current through a wire, like a copper wire, if it's decent current then the current flows uniformly through it; the current density is uniform. If the current is alternating, the current does not flow uniformly. As the frequency goes up the current tends to crowd toward the surface. It's called the "skin effect." The skin effect is a function of frequency of the electric current. It's a function of the magnetic permeability, and also the resistivity. With nickel, the fact that it has the 600 relative permeability means that the skin depth is about a 25th that of what it would be if it were copper. In other words, the currents tend to flow on the surface to a large extent. So what I can do, and I have the equipment for doing this, I can put a large AC current through a nickel rod as a burst—a short time—where the outer 50 microns is heated a couple hundred degrees centigrade above the rest of the nickel rod, and there's a very large inward heat flux. Theoretically, it should be a much better trigger for the reaction than what the Italians have done, and the actual energy input is extremely small because it's a very short duration and theoretically it should have results. That's what I'm working on and we'll see.

Oh, and by the way, the other thing we're getting is we've got a good enough thermal insulation that we should be self-sustaining. The originals for Focardi were when the fusion reaction took place they had to heat it to get it to the 500 degrees C or whatever. When the fusion reaction took place, they could substantially reduce the electrical energy. What we're doing, and this is important, the insulation is good enough that it will be totally self-supporting. We would have stabilized the temperature by controlling the thermal heat transfer.

CS: I would think that this would be the end of the game for the skeptics. In other words, there's no energy *at all* coming into this.

WR: That's right. It's not a matter of the difference of two numbers. It's something coming out and nothing going in. Math is simpler.

And the other thing that I'm planning on doing is to be absolutely open. If I get positive results, I'm going to share every detail. My feeling is that the things that I contributed I can protect with a provisional patent. My guess, though, is that the real valuable ideas are going to come ahead, and the important thing is to keep things moving and definitely not make the mistakes that Fleishman and Pons got sucked into where there was cloak and dagger, and a lot of secrecy, which backfired.

CS: Yes. And publishing it to some tabloid, right? Didn't they go directly to the media instead of to the scientific community for peer review?

WR: Well, the problem—and that problem remains—is that there are a lot of publications that say if you're dealing with anything that's related to cold fusion we're not going to publish it. So that is an issue, and that's one of the things I want to see overcome.

CS: Well, I just find the whole refusal to publish thing so unsupportable as an aspiring philosopher/scientist of my own meager capacity. I just find the whole thing completely gross.

WR: Here's the interesting thing about energy. A hundred years from now people will say, looking back, it was simple. Where is the energy? The energy is in the nuclear world, not in the chemical world. The money is in the bank, it's not under the mattress. So why did we not like nuclear energy? Well, we thought nuclear energy was synonymous with radiation. We don't like radiation. We're willing to pay a price to avoid radiation.

The assumption that nuclear reactions must produce dangerous radiation is invalid, and it's similar to an assumption I heard made in the '60s. People were talking about smog. It's interesting because this is where the oil companies probably should have pointed this out. People said if you burn any fuel, you will create smog. Wherever there's fire, there's smoke. Well, not so. Wherever there's incomplete combustion there's smoke. Wherever you burn things you'll get water vapor and CO_2, if you start out with a hydrocarbon based fuel of course. The assumption that smog was inherent in the burning of gasoline was false and that's true in the nuclear world as well. If you do the reaction of uranium 235 yesterday you'll get stuff you don't like, but there's lots more to nuclear than 235.

CS: Speaking of that, one of these things produces neutrons coming out your ears, right?

WR: The cold fusion reactions do produce neutrons, but four to six orders of magnitude below the stoichiometric, i.e., one neutron per reaction. The conclusion is that there's several likely chemical reactions; there's a main reaction that's aneutronic, i.e., that does not produce neutrons. There are some side reactions that *do* produce neutrons.

CS: What are those reactions? Because you would think that if you simply have a proton that's changing nickel to copper, there's no neutron in the normal hydrogen isotope.

WR: In the reaction that the Italians have been working with, I do not know what the neutron flux is. There's talk that there is a neutron flux and I don't know what the reactions are, but what people do see that's consistent with this, is they see transmutation taking place. They start out with the material, whether it's the Focardi type of experiments with nickel and hydrogen or the Fleishman Pons with deuterium. And you see a primary reaction in the case of deuterium reactions; you see HE4 being produced, but you also see a host of things. When you do a spectrographic analysis and mass spectrometry, you see these other nuclei being produced ...

CS: You see HE3 plus a neutron.

WR: Yes. There are a lot of things. It's complicated. So that in itself is proof that something nuclear is happening. You don't get new nuclei out of a chemical reaction.

This is going to be exciting, I feel. As I said, even if you knew that it would not be a significant source of energy ever, you'd *still* want to do the science because the science is exciting. To predict a negative, to say that something of great significance in science will not have significance in energy—that would be absurd.

I discovered an interesting thing. When I was a grad student I switched from physics into electrical engineering and I noticed that people were teaching controls and I was interested in the power side of electronics which, of course, is what I've worked in all my life. And I assumed that the control area would be important for things like communications, cell phones, and computers and all that.

But somehow I thought initially that we're missing the boat in terms of energy. Well, it turns out digital controls are important for everything; they enable us to do things with power electronics that we could never have done had we not had these control chips and the theory that goes with it. The point being that it's hard sometimes to appreciate the consequences of things until they happen. We tend to underestimate what can happen.

CS: Let me ask you this, do you know who Martin Perl is? The guy who discovered the tau lepton? He's at the Stanford Linear Accelerator.

WR: The name is familiar. Yes.

CS: In 1971 he won the Nobel Prize in physics, and I interviewed him last year for a different project. That was a fascinating way of spending 90 minutes, I can assure you of that. But it was frustrating as well because I kept saying, "Look, is there some application of what you have done or what you're doing in the area of clean energy?" And he responded, "No, it's got wonderful implications outside of theoretical physics especially in terms of medicine." And he went into a few minutes on that. And I 'went back for seconds.' "Wait a second, Doc. Are you telling me that there's *nothing* that you're doing here…."

WR: Well, nothing he could think of. But this reminds me of the great mathematician, Matrix, who was disgusted with the fact that people were always doing math because of its application to physics and the sciences. He wanted to do math that was just math for math's sake, and he developed what is known as matrix theory which of course is tremendously valuable.

CS: The guy's name was Matrix? Matrix is named after a human being? I had no idea. That's funny. Go on.

WR: So the things that you see and the things that you think are surely theoretical. They have tremendous applications. When Sputnik was launched, what were we thinking about? We were thinking about bombs. If they can launch this, they can launch a bomb against us. What else were we thinking about? Maybe spy satellites; we would think about that. I wasn't thinking about hurricane observation. I wasn't thinking about being able to have a navigational system so that I drive places and know where I was or that airplanes could go places more easily, but those are the implications.

CS: Well, the whole history of science that's the one underlying current is that the ultimate applications are almost never what they thought they were going to be.

WR: Exactly. The invention of the diesel engine; Rudolph Diesel envisioned that the diesel engine would be used in people's homes where they had shops so that they could do woodworking and things like that. It's just now a vision of what it became.

But let's go back; I'm not sure I've fully answered your question about the impediments.

I want to follow-up on a thought that I had started on earlier. I think the biggest issue in all of this is education. People are ignorant about a lot of science fields, but in some ways I feel we're most ignorant concerning energy. As an example, just the other night I was watching one of these ads trying to promote fracking as being a great thing. They said this is an energy resource that exists right here in the United States and if we utilize this we can become free of foreign oil. Well, the implication was that somehow you go from natural gas to powering vehicles and that's possible, but it's not automatic. It could be via natural gas vehicles and it could also be via electric vehicles where the electricity is generated by natural gas.

CS: And gas to liquids, and so forth.

WR: Yes. All these things need to be understood to some extent before statements can be viewed as true or false. One of the things that is so interesting is that most people think that electricity comes from oil and that was the implication, by the way, in this. We import large amounts of oil to generate electricity. That's what a lot of people think and that's what the oil companies want you to think because then, first of all, electricity vehicles don't make sense. You're just running the oil in a different place. Moving it from the vehicle to the power plant. So that's one of the areas where I've found great ignorance. The other area where I found ignorance is I ask, so if all vehicles were electric—all cars and trucks and so on—how much would we have to increase our electricity generation? People think, oh, it would be tremendous. Well, what do you mean by tremendous? Ten times bigger. And when you tell them that it would increase by 14 percent they find that hard to believe. So this is another important thing because admittedly we have to solve problems with electric utilities, but if we solve those and have clean electricity then you don't have to increase it very much to have clean transportation. So that's an important one, and again, I think there are a lot of interests that want to make sure that we don't know certain things.

CS: Right. Well, it's easier every day because most of the people don't have the education they used to. If they had shown that commercial to Americans 35 years ago a lot of people would have said: *Bull Crap!*

WR: Yeah, exactly. So one of the impediments to all of this is education and knowledge, and the ability to do critical thinking. And it doesn't mean that everyone has to agree, but at least we need to be discussing this on a more rational level than we are, rather than just what is the latest hype we saw on TV.

CS: Yes. Well, I was one of a lot of people who predicted a great onslaught of PR from the fossil fuels industries (plural) simply because, not only is there the issue that you made before (i.e., addiction), but it's also guarding against what is the obvious backlash from people. Oil companies expect a backlash from people who realize: wait a second, our kids are dying overseas protecting the channels for getting our product into the United States. At a certain point, they're going to get sick of this.

WR: Yeah. It's troubling to me, and they know what they're doing. The ads make sense psychologically and everything. They're done well.

CS: Oh, I'm *sure* they're done well. The whole world since the Second World War has gotten real good at manipulating our thinking.

WR: Another element in all of this is in addition to education there is the issue of just general motivation. If you hear about a challenge, do you feel that this is something you wish would go away, or do you feel motivated to stand up to it? All of us have both responses. When we were attacked at Pearl Harbor I'm sure we didn't jump up and down and say great now we're going to solve our economic problems. It came at a price dealing with all of that. I believe that to gain true energy freedom is going to be more of a challenge than World War II. I think that's a wonderful thing; I think that's tailor-made. If you had to write a story for the greatest chapter of America's history, that's what it would be. Here you have the confluence of things. You've got global warming. You've got the economic things, unemployment; all these things, and lousy education—not because kids are dumb. They're no dumber than they've ever been, but they're not motivated. And why would they be motivated? Now you put all of this together and it makes sense.

I discovered this personally. I was on tour for *Who Killed the Electric Car* and I went to Denver where I was there alone; (filmmaker) Chris Payne was not there and so I tried to answer the questions about the filmmaking as well as the technology. I gave a little talk first and I thought, you know? I'm going to try something. I know these people are a little bit left of center so I'm going to give a talk right of center and see what happens. It can't be that bad. They're not going to throw anything at me. So I talked about using this technology to build up the economy to help us become more competitive. I spoke about the environmental issues, but I placed them a little bit as a spin-off from the central purpose. I got a standing ovation.

I thought, wait a minute. These people didn't come to hear me talk like a Republican. They came here to hear me talk about how bad General Motors was, and now I'm talking about how this can be the future of General Motors, and they liked it. I thought wow. If politicians would discover what I've discovered then we'd be able to do something.

So I think that someone will discover that at some point. That's usually what works politically. You find a way to pull the two sides together. Right now it's just the opposite. Everything is being repulsed. It's far away from center.

CS: Well, that's what scares me. The way people get elected—and certainly the way they behave when they're elected—is to move immediately to one side or the other. And so we've lost the rationality of the middle ground; no one seems to understand that we can't just stop using oil this afternoon, and we can't use it forever.

WR: Well, I think one of the key messages to make progress is to dispel the myth that the choices we have are either clean or economic, and to realize this can all be on the same side of the fence. We can make a lot of money doing what's right. It's hard, and that's a challenge; it's not automatic. Bad technology is never going to work whether it's clean or dirty. So it's a matter of getting smart enough so you make these technologies into the centerpiece of your economy.

I think that's how the winning strategy will be posed, rather than what the hydrocarbon interests are doing. They're saying, "We're the ones powering the economy, and they're the ones that are holding it back."

CS: Right. And it almost worked. (California's referendum) Prop 23 got 47 percent of the popular vote. It came within two millimeters of working.

WR: Yep. So this is of course one of the reasons why I'm so intrigued with cold fusion. If you're asked what you have to envision to get one cent per kilowatt-hour, now you can argue whether you want it or not, but just looking at that from a technical point you probably aren't going to get there with any of our known technology. With fusion energy I think that's going to be a reality: one cent per kilowatt-hour.

Think what the implications are. Get to the point where you're using a lot more energy. We can live with that if the energy is so very clean and abundant then it makes sense to do that.

CS: I need to get you back to the office. Anything to say in summarizing where cold fusion needs to go?

WR: I think the best way of dealing with the skepticism is just to bend over backwards, acknowledge that the bar is high, and to publish papers with such detail and repeatability that people almost become bored with that. I think we get past it.

CS: This is the part that I don't really get about this thing. I would think that if there's any repeatability at all, then it's at least trustworthy.

WR: You're right. I know what you're saying. If you went to a place and a person claims to have an airplane, but it crashes a lot, are you going to say that airplanes don't work? I would say they're not good transportation vehicles, but powered flight is a real thing.

CS: That's my point. All right. good stuff. Oh, I hope I haven't kept you late.

WR: No, it's okay.

CS: Okay. Let's go. Thank you.

Craig's Interview with Ray Lane

I've had the pleasure of bumping into Ray Lane at numerous industry conferences, and have been lucky enough to hear him speak on subjects that include the financing of renewables and electric transportation. I was thrilled when he accepted my invitation for an interview, as I knew it would add a much-needed perspective of the real-world, no-nonsense exigencies of big money. After all, we can *talk* about the theory of money—but we can also look at the way in which billions of dollars actually change hands.

Ray currently serves as Managing Partner at venture capital giant Kleiner Perkins Caufield & Byers, focused on helping entrepreneurs with technological and market insight, organizational development, team building, selling and managing growth. Since joining KPCB, Ray has sponsored several investments for the firm in clean and alternative energy, including Ausra (concentrated solar power), Fisker Automotive (plug-in hybrid car), and Th!nk NA (battery-electric car).

Ray also serves as Non-Executive Chairman of the Board of Hewlett-Packard – a company I've had the pleasure of serving as a consultant on a dozen-or-so occasions in the 1990s.

CS: Wow, this place is a beehive! I got here a bit early, and I was sitting outside in the lobby with dozens of nervous entrepreneurs. Outside of the Kleiner people, I may be the only calm person in the building.

And thanks for the opportunity to speak with you; I've been looking forward to this.

That book you're holding is what I did in 2010, and the reason I'm here is because now it's 2011, and time for another one.

RL: You're only as good as your last... yeah.

CS: Exactly. So that was a compilation of interviews with 25 subject matter experts on the breadth of the technology, the economics, and the politics of renewables. Now I want to drill down into the economics, because what I learned from doing the last project is that there are eight or ten really good ways we can kick this thing technologically. But finding the political will and the economic horsepower behind it is another issue.

When we met at the Detroit Auto Show late last year, I told you that I respected you for what you said on stage close to the end of the presentations ... after the platitudes of the governor of Michigan and some people from Ford and Toyota, and you said in so many words: "It's time to stop kidding ourselves, telling each other that we're doing a good job in clean energy and electric transportation, because it's clear we're not."

RL: Thank you very much.

CS: So do you mind elaborating on that a bit? In other words, you said we did a good job with the Internet and that's wonderful. And communications, networking, and IT—and for the last few decades we've done a good job in leading the world. Now we need to step up to the challenge and for whatever reason we're failing at this. Can you just elaborate on that?

RL: Sure. I think the comparisons to the Internet are full of errors. I don't think that energy works the same way as software—or more broadly—digital business. Computer technology, software, internet, social networking—that whole kind of value chain is a unique business compared to almost any other industry. In fact, I can't think of another industry that works the same way. In software, you can take a few months to develop a product, distribute that product, and get people to actually come and use it for free or a small fee, and you don't have to do much heavy lifting to get value from it. And then it becomes kind of a circle; it becomes a viral network that continues building. Now a lot of companies obviously fail in that environment, but many succeed—and so you have low capital expended. So even if you look at Google, Amazon, Ebay, some really highly valuable companies today and look at how much capital it took to build those companies, it was relatively small. Not even *relatively* small; it was actually *very* small compared to anything in any other industry. So when you look at building something in new energy, or building something in... you pick the industry... you've got to pay attention to the amount of capital that goes into it and the physical infrastructure you build. The plants and factories that have to produce the products—it's just a lot different. Now, there are a few exceptions in the industrial business, like semiconductors. But even with semiconductors, you may have to get to building a fab; it's a billion-dollar or a two-billion-dollar kind of a thing. But generally, in our digital practice here, we'll invest a few million dollars in companies and see if they get traction and know if they're going to be successful before you invest five or ten.

CS: I'm with you. And you're saying that this paradigm doesn't translate to the green space.

RL: Right, it doesn't translate at all in the green market. There may be a very few, but if the rule of thumb is 80 percent of the cases in digital, it may be five percent of the cases in new energy.

So that's one issue in trying to draw that comparison. Now, back to your original question. I think the failure is that we don't yet have a national agenda. We have not taken this on as a priority one issue.

CS: In the public sector.

RL: Even the private sector. But yes, it needs the public sector to make it a national issue. And why does it need to be? It gets very confusing and complex when we say we're doing this because we want to save the planet, i.e., that it's a carbon emissions agenda. Of course then you have another agenda which is oil and our dependence on foreign oil and a national security issue. And then you have other kinds of issues like the economics of technology replacement. We haven't pulled this all together to say the reason this is important is that it is a new era of industrial growth that will create jobs in the future. We haven't done that yet.

CS: But let me just make sure I understand. That is purely, it seems to me, a public sector thought process.

RL: I disagree. For instance, why do GE or Wal-Mart or various other companies have such an agenda about being green? Do you think it's just because they are good citizens?

CS: No, that's my point. But they're not into building a national agenda, or creating jobs either. As a matter of fact, most of the jobs they're building aren't in the United States. But my point is if your motive is profit; if you can do the same thing without creating jobs – in the U.S. or anywhere, so much the better.

RL: I totally agree; I misspoke. They're not going to be altruistic about making U.S. jobs. The government can certainly help that; the government can say we'll give you incentives to put those jobs here.

China is a major factor. It's not so much an economic decision. It's not because of low labor rates. It's because they find an environment where they can do something quickly. I'll give you an example. Steve Jobs builds iPads in China. And when he was asked why he didn't build them in America, everyone thought he would say it's because the labor rates are so cheap over there. He said, "In fact, the labor rates are about the same. Maybe a little bit less, but it's not enough to make my decision to build them there. What makes the decision is that I wanted to get four million iPads out the door quickly and in China when they start building a factory or a building, they're moving in and manufacturing iPads on the first floor while their building the second floor. Permitting took three months. Here, you try to do that in California and it would be three years just to get a permit."

When the President used this Sputnik moment thing, it's nice rhetoric, but we don't feel that impending doom yet. I don't think it will be the planet getting warmer; that's just too far away to produce impending doom on a public agenda.

CS: Right. We have plenty of impending doom on our doorstep this afternoon.

RL: Yes. Oil dependency could work. With oil about to go over $100 a barrel again; if it can sustain that, if it could really stay above $100 a barrel and we get over $4 at the pump, then I think you start getting a little bit of urgency. But to me the urgency will become much clearer when we see China's economy, and you see the contribution that the alternative energy industry is supporting in China. So I think that's the failure. We just haven't developed the national agenda. When we put our minds to something, there are lots of examples; building an atom bomb or the national highway system.

The gas pipeline system is the best in the world. It wasn't done with government help; that was a private equity venture and it enables very, very low cost gas in this country – it's about a third of the price of any other country, because the cost of gas is all transportation. It's not the gas itself; it's the transportation of the gas that drives the cost. So we need to get a national agenda. We need leadership from the president right now. If it's a new president in two years— whoever the president is, he needs to have a national agenda to convince the public this is not just about a warming planet. It is critical to our growth. We have to have our own energy for growing the economy. It's an economic issue, not a global warming issue.

CS: I'm with you. Let me tell you why in a sentence or two why I think we don't have that and then I wonder if you can just simply react to that. First of all, we have elected officials whose jobs come up for renewal every two years. Even if you do impute moral goodness to those people, I'm not sure it's realistic to expect them to take actions that are essentially career suicide. In other words, a politician's making a decision whose benefits are not going to be felt in that election cycle is simply not going to happen.

On the other side of the coin, we subsidize fossil fuels several times the degree we subsidize renewable fuels. Everybody talks about the subsidies for wind and PV and so forth.

So the reason we have artificially inexpensive oil is simply because it's coming out of yours and my pocket.

Do you agree with what I said? And if so, how do we get there from here?

RL: No. I don't agree with the first premise because I think the assumption is that it would be political suicide to get behind an alternative energy agenda. So it can be couched in terms of our future economic success—that we cannot grow without clean energy and clean energy will lead to jobs and profits. There is a way to position this— and national security doesn't sound like we're simply hurting our economy to save the planet. And there are people who don't believe those 1,000 scientists that say the globe is warming because I got ten feet of snow today. Okay?

CS: Exactly.

RL: It's just a low IQ. We believe what we see on TV. So I think there is a way that you can put the story together so that people can generally agree—and it obviously has to be bipartisan. But it will never ever fly on an environmental agenda; it must be an economic agenda.

Your second thing on subsidies is absolutely right. We have to change the system. Obama has recommended not providing the tax breaks to big corporate oil and the Republicans are fighting it. I don't get it. I'm a Republican. I'm the only one in the building. Okay? I can't defend corporate tax breaks for big oil. I just can't. I don't get that.

CS: Right. And that's only one of about a dozen or 15 types of subsidies.

RL: Exactly. Maybe if you go back 50 years it made sense. It doesn't make sense anymore. The government needs to be helping new industries, not old industries. This gets into a much broader issue of the U.S. position in the world. We are a fat and happy society. Yes, we talk a lot about our problems and our jobs and everything, but today we have an entitled society that doesn't want to give up those entitlements. So whatever we have, we're not going to give it up. We don't like the house prices going down; we don't like our corporate tax breaks to go away. We want more, and we say that it's all about me.

That's the first step to decline. Maybe 10 years ago, you might have described the U.S. position in the world as the most powerful country in the world – and the most admired country in the world. You would have said that we have a political system that seems to have stood the test of time: Jeffersonian democracy. And generally, you would say that we're good—helping the world. Today, I don't think anybody is afraid of us; I really don't think we have the fear factor going anymore. After coming out of World War II everybody was scared as hell by us. Now no one fears us. We have the wrong political system to move society fast; we're in gridlock. I'm not saying we have to throw away our democratic system, but we cannot keep up with China. China, if they develop a national agenda they just simply implement it.

It is pretty predictable right now that China will be the largest economy in the world in about ten years—maybe 12. I tend to think faster rather than slower. So I think it's a decade—maybe a little longer—that China becomes a bigger economy than we are. Okay, so how do we feel being Germany – a nation state that doesn't have the influence in the world? We may not have the currency that's a standard in the world. That's where we're headed unless something changes. So it's a bigger agenda, but we have to wrap our heads around this impending problem and get all the wood behind one arrow and say this is really, really important to the country. Energy is growth. You cannot grow without energy.

And China can do it by burning coal. We need to decide if we're going to continue to burn coal. I do believe that the kind of new energy environment we have in the next ten years should include clean coal, nuclear, and gas. I don't think we go from burning fossil fuels to none overnight. It can't be done. So it's a thirty-year transition and maybe it never goes away fully, but I think if we could get the world into 50 percent clean energy and 50 percent fossil fuels and the coal is using technology to clean it up, gas is already fairly clean, that we would be so much better off and we can get our cake and eat it too.

But we can't. We have probably 30 states—60 senators that come from coal states. And they say no... not only no, but *hell no*. If you want to use coal to turn into diesel oil, that's OK with them, but it's a *terrible* decision. We need a clear, simple path forward to say we are going to do this by a certain date. And everybody gets behind it. Congress gets behind it—rather than these short term partisan agendas that just tear us apart.

CS: That's exactly right.

RL: And we'll wake up some day; I think it's going to be no longer than five years from now and say, "Oh my God. China. We can't catch them." They will be producing products that they sell to us. We thought it was going to be the other way. Five years ago the rhetoric is we'll do the innovation and we'll sell clean energy products to China. It's going to be the other way around.

CS: I'm afraid you're exactly right. Okay. Well, we'll come back to this energy thing, but let me ask you if I may—and this is a delicate question; kind of a philosophic question I guess. Venture capital is obviously about profits. You're here to make money for your LPs (limited partners). I would suggest though, having been a marketing consultant for 30 years and worked for a lot of venture-capitalized startups, that it's a damn good thing that you folks make money because without that, there would be a lot of ideas that never got off the drawing board. So in other words, can you speak if you would to the kind of philosophy... why do you feel good about your job?

RL: Well a Kleiner Perkins' answer and my answer would be a little different. At Kleiner Perkins we have a philosophy of building big companies. We like big, disruptive ideas. That's very different in the industry. There are 900 venture capital firms; there should be 300; there are way too many. They were all created during the '90s when it was easy to kind of invest in Internet technology and make a lot of money very quickly. That's not what venture capital is about. Venture capital is a long-term gain. When we raise a new fund we tell our limited partners it's ten years. They sign a ten-year contract. So it's ten years they're going to be paying fees, and ten years before they expect returns.

Now the industry has trained the limited partners to see returns in probably five or six years because a lot of it is prompted by digital, IT investments. But in the energy world I think it's probably more like seven or eight years. You're not investing money to get it back in three years if you want to invest in venture capital. You are taking a lot of risk. It's the riskiest type of capital.

So we choose to say that we don't want to just hit singles all the time. Our job is not just simply to provide modest returns for limited partners. If you take that philosophy, you are really a financial investor and you have to beat all the alternatives that are out there. So you get this IRR (internal rate of return) mentality that says you need to keep your IRR in the 30+% range and that means you can only invest in safe companies: low risk, fast return. That's not our philosophy. We say every fund is going to have about 40 companies in it because we have to diversify the risk. Every one of those companies when we invest in them is going to be disruptive by a ten X factor. Out of 40, five are really successful, another five are modestly successful, and the other 30 almost don't count. It's not for the faint of heart, but you produce companies like Google and Amazon.

CS: Ha! Yes, it sure is quite a list.

RL: It's a good list, but there are 550 companies that have produced 50 companies that have succeeded. And so why do I feel good about the job is that we are creating big change that delivers on value. It delivers on profit. But it delivers value to society. It's created jobs; it's created new businesses. Google has created 20,000 new jobs and Amazon has created 20,000 new jobs and Sun has created 30,000 new jobs. It's the job creation. Kleiner itself has funded companies that have created over 500,000 jobs.

CS: That's unbelievable. And I would argue, and I'm sure you would agree, that the value to the seven billion people on this planet of a company like Google far exceeds the 20,000 people who work there.

RL: Exactly. You're right.

CS: Post-Google, it's a different world.

RL: Absolutely. It's a different world. Access to information. You could argue that for Ebay. You could argue that for Amazon; any of these types. There has to be basic economic value to people that are using the service otherwise it just doesn't work. We focus first on companies.

I understand the business well after being in it for ten years. But I didn't grow up in the business; I grew up running companies and I like building and scaling companies that have something of value to sell. So if you do that right, you return a lot of money to your limited partners and that's what we focus on. I like the fact that we always take the risk of disruption. We're not afraid of doing that.

CS: Yes. And I have a couple of questions on that. I woke up in the middle of the night last night. I had fallen asleep watching PBS, and Nova was on at three o'clock in the morning and believe it or not, it was on clean energy and they're talking about the (Kleiner portfolio company) Bloom Box! And I go: This is an unbelievable coincidence. I'm going to be in this guy's office in a couple of hours. But talk about disruptive. That *does* seem to be the key underpinning of this.

RL: Exactly.

CS: It's not for the faint of heart, but when you hit a home run it goes way out of the park.

RL: That's exactly right.

CS: Any news on the Bloom Box (a fuel cell that can use a wide variety of inputs, including liquid or gaseous hydrocarbons produced from bio sources, to generate electricity on the site where it will be used), by the way?

RL: No. It's just that they have a huge order book. They have installed a lot of these things. So I don't know how many customers they have now, but it's a lot. So they're doing very, very well. We expect this thing to be, if not the top... we always measure our expectations on our companies, on dimensions of how much profit they'll return. So when they go public or when they get bought or whatever, what do we think we'll realize based on their value and our ownership—what they would return to our limited partners, versus the probability of returning capital at all. And Bloom has always been kind of the top of that. There are probably ten others that are surrounding them, but we still have enough ownership in Bloom and it's doing well enough; its value is over a billion dollars already.

CS: A lot to like there.

RL: A lot to like, yeah.

CS: So here's another question about venture capitalism just generally. Everybody, I think, understands the platitudes like "I'd rather have an A team and B idea than a B team and an A idea." And certainly that you take risks that you understand, etc. But are there any other pieces of advice that you would give entrepreneurs who want to approach Kleiner.

RL: It's pretty straightforward. At the end of the day there are a lot of things we measure, but there are really four things that we measure hardest. If it doesn't meet one of these four things, it gets eliminated. One is it has to be a big, big market. So we don't want to go into small markets; we can't control that. It's the only thing we can't control. So if we fund a company that's going out to a small market, it might be a small company or it has to take a lot of share of that market to be big, and either one of those is bad. Second, you have to remove the technology risk early. So with the first money in you want to remove the technology risk. If you're putting $50 million in the third round and you haven't eliminated that technical risk, you're in trouble. You have to do that.

So you have to get that behind you and not be taking technical risk when you have a lot of money in the company already.

The third is the team. So is this an experienced, savvy "A" team that's really smarter than the rest of the competition.

And the fourth is the financial risk. Do we see a way to fund this all the way to profitability? That's critical in green because here we're talking about real money. We did have several of these companies in the bubble period of green, in the'07 time period, where we liked the idea so much... it was so bold ... and we knew we'd have to build factories or plants, but we didn't think ahead about how will that be financed. There was plenty of capital back then. We didn't have a recession yet, but the recession really set all the private equity back. Capital was really hard to find.

Now we have to think about how we fully fund these. Will there be big capital? It's not venture capital. Will there be big capital to build these plants? You don't want to use equity capital to build plants. So will there be non-diluted funding? Will there be government funding? Will there be private equity funding? Will there be oil and gas kind of money that funds all these projects that all they're looking for is kind of an IRR of a certain level. It's pretty low; 15 percent is fine. During the recession, all that money dried up. It just went away and it really busted the bubble that existed with green tech.

We have built a hell of a team. This is the best green tech investing team in the industry. We have half a dozen guys that can go down to the science level and really understand when an entrepreneur explains a concept, who can poke holes in it at the chemistry level, at the physics level. And I've told them that I want to be the best post-recession green tech investor.

That means we have to pay attention to all the rules that we're dealt with. We don't have enough regulations to propel us forward; we thought there'd be better regulations.

Prior to the recession, we thought we'd have some kind of national carbon cap bill or energy bill or something like that. We don't have that. We can't depend on the senate; we never wanted to depend on the senate.

And we have to be comfortable with commodity risk. Oil has moved between $140 and $40 and gas has moved between $12 and $2 or $3. So we've seen incredible fluctuation of volatility in commodity prices. We have to know where the capital is going to come from because most of these companies will take $100 million of equity and some of them $200 or $300 million of equity to build the company. That's very different than investing in software or an Internet project. So we have to be comfortable with all of that.

We're trying to drive this practice into recognizing those factors, as opposed to simply looking for a cool technology. If you're investing in cool technologies—and I can point to a number of venture capitalists that are doing exactly that – without thinking about the problems that will occur three or four years from now – when you try to scale it up, you won't be successful.

CS: I see—a kind of "Valley of Death thing," in other words.

RL: Yep. Absolutely.

CS: Okay, I'm with you. Let's go to capital formation and the kind of trajectory for where you see this going as it applies to green tech – but also more generally as well. People consider that capital formation has been pretty feeble of late. There's a trillion dollars of private money sitting on the sidelines. What's up with that, and where do you see that going?

RL: Well, there is a big Valley of Death here that is establishing the proof-point for a plant. If I have money that I want to put into a project and somebody comes along and says we're going to build a natural gas-fired power plant, I know to the penny what it's going to take to build that plant and what the return is going to be. So I have almost a guaranteed investment projection and a return projection that I can give my investors.

If you're going to build a solar farm or you're going to build a wind farm—wind is almost getting there actually—but if you're going to build these things, or say a gasification project or a biofuels plant, you don't have that first proof point. Getting that first commercial plant is critical and all this money sitting on the sidelines won't do it. It's a lack of bankability. They're just afraid to take that risk; it's not what that money is for. The private equity money is low-risk money. They don't want to take any risk. So they don't want to get into a project that says: I've seen it work, it should work, everything says it will work; but you get half way through it and it doesn't work. And they don't want to take that risk. So please come see us after you have a first commercial plant and we'll fund your next five. That is a lockup right now.

And that's where government can really help. A government loan guarantee could help build the first commercial plant, and that's what we ought to be using government money for. Not for building what private industry knows is a guaranteed return. So if we really want an alternative energy industry in this country, let's take that on and recognize that 20 percent of them are going to fail. The government has to be willing to take risk, and they're going to see failure; they need to build that into the economic model. So whatever interest rate they charge, whatever terms they create, assume 20 percent of these things are going to fail. And that's the only way around it that I see.

CS: Is this what the DoE is attempting to do under ARPA-E?

RL: No. ARPA-E is really early stage high risk. So they're putting small dollars to work; say $2 to $5 million to get a technology out of the lab. I'll give you an example. At Carnegie Mellon a professor invented a new battery that we put some seed capital in. They got an ARPA-E grant of $5 million and the red tape that comes with it is unbelievable.

CS: Oh, I bet.

RL: For a little tiny company that just wants to work in their lab, they don't have time to send them a document or paper to get the next payment and all of that. But that's what ARPA-E is all about. It's like what DARPA did with the Internet; it's very traditional; the government is very good at it. We need to continue to do that. I'm talking about putting up big money; $200 million, $300 million, $500 million that they would put as a loan guarantee or a direct, low-interest loan that would get the technology that has been proven at the pilot level into its first commercial plant.

CS: I suppose this is an example of what you're talking about (pointing to a drawing of a car on the wall). Is that the Fisker Karma?

RL: It's a Fisker, but it's called Next. We don't have the loan yet. We expect it in a couple of weeks. That's a direct loan from the DoE, but they haven't made one since Fisker; over a year ago. They don't know how to take risk. They don't know how to assess it. They've got a lot of people; 160 people crawling all over these deals looking at them, but they're not able to squeeze the trigger on a lot of these and that's what their responsibility is. And let's just say

Solyndra is a good example. We knew Solyndra would fail two years ago. We told the DoE, but they didn't listen.

CS: That was like $600 million.

RL: There's no way that Solyndra could get their costs down. We knew that. I have a technical team that could just simply look at that technology and say it can't compete.

CS: Really?

RL: Cannot compete in the PV market.

CS: This is CIGS (copper indium gallium diselenide), right?

RL: They're CIGS, but it's a different implementation of the tubes and they couldn't get their costs down. There's no way they could compete in this market. They're talking to bankruptcy lawyers.

CS: Wow, that's terrible.

OK, having said all this, let me ask you: We know that renewable energy is going to happen. We're not going to be driving Hummers and burning coal 100 years from now. I often say that the real questions are when it's going to happen, and who's going to make a buck in the process. We're only a few years away from grid parity, at which point an incremental kilowatt-hour of electricity is going to be the exact same price whether you do it with coal or wind. If we're that close to grid parity, why is this moving so slowly?

RL: First of all I don't agree with the premise. And therefore, I don't think it's going to happen anyway. If we just let the market forces work, I don't think it does happen.

We have cheap energy in this country and we can't control the price of oil. But we can certainly control the price of electricity. We just keep burning coal. I think it will be a long time before grid parity happens. PV will not get down to coal. It *will* get down to clean coal or gas. It depends on the state you're in, but today PV is probably in the $0.12 to $0.15—if you really scale it up and use CIGS and get a lot of efficiency. That's not coal. Coal is $0.03 or $0.04. Clean coal is $0.06 or $0.08. So it does need help; it does need a push.

These big coal-fired power plants have been written off long ago; we did a lot of coal. We don't have to dig very deep in Campbell County Wyoming to get a lot of coal. It's right there on the surface and it supplies half the energy in this country. Now, if we decide that there's no free ride anymore—if we say, "You want to burn coal you're going to have to pay to clean it up—before or after—you can only build clean coal plants, or you're going to have to have scrubbers or something like that" that makes this more interesting. You may put a tax on it.

And then we refuse to build nuclear plants. Nuclear can actually compete with coal. It can actually get there today. We know that. We can build a nuclear plant today and deliver the power at the same cost as coal, but no, we don't want to do that. We don't want to take the waste from the nuclear power plant. No one wants to give up the entitlements. Nobody wants to kill birds with wind turbines. I was just in West Texas last week. We came in at night, and it looked like we landed on Mars. There were these red lights all around me blinking in the same sequence; it was eerie. The next day you get up and you see all the wind turbines. And everybody out there is complaining. Damn wind. I say: you know, it's not all that bad. It shows progress. Yeah, maybe if you're on a ranch and you want to see nothing but just country and all that, but no one wants to install these things. They're the closest to grid parity. But it's intermittent. You cannot dispatch energy with all wind. You can only create watts onto the grid that are supplemental.

So I don't think we get to grid parity without some help. I think every entrepreneur; every venture capitalist would take a deal where the government gives us five years of help. That's all we need. So in the transportation sector, give us five years of help; tax breaks on buying electric cars. Batteries are more expensive; the technology to produce an electric car is more expensive. So give a $7,500 credit for a car, and let drivers get in the HOV lane.

All of that is a great model for assistance, but then take it away. If a company cannot compete without subsidies then it shouldn't exist. Because our energy prices are so low in the United States, we've got to have a way of getting enough technology moving, enough companies that are approaching scale that then we can let go of subsidies. Bloom doesn't work without subsidies today; the economics just don't work. So the customers that are buying it are saying: OK, I see the price; I understand what it's going to cost me. And because of the subsidies I am basically at parity in California. Now, if I'm in Nebraska, no way. But in California I'm getting clean energy at basically the same price as I pay for either gas-fired or coal-fired. Half of California still is coal-fired; the coal plants are in Arizona and Nevada. So they can basically say at the point of use I'm paying the same thing for Bloom.

Subsidies will go away. Well, Bloom knows it must have its cost down when those subsidies go away, so it works. That's the way it should work; the subsidies that have a fixed date of termination I think is the way to do this.

CS: Yes indeed. You alluded to something I want to talk about: the externalities. In other words, you want to build a coal plant, that's fine, but somebody has got to pay for the cost of cleaning this stuff up—and it shouldn't be our grandchildren.

RL: Right.

CS: When I first started talking about this a few years ago people looked at me as if I were crazy. Recently, though, people have started to realize that some of these externalities are clearly identifiable, as well as measureable. Harvard Medical reported that we spend, depending on what you count, between $500 billion and $700 billion per year in dealing with the externalities of coal alone, most of which is asthma and other forms of lung disease, associated directly with the aromatics. 13,200 die each year from this cause in the US alone.

RL: That's right.

CS: Do you think the notion of internalizing the externalities of the energy industry has legs? Is it going to work? Perhaps a carbon tax?

RL: Yeah. But I think it again goes to our political system. If the U.S. were a corporation and Obama were the CEO, he could say I'm the boss and here's what I think our full cost of ownership is. That's the way corporations work.

We have a company here called Hurrah that does exactly this. It measures your full cost of the energy you use, and helps you measure that cost of energy, and also reduce carbon omissions. But it doesn't measure the healthcare benefits and all of that. But if the U.S. were a corporation and he was the CEO, he would do that. He would say we spend money that you call an externality that ought to be included in this, and so if you knew you could save money in healthcare by cleaning up coal, you would do it. You would make it a business decision.

But in no way does it work that way, and so I think my answer is no. I don't think it's going to be measured project by project. If an investor or a project owner sees the economics of putting up a gasification plant or putting up a clean scrubber or something like that, then they'll do it.

CS: Ah! I remember Hurrah now. Is the CEO an Indian fellow?

RL: Yep.

CS: He had a great article in *Entrepreneur, Inc.* or something like that. You must have seen it.

RL: Yeah.

CS: That was really fantastic.

I think the reader of this book is going to want to know: what can I take away from this chapter with Ray Lane in terms of moving my own idea, at whatever level it is, into the real world?

RL: Well, there are a lot of ideas. Ideas are pretty cheap actually. So you can say: what if we did this? You get very creative and very innovative about an idea that is not well thought through, but here are some things to consider. Is it going to be a big enough market? Is the risk removable? Can you scale it up? What are the economics? Is it disruptive? So, if it meets all those tests and you think it through that way then it is absolutely fundable and could be a valuable company.

Look at some of the companies that we're really excited about here; look at Fisker Automotive; we're very, very excited about them. It's a great product. It will create a lot of jobs. We bought an entire plant from General Motors. It will create jobs in Delaware, and it will create a lot of profit return for our investors. We have an early stage battery company we invested in out of Carnegie Mellon; a professor at Carnegie Mellon invents this new battery that's nontoxic, low-cost, that basically will make solar and wind and grid backup much more viable. We have thin film solar and a CIGS play, we have next generation high-efficiency solar at the price of CIGS. We get into these big disruptive projects and even though we know that they're going to run into problems along the way, we like these big disruptive ideas.

But they do require a lot of thinking. The idea itself might be great, but how will it become a reality? How will it become a real business with real economics without subsidies—and how will it get funded? And thinking that through in this business is as important as the idea itself.

CS: I completely agree. By the way, you may not recall that when I bumped into you in Detroit I asked you to help me contact some people at Ausra, and eventually I got David Mills to sit down and do an interview with me. What a brilliant guy. That company obviously was sold to Areva. So what happened to your investment?

RL: Oh, we made money on it. We got a good return, though not a great return on it. Areva is pursuing the four or five projects, but they have the capital to do it. You either accept the offer and take all that risk off the table and transfer it to somebody else, or you have to have the confidence you can go out and raise the big capital in order to produce these solar farms. Bright Source has chosen to do it the other way. Bright Source is basically saying that they're going to choose to make this a big company. At the end of the day the venture capitalists in Bright Source will have had a lot of money in it, so it better work. I think Kleiner Perkins had $20 million or $25 million into it.

CS: Yes, that's what I recall.

RL: My guess is the venture capitalists at Bright Source may have three times that in, and they're taking a billion dollar government loan. So the pressure of that loan... if you take that loan, it better work. You don't want to upset the government on the loan. So they better be sure it's going to work.

I think both of them are good. We took the risk off the table and made some money and now we move onto another project, where they are going to be in this for years. Now they may choose to take it public earlier—start getting their capital out before they ever build a project. Again, it's just an assessment of risk.

CS: The reason I ask is that I really like CSP for so many reasons. One is the storage obviously of energy as heat is a fraction of what it is as electricity. So using this in combination with molten salt and so forth is really attractive on the long term. If you're looking at solving a world energy issue, you're going to need something like this.

RL: Yeah, but see we were violating one of the rules I told you about. So we had $20-$25 million into the company. There was a total of $150 million capital and we had not removed the technical risk. So we built a five-megawatt facility in Kimberlina, California to demonstrate that the mirrors work. We had never demonstrated the storage. No one has.

So there's still a lot of technical risk and you're pouring in tons of capital. We chose to say Areva could do this so much better than we could. Ausra is doing well. It continues to operate, but it will be well capitalized by Areva.

CS: Good. When I spoke with David we spent half the time talking about how capital intensive CSP is. I asked,

"Well what's your cost per watt?" He says, "I don't know." I was shocked. "What do you mean? The wind guy can tell me." He said, "Of course he can, because they have a three decade head start on me."

RL: Yeah. And the other thing is that we had a split camp here that believed PV would get lower in cost because it had physical laws that it was taking advantage of. Getting the solar cells smarter and smaller and more efficient. The scale in PV would help them; scale doesn't help CSP. The process of turning thermal energy into electric energy has a limit to what the productivity is.

CS: This has been great. Any concluding remarks?

RL: Well, you said this is going to happen anyway. I think it is going to happen. My belief is that it going to happen, but it's not going to happen without proactive political capital. All of that has to be behind it. I'm very happy to see that corporate intentions are not backing off. It would be easy, I think, for a General Electric or a Wal-Mart or a Coca-Cola or these others that have a really clean agenda to say it looks like this had a little bubble and everything seems like it's subsided, and to just simply back off. That would be big trouble if they did.

I think they've got to continue to see this as an important issue to the country, an important issue to them for creating profits, jobs, or however way they see it. They have to see it as an important issue to them. Energy is how they will get growth. And right now if they continue to see an environment where we have fluctuating prices like we've seen and we can't control our energy future, then that's a big agenda item for them.

CS: I completely agree. And certainly GE clearly wants to own the world as it goes green. I wouldn't have said the same thing about Coca-Cola, but I'm thrilled to hear you have a similar view.

RL: They are. They're a big customer of Bloom, but they use a lot of energy and a lot of water. So they have to be. Safeway is the biggest energy user in California. All of these big energy users are looking at how they can cut their energy use or make it cleaner. And I think that's really important. Right now they are the hope. The corporate side is the hope and now the government just needs to get something behind it.

CS: Terrific, Ray. Thanks very much.

Craig's Interview with Jason Scorse, Ph.D.

I was lucky to happen across Dr. Jason Scorse in my quest to interview an economist who could shed light on the migration to renewables.

Jason is currently Associate Professor and Chair of the International Environmental Policy Program at The Monterey Institute of International Studies, a graduate school of Middlebury College. He has consulted for numerous environmental organizations, including the Natural Resources Defense Council and the Sierra Club.

I became familiar with his work when I found a video in which he discussed his book, *What Environmentalists Need to Know About Economics*, published by Palgrave-Macmillan. I like his conversational style, but note that he packs the rigor and discipline that makes his line of thought so compelling.

> **CS:** Thanks so much for meeting me, Jason. I'll just jump right into this.

Where my last book was a compilation of interviews with subject matter experts on a gamut of renewable energy issues, this one asks: Why can't we have it? Why, specifically—technologically, economically, politically—is this so difficult?

I've listened to your wonderful talk: *What Environmentalists Need to Know About Economics.* Did you want to start by summarizing that?

JS: Sure. What I was trying to do with the book, *What Environmentalists Need to Know About Economics*, and my talk on the subject, was to lay out the case in very simple terms for the lay audience—and also for more sophisticated people—NGOs, political staffers, and students—that well-functioning markets are really the environment's best ally. The superficial view that economics is opposed to the environment because of the commoditizing of nature, and money's taking precedence over everything, is a very simplified and erroneous view of economics.

CS: That's really counter-intuitive. The common wisdom is that you've got environmentalism over here and then economic stability, or coming out of a recession over there.

JS: Right. That was exactly the notion I wanted to dispel. The key here is the well-functioning markets. If we look at the world today, for jobs and for the environment, the problem is distorted markets. In the case of energy, specifically, you have the issue of national security; I would say our national security has suffered because of the distorted energy markets in particular. The point I was trying to make is that well-functioning markets—markets that adhere to simple economic criteria, actually will produce a lot more jobs because it's the renewable energy specifically which is being under-invested. It's labor intensive, and a lot of it can't be outsourced. Some of the elements can, but a lot of it can't be. And many of the distortions in the energy markets, in particular, are leading to entire development patterns that are very sub-optimal. They lead to all types of inefficiencies, and then have big productivity and economic growth impacts down the line.

CS: Okay, well let's unpack this if we can. So you're talking about markets that are not efficient—that are not happening according to what would normally happen if there were a whole bunch of people with a bunch of hens laying eggs, bartering with a bunch of people growing flour. But according to the lecture, there is no such thing as a free market anyway. We say we have a free, laissez-faire market, but that's not the case. What specifically has gone wrong here? Why are these markets not operating optimally?

JS: Let me take one general point and I'll get specific. The key that you focus on about free markets being an illusion is the right way to think about this. The whole concept of free markets is a distraction. What we should be thinking about is well-functioning markets versus not well-functioning markets.

CS: Okay. So you're saying we have poorly functioning markets. Can you give me an example, please?

JS: Yes. In fact energy is probably the prime example. We have fossil fuel based energy being subsidized in two ways. One is directly. We have the fights right now that are currently in Congress over direct subsidies, the tax breaks for oil drilling, we have leases for oil development, both offshore and onshore, that are below market price for the land and the leasing; we have below-market royalty payments. We also have the subsidization of all types of infrastructure and transportation that rely on fossil fuel, which then gives a boost of the demand for fossil fuel.

I would say more importantly though, is that there are two types of the subsidies that economists identify. One is active subsidy. So what we typically think of and which is what we are trying to address in Congress now: paying companies money to do things. And those are certainly significant, but the biggest type of subsidy for fossil fuel is the passive subsidies. The way you can think about passive subsidies is not charging a company for the damage it creates. A very real world example would be if a company came into a city to create a development and they had to buy the land and they pay the market price for the land, but then in the construction process they dumped all types of toxic materials, left all types of garbage everywhere and didn't pay for it. That would be obvious; we'd say they got an underpriced asset, and the city has to pay for all this toxic waste. So we can add up that cost and whatever, how many millions of dollars, we'd say, "That was a passive subsidy to that industry because they didn't have to get charged." It's a little more loosely defined in terms of fossil fuel, but it's the exact same concept which is the passive subsidies for climate change damage, for national security payments to protect the oil lines, and then for just basically physical health damages.

CS: Yes, internalizing the externalities. But to be fair, before you can charge somebody for it, you have to identify it, and then you have to quantify it, and then you have to pass legislation to pin these costs on an industry that has the world's best attorneys. So this is problematic.

JS: Well, yes. A couple things I'll say to break that down a little. First of all, a lot of work has been done in identifying the costs on this. The damages directly, like you said, pollution from burning coal, even burning natural gas, from burning oil, all the fossil fuels. We've been studying the actual physical health damage from air pollution for decades, and we have good estimates. If the industry wants to argue, we can take the conservative estimates; we don't have to take the high-end estimates. You take the low-end estimates; it's still significant, and we have good data. The military estimates, the actual amount of money we spend on the military to protect oil pipelines and the kind of political instability that comes with that—some pretty good studies that have come out on that too; again, take the low-ball estimate.

CS: Yes, but doesn't that get into the politicization of do we fight for oil? There are credible people who say we don't.

JS: I think the right way to think about this is not to say that we went into Iraq, or Afghanistan or anywhere because of oil. The right way to think about it is, would we have gone into Iraq if there weren't oil? Clearly the answer is no. There's just no question that we wouldn't care about the stability in the Middle East if the Middle East weren't the center of oil. Just because a statement is not true doesn't mean its converse isn't. My point is not to say that every dime that's spent on the Middle East is spent because of oil, but there's a percentage that is. People have made estimates of this, so that's not that difficult.

CS: Okay. So going back to your idea on the improperly working markets, and I'm sure there's a better word than "improperly" …

JS: Just market failure.

CS: Market failure. So are you suggesting that these subsidies are the cause of that failure, or is there more to the story?

JS: Yes. There are many components, but certainly the mass under-pricing of fossil fuels is the primary component of market failure. Again, let me just also point out, the social cost of carbon is the attempt to look at what the incremental damage of every bit of carbon pollution adds to global warming. Again, well-studied, the top economists, entire governments, the UK is on this, many European organizations have done this, big think tanks have done this. There's a whole range of estimates out there. We can take the low estimates, but my point is that the numbers are actually there. This isn't stuff that's esoteric and we're pulling numbers out of the sky.

CS: Okay. Let me ask you to give me a chronology of what would happen over the next couple of years if we were to pull those subsidies and create a level playing field in which all the externalities were internalized, remove all the cheap BLM land leases and so forth. If all of that went away this afternoon, what specifically would happen to the price of gasoline?

JS: Sure. So, the first thing is economists advocate spacing all of this out over time. We don't want shocks to the system; we don't want gas going from $4 to $10 within six months, right?

CS: Yes, but let me ask you this. There are people who say that wouldn't happen anyway because oil is bought on a world market. Therefore, all we're really doing is transferring $70 billion a year of wealthy taxpayers to shareholders of oil companies. There are people who say that we wouldn't change the price of gasoline at all.

JS: But remember, we would be doing it at the level of the United States. We wouldn't be affecting the world price here. We would be taxing carbon emissions at the source in the U.S. That would definitely affect the price and that would be passed on to the consumers. In terms of specific estimates of the price of electricity, the price of gasoline;

my guess is if we were to tag a $30 per ton price on carbon emissions, you're looking at gasoline going up in price at least a dollar or two, and you're looking at electricity going up a few cents a kilowatt hour. You're looking at a 10 to 20 percent increase in fuel costs in the United States over time.

The key point, though, is that the money that would be generated from that could be refunded to consumers in a broad-based progressive way. So we could give back a lump sum payment, where everyone gets a check, say a $1,000 refund at the end of the year. We could tweak that a little so regionally people who are in coal-dependent states get a little more, since the demand for those fuels would decrease. We would see a shift towards alternative sources.

CS: Well, it's certainly true that this non-level playing field winds us up with private investors who are very nervous about putting money into something where the cards are stacked against them.

JS: Yes. Interestingly, I am sure you are following the price of wind energy coming down dramatically. In many places wind can compete now with fossil fuel energy. Solar PV is still higher in most places, but given Moore's Law on the trajectory, the predictions are that within 10 to 20 years solar power could be significantly cheaper than fossil fuels. So in some sense the hey-day of renewables is coming, no question, in spite of having the worst energy policy you could possibly have imagined. You couldn't craft a worse energy policy than we have in the United States, and in spite of that we might have renewable energy coming quickly. I think your point is, and the economist's point is, we're going to get there. We're going to get to decarbonized fuel. The question is when, and how much damage, and how much transfer of wealth to the Saudis, the Iranians and the Hugo Chavezes of the world. My point has always been that we can get there quicker, and give that money to us, and give the jobs to us—or we can give the money to the Saudis, we can give the money to the Chinese, we can kill a lot more people, we can make climate change a lot worse, and we can lose a lot more jobs. We're going to get there, but the question is: Do we get there in a way that benefits us, more or less? That's the variable of interest.

At 2050 we're going to be there. The question is, are we there at 2030 or 2020? By 2050 we're there, or we're gone.

CS: OK, please tell me a little bit about job creation in the US, versus off-shoring jobs. What does all this mean? And please be as specific as you can with respect to the quantification of jobs: blue-collar, white-collar, green-collar; whatever other color.

JS: Well, the first thing is that we have to separate the markets. Take transportation and displacing oil markets; this means the electrification of the transportation system. We're starting to see the beginning of this with the Nissan Leaf and the Chevy Volt. My prediction, and the predictions of most economists who study this, is that a significant increase in the price of gasoline and fossil fuel energy would make electric vehicles much more attractive financially. Right now, you have an added up-front cost, but you save on electricity; it's still a toss-up even with $4 a gallon gas. Once you start getting $5, $6 a gallon gas and you're getting better battery technology and longer life, it actually becomes cheaper to own an electric vehicle, even with these higher sticker prices. That technology is extremely dependent on U.S. manufacturing. And in battery technology, the plants are opening up around the Midwest, and they're opening up on the East Coast; we're talking about producing hundreds of millions of batteries. That's tons of new jobs.

Also, we would need the renewable energy to power them, which means reconfiguring the entire grid, which means wind and solar. Again, even if China has a leg up on us and Germany has a leg up on us, a lot of panels are being produced overseas, which don't have to be. We can catch up, but currently we are importing a lot of those. Even so, the construction and maintenance of this is all domestic. The entire reconfiguration of the grid is a massive jobs bill.

I would say also if you talk about electrification, we're talking about smart grid technology. This means installing new meters in every single home in the United States that can then read and monitor the power for the individual. So you know how much power your dishwasher is taking, and how much your laundry is taking. Then Google is optimizing your energy use. A computer program can look at your energy use and say: given that energy is cheaper at this time of day, if you switch your dishwashing to here, if you charge your car at this time, you can save 30 percent on your energy over a year with a family of four. Especially in a place with high electricity costs, you can save thousands of dollars a year. That technology, putting that infrastructure in, the programming, the software, the hardware, the meters—it represents millions of jobs. We're talking about a paradigm shift, a transformation to a completely new energy system for 350 million people. The sooner we do that, the sooner we can develop that software here, we can make the hardware here and get those jobs.

I want to be clear: I don't think we should oversell this. There's a danger of overselling green jobs and then if all of a sudden half the new jobs created aren't in the green sector, people can say, "See, you oversold it." But I think it's significant. We're still going to have a lot of jobs in agriculture, construction, in basic IT. Military is going to be a huge employer. All of these need a boost given the hit we took in 2008, but I think there's no question that green jobs are a major component. Again, not only does this stuff require a lot of jobs when it's built, but the maintenance and the continual updating of this—it just needs people, it needs bodies.

CS: It needs bodies, but I'm wondering at what skill level. I'm not an expert on this, but it seems to me that most of these things are what would classically be referred to as blue-collar jobs.

JS: I would say it's a pretty good mix. The blue-collar jobs in terms of basic manufacturing would be insulation, solar panels, wind turbines, putting in the new meters, putting in all the new transmission lines that are going to be needed, all of the switching stations, all of the sensors, the monitors. Also the retrofitting, this kind of Cash for Clunkers program, which, by the way, is one area where it hasn't been as big a success. There have been some bottlenecks in that system. I think it still has a huge potential, but that's literally paying people to go and re-insulate your house and do the infrared sensing and figure out where your leaks are and literally putting in new foam in your attic and stuff—all blue collar. But the beauty of this is, it's very sophisticated technology and we need the software and the engineers and the switches and the routers. This is very high level so we've got a lot of high-end, white-collar stuff on the back-end of this, too.

CS: So you sound pretty bullish on this thing overall. It's funny; in that lecture you gave, and I don't know how long ago this was... It was right after your book...

JS: This was just six months ago.

CS: Yeah. So you sounded... maybe you sounded angrier? You seemed to be saying that environmentalists were despondent, were dejected, had taken a kick in the teeth. We need to regroup and be able to articulate a message that is the core thing anyway. In other words, the mother discipline on this thing really is economics.

JS: Yes. My anger is mostly directed at this: The right wing has hijacked economics and misrepresented it, and has basically lied. And the inability of real economists and real environmentalists—not these people who are on the payroll of the oil companies in Exxon and the Koch Brothers—to stand up and make the counter argument. Again, I love talking to Republican audiences and conservatives. I say, "You guys should be the ones who are most angry. These people have hijacked your ideas. We should be in the heyday of conservative economics right now, because we should be working to get markets operating efficiently, which will benefit the environment, benefit national security, benefit jobs. But your ideology, true conservative principles, have been hijacked by these tea party ignoramuses and these right wing think tanks." So I think the coalition is there. The real conservatives, the true Republicans are there. The problem is that we don't have the counter-argument telling them they're being lied to by these propagandists on the right.

CS: Please explain this to me. When you refer to hijacking, to misrepresenting the basic principles of economics, can you give me an example?

JS: All this Americans for Prosperity, the Koch Brothers, FreedomWorks by Dick Armey—all these fake grassroots organizations that are founded by billionaires—are masquerading as economic populists. We're just coming out of a major financial crisis brought about by deregulation of the financial industry, and a lot of people are angry. Median wages are stagnating, especially among blue-collar people. We have housing bubbles in places. It's very legitimate anger out there. The origins of the crisis actually are somewhat bipartisan. I would say the Republicans were the forefront of the deregulation of the financial industry, but certainly Clinton signed on, and it has been a bipartisan thing. So these big industry groups have done something very brilliant; they've taken all this right wing populist anger and directed it generally at government. They say it's the government's fault, that we need to get government off the back of industry, and that government is actually in cahoots. So what they're doing is using this kind of populist rage to try to argue for less government when in fact they're just arguing for fewer things that hurt their bottom line.

It's a very clever way of taking populist anger, and directing it at government, to fatten their wallets. These people are laughing all the way to the bank. The Koch Brothers, Dick Armey—these guys couldn't give a rat's ass about any of these hard-working people. Everything they're doing is harming these people, but again, they've been very good at channeling this rage to this kind of general hatred of government in a very kind of sophisticated way. And unfortunately there are a lot of the low-information voters, people who don't read enough, who don't have an understanding of economics, who don't have the wherewithal to really see that they're being lied to.

CS: It will be interesting to see where all this goes; personally, I go back and forth on it. For instance, I've written a whole bunch of things on electric transportation. At a certain point, I thought that there really was essentially a divorce between big auto and big oil. But I've been seeing this dribble along. And I've always said that there's nothing really "in it" for big auto to do this. If you're the vice president of anything at Chrysler or whatever and your 401K is rooted in essentially profitability that you can extract from a customer who wants to buy a new overpriced gas-guzzling piece of junk every three years from you, there's nothing in it for you at all to advocate for electric transportation.

JS: Well let's be clear, here. Big auto made some terrible mistakes and were really counterproductive for much of the '90s. You think about the SUV craze that was taking off. SUV's are a big hunk of metal. There's nothing sophisticated in the technology whatsoever. They were selling these things, and they were making the highest profit margins of any vehicle. People were lapping them up because all of a sudden it gets associated with status, they're safe and everyone wants to be a soccer mom. So in terms of short-term economics, they were doing the entirely rational thing. It was the highest profit margin, and there was no indication that gas was going to get more expensive; the taps were flowing. Clinton and Gore completely failed to do anything with the gas tax or to do anything about climate change. So from a short-term perspective, they were doing it up; their stocks were soaring. They didn't take the long view and this is where they got into huge financial trouble.

CS: But was this surprising? Had they ever taken the long-term view?

JS: Well the issue is, now, in order to get bailed out they were required in some sense to take the long view. The Obama administration made pretty strong conditions that a) you're going to have to start focusing on more electric vehicles, and b) we're going to beef up the CAFE standards—which they did, in the biggest increase of CAFE standards in history. They're going to increase those again, and I think that the auto industry has been chastened to some degree by the fact that they did take a hit. And if they don't stay up on this, the issue of whether there's going to be an administration friendly to them, if they get hit again is certainly up in the air. The best thing we can do though to make the auto industry think long-term is to put a price on carbon emissions and make the electric vehicles attractive.

Make electric vehicles powered by wind and solar something that consumers want. They're going to follow consumers, consumers are going to follow the incentives, and the incentives have to come from the government at some level. Now again, in 20 years if solar power is so cheap that you can ride electric vehicles 500 miles for five bucks, it's not going to matter what the government does. So again, ultimately technology is going to win this. The question is, in a short—to medium-term, can we accelerate that?

CS: Yes. And going back to your lecture, I think you did a really good job laying out the conditions under which government really needs to intervene in certain situations. Can you take us through that?

JS: It's externalities, property rights, perfect information, competitive markets, and full complete markets; those are the five criteria for deciding whether the government should intervene. I make the case, for example, that government should get completely out of the housing market. Just so I can get some conservative bona fides here, I agree 100 percent with conservatives who say that the government should have no business in the housing market. It should be completely privatized; we should deleverage Fanny Mae and Freddie Mac, and if you can't afford to put 20 percent down and buy a house, you should rent. End of story. The government should not be supporting housing. As policy it serves no social benefit.

In fact, we could maybe make the argument that in this economy we need people to be mobile. Being stuck in a mortgage is actually bad for the economy. More people should be renting so we can get people mobile and going to the hot spots, and if climate change is really bad and storms are threatening you, you're not in that house with a mortgage that no one wants to buy and your insurance premiums skyrocketing. If you're renting, you can leave. If anything, I think we should be promoting mobility, which would be again supporting the housing market. This is where conservatives are right. Real conservatives are right about a few things. They're right about the environment, but unfortunately their voices aren't being heard; real conservatives are right about the environment, but they've been hijacked by the fake conservatives.

CS: Yes. Doesn't the definition of "conservative" mean "one who conserves?" Shouldn't a true conservative be concerned about conserving what we have?

JS: Absolutely. Let's remember, true conservatives, Teddy Roosevelt, started the National Park System. Ronald Reagan, I have a lot of beef with some of his environmental plans, but he signed the Montreal Protocol and used straight economic cost-benefit analysis by the Montreal Protocol. Richard Nixon started the EPA, the Clean Water Act, and the Clean Air Act. George H. W. Bush used market principles surrounding sulfur dioxide in the Clean Air Act Amendment for the cap and trade. So most of the real big innovations around policy came in Republican administrations. Let's not forget, in 2008 it was a Republican platform. John McCain was a champion of cap and trade until all of a sudden everything Barack Obama does is somehow bad. As soon as it has a 'D' on it, now it's a bad idea, even though it was your idea a year ago. So let's just remember, we don't have to go back 30 years to remember when conservatives believed in this stuff. Just look into the 2008 Republican platform.

CS: Wow, that's very good. I'm just thinking that your students... oh, of course you have graduate students, you don't have undergraduate students.

JS: All graduates.

CS: Yeah, right. But I was going to say, they must like you, because you really do speak very cleanly.

JS: Well, thank you. I hope they do. I'll see my evaluations in a couple months.

CS: You say we're going to get there in 2050, and I happen to agree, if we don't kill ourselves first, given rogue states with nuclear weapons, global climate change, and half a dozen other frightening concepts. A friend of mine had a conversation with his son not too long ago where the son asked, "Dad, what do you think it's going to be like living in 100 years?" The father is very decorous about not saying "We're doomed." But he was thinking to himself that there's no way in the world we're going to have a civilization here in 100 years from now.

JS: I'm much more optimistic. Let me break it into two parts. There are two existential threats to civilization. One is the threat of climate change. When I say we're going to get there in 2050, we might get there too late. Let me be clear, I'm not being Pollyannaish about this. The technology will get us there by 2050, but we probably need to get there by 2020, 2030, in order to avert the worst consequences of the climate change. My point is that this is the crucial decade right now. Again, these fake conservatives and this tea party who are under this spell of this right wing industry and big money, these people really threaten humanity's future. These people who have inculcated masses of people to believe that climate change is a hoax and all this; this is really a big threat. This is an existential threat to civilization.

I don't use the word 'evil' lightly, but most of these people know better. Most of these people know climate change is real, but they want to make a quick buck and they want to lie about it. They want to block legislation that's going to hurt their profits. When you're knowingly harming civilization and the long-run trajectory of the human race in order to make a few billion more dollars, there's not much more evil than that.

I don't throw the word "evil" around lightly, but that's evil. So we're dealing with some very evil forces right now that might win. They're winning right now, but I think we will defeat them. The other one is the terrorism threat. A WMD going off in a major western city…

CS: Like New York City. It doesn't even have to be a big one. A small nuclear weapon in Manhattan would destroy our economy.

JS: Exactly. That's why I love to be working where I do, because we not only have the top international environmental policy program, but we also have the only terrorism studies program. Let's be clear, here. There are two things that are working in our favor. One is technology. Technology in 100 years is going to be mind-boggling. People will be living to 150-200 years routinely. I think we will defeat scarcity as a concept. I tell my students that this century is going to be the end of scarcity. We're right now working on how to defeat scarcity as a concept that humanity has to deal with, and we will do it if these two existential threats can be kept in check.

Also, from an American political perspective, this might sound crass and a little insensitive, but the tea party and this kind of real right wing push is really the last gasp of a very older generation that's racist and hates change and hates the direction that America's going. It doesn't like the more secular worldview; it hates the fact that we have more people of color in society, and there, the demographic is over 65. These people are going to be dying off, just by natural causes, over the next 20 years.

The young generation has its share of crazies, but much less as a percentage. The young generation is smart, they're savvy, they're tolerant, they know people of all colors, they know people gay and straight, they grew up in a world of social media and they really care about the environment. Once they come along in 20 years, we're going to be good. So really, what I look at is this 20 years. It's dealing with this last gasp of right wing paranoia, and it's dealing with these transitions right now that are being blocked by these big industries making record profit. So we have some big forces to overcome, but once we overcome them I think the future's very bright. I'm very optimistic, actually.

CS: Wow. That's good news. I had only two courses in economics as a young man, and one of them essentially defined economics in terms of scarcity. It's about the allocation of...

JS: Scarce resources.

CS: Right. So, first of all, how real is it to get rid of scarcity in a meaningful way? Then, let me ask: Is it *good?* *I.e.,* don't people need challenge? And what will be the social fabric with which it will be replaced?

JS: That's actually the subject of a novel I'm working on. So again, I think the 21st century will be characterized by this larger push to eliminate scarcity worldwide, which will mean bringing up the billions of people in poverty to a middle class standard of living, and then dealing with these existential crises that we've talked about. The next challenge, the challenge of the 22nd century, will be profound in that it will be dealing with a world in which we don't really have to work that much and one in which there isn't want, in which there are 10 billion people living full lives of 150-200 years.

What's it going to do to the whole family structure? When you're living 150-200 years, the whole nuclear family having a one-partner monogamy is probably going to be rethought. The entire western project that's been built along a nuclear family—that's already seeing itself frayed by the divorce rate and all types of things – is going to be blown out of the water by the next century, and by all this time on our hands. What are people going to do? I mean our entire consciousness since we came out of the primordial soup has been about fighting scarcity, about overcoming challenges, and those are going to be largely absent. It's going to be a profound reworking of what it means to be human. I think it will be no less challenging; in fact, that's the irony. The lack of challenge will be the next challenge. That's the Catch-22.

CS: Well that's precisely what I'm asking. Is it good? I can't see getting up every day and not having a challenge.

JS: Again, not to get too sci-fi on us, but there's this whole universe out there. And we'll be living on Mars by then and we'll be exploring new solar systems and maybe that will be the new frontier. Not to get too Star-Treky, but maybe that will be our new sense of awe, in pushing human limits and athletic pursuits and in terms of just art and music; maybe we'll push new frontiers there. So I think they'll always be frontiers, but it will take a major reorienting of our priorities.

People like me won't be needed 100 years from now. If people like me are needed in 100 years, then my discipline will have failed and we are going to have much greater problems. So I tell students that as you're working, always think about that second career you wanted because my job is a terminal job. I want to finish the project and be done. I don't want there to be environmental economists 100 years from now.

CS: Okay, but given where we are now, we have a billion and a half people who can't get a clean glass of water today, and mass starvation, unbelievable political unrest and lack of basic sensitivity. As a matter of fact, I have a question in a recent survey I conducted with the subscribers to my newsletter. I asked people to rate their level of agreement on a scale from one to ten on various things having to do with existential threat of exponential growth in populations and shrinking traditional energy resources. One of the things I asked them to rate was the notion that this is going to cause mass suffering and the extinction of billions of people.

JS: My view is that I don't think population is a central focus for environmentalists, except in one way that is really productive. The bottom line is that we should be actively working for a sustainable world for everybody and we should be actively hoping and being happy when the poor in China and Nigeria and Brazil and India have refrigeration and have medical supplies and have access to computers and have leisure time. This should be celebrated. Environmentalism tends to want to put the brakes on that, and bemoans the fact that people are getting wealthy and getting more consumption. I don't subscribe to that; I think it's a very negative form of environmentalism.

CS: Well, of course, but also notice that the world population doubles in size every few decades. In other words, when we're at seven billion... when we were at three and a half billion—it was within my lifetime, wasn't it?

JS: Yeah, it's decelerating though. The UN population projections were originally peaking at nine billion in 2050.

CS: But what would cause it to peak?

JS: Well, two things. One is that, in the western world we're having actually negative rates; we're not even going to have replacement rates in most of the western world. In fact, the U.S. is one of the exceptions to the rule, because of huge improvements in infant mortality and female literacy and overall wealth. People who are wealthy don't have six and eight kids. Women who can read don't have ten kids.

CS: Yeah, but we have a bifurcation of wealth. The richest one percent owns more wealth in the United States than the bottom 90%. And God knows what it is outside the United States.

JS: But it's converging.

CS: Really?

JS: It is converging. We're getting higher per capita incomes around the world. I'm not trying to say there's not a big gap of wealth in the developing world, but actually U.S. inequality is eclipsing developing world inequality; and remember, inequality doesn't mean the poor aren't getting wealthy, right? So that's another thing. Yes, we have billionaires in China; we also have peasants who now have refrigerators, right? So they can both be moving in the same direction even as the gap is growing and we need to be cognizant of that. The UN just updated its findings and sub-Saharan Africa is not predicted to grow as fast, because of a decrease of fertility. We're looking at peaking at about ten billion in 2100. So it's an extra billion.

CS: After which, what will happen?

JS: The population will stabilize and/or decrease. So we're not at a doubling any more; we have decelerated. Now that's still three billion more people, and it's mostly in developing countries that are going to be going from zero to huge wealth. So it's a big increase in consumption and it's the biggest challenge right now in the world: how to get three billion people to a middl-class life and not overwhelm the planet in terms of the resources; that is the challenge. But again, I think we're up to it and we have to embrace it. We can't say, "Oh, you can't come into the rich people's club."

That's not the solution, to not let them in. First of all they're not going to listen. Message for environmentalists: the Chinese and the Indians aren't waiting for our okay. That train has left the station.

It's up to us to try to help them do it, and the best way is for us to lead by example. Try to create the technology to make them leapfrog. A perfect case in point is the cell phone. We created the cell phone in the developed world, and now they're leapfrogging. This has saved the developing world trillions of dollars in infrastructure investments; they don't have to build landlines all over China; a few satellite connections and *boom*—they have communication. Let's do that with medical devices. Let's do that with solar. Let's do that with everything. Let's create it and then sell it to them and let them leapfrog. That's the way we can promote their development.

CS: That's terrific. Let me go back and talk about a few more current issues. Carbon trade died, but what do you think is the trajectory for a useful carbon pact at some level?

JS: Well I think ironically, the deficit might be part of the solution here. A long-term deficit is a problem. Obviously the short-term deficit is exactly what we want; we want more short-term deficits now because we need more stimulus to help these 15 million people out of work get jobs. But long-term we have a deficit issue. Look at the work of (Yale University economist) William Nordhaus, who works on climate change policy. He has done a study suggesting that a moderate carbon tax would help in this power sector we talked about earlier, and would also raise hundreds of billions in revenue. We could use half of it to give everyone a lump sum check—everyone gets a tax credit, and then use the other half to pay down the deficit. It's probably the best way to generate revenue to decrease long-term deficit.

In a way, if we can get some serious conservatives on board, we could have a win-win situation here. People wrote a carbon tax off a long time ago, once the Republican party went crazy, but now that we have to come up with ways that would generate revenue—and real conservative economists think this is a good way to do it. We might see traction over the next five years on this. I wouldn't put money on it, but I think it would be a great policy and conservatives should get behind this. Again, my point is that real Republicans, real conservatives, should be loving this. It's exactly what textbook economics says. Let's tax bad behavior and use the money to take taxes off labor income. We don't want to tax labor; labor is good. We want to tax pollution; pollution is bad. It's textbook economics.

CS: Yes, right. Which is what, to me, makes the whole thing of the subsidies for fossil fuel so Orwellian, really. You're giving people money to create a social nuisance.

JS: It *is* Orwellian. It's paying people to do bad things. It's called "perverse subsidies." So here's your litmus test. Any Republican, any conservative who justifies subsidies to the fossil fuel industry doesn't believe in market principles; they're a socialist. They believe in paying big business to do things—and not only to do things, but to do bad things. It's one thing to be a socialist... I don't think socialism is a bad word. It's one thing to pay to do good things, to pay healthcare for people, to build roads; they're a good social good. But you're a real *bad* socialist if you want to pay fossil fuel costs.

CS: Perhaps I should have begun with this, but do you mind telling me your background?

JS: Yeah, sure. I did my undergrad in environmental studies at UC Santa Cruz, and then I wanted to kind of be out in the real world for awhile before going to grad school, so I did a variety of projects. I taught junior high school for a number of years, but I knew I always wanted to go back to school. So I waited until the time was right and then I went back and did my Ph.D. at Berkeley in environmental policy, environmental economics. I also did my minor field in behavioral economics. It's kind of the new up-and-coming field on psychology and economics, regarding how people act irrationally and how to deal with that. It has great applications for the environment by the way, which I incorporate into to my class. Berkeley has the top environmental economics program in the world, and I was extremely fortunate to have amazing professors and to do some really good research there, and then really lucked into this position at the Monterey Institute which is now a part of Middlebury College, which has the oldest under-graduate environmental studies program in the country.

CS: I knew it was a terrific school, but I didn't know that.

JS: Bill McKibben, who has been one of the big champions of climate change policy for decades, is a resident scholar at Middlebury. So it's been kind of the perfect marriage. We have the graduate international program in environmental policy. They have the undergraduate and more domestic focus, but then we have Bill McKibben there. So it's been an amazing kind of marriage, and this is our whole outlook: *be the solution*. We want to train and educate people to solve the world's key challenges. None is bigger than the environment and terrorism, which are both the things that our school works on. I'm just really blessed to be part of a group of people that's really on the cutting edge of this stuff. So I'm very humbled by where I've fallen and I'm just trying to do some good work.

CS: That's fantastic. Do you happen to know (Associate Professor and Director of the Monterey Terrorism Research and Education Program professor) Jeffrey Bale?

JS: Yes, very well.

CS: Yes, he's a good guy. I've spoken with him several times.

JS: Yep, I know Jeff very well. He's on the forefront. What I really like about Jeff—and this is a parallel here— is that Jeff is a true kind of liberal libertarian in the truest sense of the word. He hates all the politically correct stuff. He'll criticize the left when the left needs criticizing. I think the left has been very weak on framing things, on being skeptical of economics, not embracing economics, and not understanding economics. That's created this vacuum where the right wing has filled in, and all these charlatans have come in because the left hasn't mounted a good offensive.

CS: Well I'm so glad that you brought this up because economics has been largely discredited as a science, it seems to me. Perhaps "discredited" is too strong a word; let's just say that it hasn't been a great couple of years for professional economists generally, perhaps for having failed to foresee what happened in 2008. Do you agree? Do you want to elaborate on that?

JS: Well look. In the macroeconomics and finance profession there were huge failures. It's just shocking to me that some of these people are still in polite company. Alan Greenspan presided over the biggest housing bubble in the history of the known world—and not only did he not see it, he actually actively said it wasn't a bubble. He is on record for being the most spectacularly wrong person in the history of the economic profession, and yet he's still brought in to sit on Sunday talk shows. This guy should be laughed out of the room. Tim Geithner, Ben Bernanke, and people in the Obama administration – their records are much more mixed. I think they made some huge errors, but at least they've gone a long way to correcting those. Let's be clear though, there are a lot of economists who saw this coming. Paul Krugman was sounding the alarm well on. Roubini at NYU was sounding the alarm. I think Dean Baker was sounding the alarm. So there were some really top economists who were sounding the alarm.

Unfortunately, the people in power had been hijacked by this idea that markets are perfect. Greenspan actually ended up admitting this in congressional testimony: "I never thought markets could fail," as if he had never studied the Great Depression or anything.

So, unfortunately, my profession took a rightful hit. Now let's be clear that that's the macro on the finance. On the economics and environment stuff I think we've been pretty consistent. If you look at the work of (Harvard economist) Robert Stavins over the last couple of decades, he's been really consistent. Larry Goulder at Stanford, Mike Hannaher at Berkeley, my advisor; for decades they've been calling for the type of policies that I'm writing about. We've been pretty consistent, but yes, the economic profession has egg on its face. There's no question that the people should be held to account who got it so wrong. I'm as mad at them as the person on the street; I'm not an apologist for the profession.

CS: Okay. Do you mind giving me a couple paragraphs on behavioral economics especially as it applies to environmentalism? First define it if you would.

JS: Yes, absolutely. Behavioral economics really started with two psychologists who worked in tandem: one Israeli and one American. Amos Tversky and Daniel Kahneman, who ended up winning the Nobel Prize. Daniel Kahneman won the Nobel Prize; Tversky had died a few years earlier and they don't give it posthumously, but he certainly would have won with Kahneman. Kahneman is a psychologist at Princeton, and they basically studied deviations from rationality. They created an amazing architecture for how people think in the real world that has led to this whole new field called behavioral economics. It has really taken off at Berkeley, which is its center. Matt Raven and George Akerlof, who then won a subsequent Nobel Prize a couple years ago, created the first field where you can get a Ph.D. in behavioral economics, with the words printed on your diploma.

I'll help to make it concrete, so people can understand. One of the key discoveries of Kahneman and Tversky was this thing called "loss aversion," meaning that the impact of losing something is much more impactful and has greater magnitude than the benefit of gaining something. This has huge public policy implications. The implications are, for example, that if you ask someone to take money out of their paycheck to put it into a 401k, they're going to feel a big sense of loss. They're going to feel, "Wow, I know I should do it; I know it's good for me, but taking that money out of my check is going to really hurt me." And so what that has in terms of public policy implication is if you set up a retirement plan so that a person's future raises go toward their 401k, people will like that a lot more than taking it out of their current income stream.

So you can do the exact same thing and get the exact same money going into a 401k account by changing the way it's done; people will sign up for it more easily. So, again, it's little tweaks like this that work on people's psychology, getting them to do good things. I'll give you two examples of work in the environmental realm.

Let's take the example of organic food. You go into the store and you see food that's unlabeled; it has no label, say an avocado has no label. Then you see an organic avocado labeled organic, and say it's 50 percent more. So you're thinking in your mind: should I do the good thing and spend extra money to buy the organic avocado? So again, remember, here it's now a potential benefit. Some people do, some people don't. Now let's take the exact same scenario and leave the organic avocado unlabeled, and the conventional avocado says "grown with pesticides." Nothing's changed; it's the exact same avocado. All we've done is change the label, but now it's framed as a loss, because the organic is unlabeled and the one with pesticides is labeled and so you think, "Oh, this is going to harm me. It's going to hurt me." That's going to make more people buy the one that's organic. You've done nothing; you haven't changed any production processes, you haven't changed the prices, you've done absolutely nothing, but I guarantee you, you would have at least a double increase in the purchase of the organic by just changing the labels and changing the psychology of how people view the product.

Now traditional economics doesn't see this. Traditional economics looks at prices; it looks at information. It doesn't look at the way that information is presented. So again, if you want to double organic production then change the label. Now, of course, your conventional producers would never allow that. They will give congress hell not to have it changed so that organics are the default and they're the one that's labeled grown with pesticides. Politically, that wouldn't happen, but I guarantee you that would change the purchasing of organically grown food.

The second example, is called "status quo bias," which means that people tend to *keep* doing what they've *been* doing. The inertia against change is very strong and hard to break, even if it's a rational interest to do so.

So you ask people, "If green power were offered to you, full renewable power, that was say a ten percent premium on your electricity bill, would you sign up?" It has all these benefits, you help climate change, etc. You get rates in the realm of 80 percent of people say "Yeah, if it were a small fee, I would." Between two-thirds and 80 percent. You then offer renewable power to people and you then send them a notice and say, "Here, we're offering a green power, would you like to sign up? It's only this much more a month." You get rates of uptake five to ten percent max. So you have this huge disconnect. Two-thirds or 80 percent said they'd do it, you offer it to them, most of them do not accept it—why is that? It's because of default bias, or inertia.

You could change it so that when you get a new account with PG&E in California or whatever it is and other states, the default was you're automatically enrolled in the green power, but you then had to ask to be taken out. You say, "If you want to save money and go to the dirty power, your bill will be ten percent less; just let us know." You're going to get that 80 percent. Why? Because it was the default. People, when they get the thing in the mail, they'll say "Yeah, yeah, I'll do it," but they never get to it, they procrastinate. If you're automatically enrolled, people do it. The second though, is to see how the psychology changed it. It goes from, "Should I do something that I'll feel good about?" to "Do I really want to change to something bad?" The psychology changes. "I'm automatically enrolled in this. I kind of feel bad, switching to dirty power. Just to save a few bucks, do I want to pollute the earth and poison people?"

So again, traditional economics doesn't see these distinctions. Behavioral economics is now the understanding of how people think. These things have big impacts on consumer behavior; they're not trivial. These are things that can move tens of millions of people in a very constructive way. A lot of times they're win-win situations, like the 401k example I gave you. People are under-saving in America; this is one of the big tragedies right now. Given that Social Security and Medicare might not be as great as we hoped, people need to have a big 401k, yet people under-save. The average 401k is half of what it needs to be. Changing the incentive structure to get people to do things is going to really help them to act in their own interests. It's "nudging people." You don't want to be coercive; you don't want to be paternalistic. You want to work on people's good instincts to nudge them in the right direction to do things that are beneficial to themselves. That's what this is about.

CS: That's good. And I'm sure there are hundreds of examples that are along the lines you've given.

JS: There are. I could send you some papers by the way if you want.

CS: Yes, I'd like that. And I bet there's more to it than opt-in and opt-out, i.e., inertia. In other words, the fact that you have to make a change to do something is going to make it happen less frequently than the fact that it is the default. For example, whenever Facebook wants to do something to be aggressive, they make it the default. Yeah, you can share your information.

JS: Well, let me give you an example of that. They found that if they send people their electricity bill and show the average electricity use of their neighbors, and if it turns out theirs is higher, you get a positive effect. People feel a little bad; they go, "Wow, my neighbors are using less, maybe I should turn off the lights," and you actually get a one to three percent reduction. So that's again not a default issue, but a kind of "good peer" effect. That's one to three percent nationally, a huge amount of energy.

CS: You know I often wonder... On the first example you gave of the avocados, the good that accrues there is to you personally, your health, your life expectancy and so forth.

JS: Also to the environment though, right? Because organic means fewer pesticides in the environment.

CS: That is true, but I would argue that most people who shopped...

JS: It's mostly for health reasons, but it can then have the secondary benefits.

CS: Yes, that's true, but we can at least imagine a situation where the good that accrues is to all seven billion of us simultaneously versus me the person.

JS: Yeah. Certainly with the renewable energy stuff that would be the case.

CS: Exactly. In terms of the psychology of the masses, it's an interesting thing to understand how the world is changed, or at least how our society in the United States has changed in a few short decades. It seems to me we've dug in our heels and we're much less interested in doing the right thing if it doesn't benefit us personally. Is that true?

JS: That's a big, big question. There are certainly segments of the population for which this is true, and it's, I'd say, understandable. Here are people who are overworked, two kids, working 80 hours, or sadly, uneducated. Or that small percentage that just wants to thumb their nose and wants to drive the Hummer and eat three Big Macs a day and turn on the air-conditioner and just give their middle finger to the planet and all the hippies or whatever. There's a certain percentage of the population that's probably going to be hard to change—some for understandable reasons, some for not-so-understandable reasons. I tend to think especially the younger generation that really wants to do the right thing and is willing to make some sacrifices, willing to make some changes.

But it's understandable we're self-interested beings. People want to see some benefit for themselves. It's a little too much to just ask for the warm glow, altruistic affect to be enough. I'm that way. I'm not a saint; no one is a saint. I love what I do. I get a lot of personal satisfaction out of it and I consume a lot. I travel a lot. I have fun. But I think technology is really enabling us.

Just to give an example, I'm really working a lot on ocean policy these days. Being in Monterey, we want to have a great international marine policy institute and program. Monterey Bay Aquarium started the Seafood Watch program where you have these cards that show you the good species to eat, and it shows you red, yellow, and green like a traffic light. They've given out millions of these cards, and people use them. They now have the app you can download on the iPhone and the Android. You're in a restaurant or you're in a store, you type in the name and it tells you whether or not it's a good species.

Another one of my professors at Berkeley started what's called Good Guy; it's also an iPhone app. You can scan barcodes when you're at a store and it will give you detailed health and environmental information. So right on the spot you can find out if it's good. This technology is expanding on an exponential pace and so it's going to become easier for people to make good choices.

I think though, coming back to politics, the biggest choices we can make are on our elected officials. I think my biggest disappointment with the Obama administration has been his environmental record. I think he had an amazing opportunity with the oil spill, with the coal mine disasters, with China picking up the pace on all these green jobs. He had the softball down the middle of the plate and he didn't take that opportunity. I think he's gotten plowed by these fossil fuel interests and by the right wing; these are powerful people with a lot of money. We need to have his back, but we need to demand that he step up. That's my biggest disappointment with him so far.

CS: Well, I voted for him, and I can't imagine that I'm at all unique in my supreme disappointment. In other words, we all actually believed this. I feel rather like an idiot for having believed it.

JS: Yeah. Well, he's battling immense odds. He came into one of the hardest situations ever. The things he's done are huge. Take healthcare reform; it's huge stuff. This is paradigm-changing stuff. We're not going back to 30 million people being uninsured, and that's just the beginning step. We're going towards universal healthcare.

And let me tie this into the environment. I'm writing a paper right now and I wrote a blog post about this. My thesis is this: the reason people are very skeptical about environmental stuff right now in America – the reason that it's number 16 on their list—is because of economic insecurity. People don't want to worry about energy prices changing, and gas, and food prices when they're already worried about healthcare costs and getting a job. So the healthcare legislation that he passed, which is only going to get stronger with time, which will finally give people peace of mind, will then make it easier to pass environmental legislation.

Progressives need to understand that you have to give people economic peace of mind if you want them to take risks on environmental policy. We have to think about this big picture long-term. When I get mad with the left, especially the people who sat out in 2010 and let these tea party idiots take over, is that we've got to think long view. This is a war of ideas. This is a thing that's decades long. We can't just get discouraged if we don't get everything we want. That's immature, that's how children act. We have to be the adults in the room and take the long view. We will win this war of ideas, but we have to have some stamina.

That's my pitch, man. [chuckle]

CS: Well, I tell you what, I'm very grateful to you for having done this.

JS: No, my pleasure. Feel free to use anything I'd said liberally, no pun intended. It was good meeting you.

Craig's Interview with Woodrow ("Woody") Clark, Ph.D.

Woody Clark is another of these supremely visible figures who is impossible to miss when one attends industry conferences. He has a warm, approachable – and often hilariously funny speaking style that belies the depth of his understanding of complex, multi-disciplinary issues.

Woody is an applied academician, a long-time advocate for the environment and renewable energy, and an internationally recognized author, lecturer and advisor on sustainable communities. He was a contributing scientist on the United Nations Intergovernmental Panel on Climate Change (UNIPCC) that won the Nobel Peace Prize in December, 2007.

CS: Thanks for the opportunity to meet and talk, Woody.

My first book was kind of a survey of renewables – 25 interviews with subject matter experts for somebody who wants to understand the subject at a 50,000 foot level – the political, economic, and technologic implications of all this. People want to know: why isn't this happening faster? Why are we so married to fossil fuels? What are we going to do about peak oil, national security, borrowing a billion dollars a day, the healthcare impacts of fossil fuels, global warming, and so forth? The current project gets more into these "tough realities."

WC: Okay. This is timely for a couple of reasons. Number one, we have a new governor in California. So, much of what I may be saying to you is directly relevant to what's going to happen in the next few years. Number two, California as you probably well know is now called an island nation; it's now totally independent from what happens in the other parts of the United States, in terms of politics and where things are going; not just job creation, but in all different areas. Not just renewables, but everything.

Number three or four are when you look at the global picture, California stands out from the rest of the United States, but it's still not there, and I'll get into some details. And the fourth thing, which is really important, is that people throughout the world want to know what is going on in America – because they're not understanding or cannot believe what they are seeing and hearing. The point is that people around the world disagree with much of what America appears to be doing: drilling for more oil and gas offshore and in Alaska; shale oil exploitation and now even nuclear power stations despite what happened in Japan in March 2011. And then, if you look at the local communities and cities for renewable energy, this is really critical because of the different perspectives and debates, that are really non-possibilities in regards to the environment. When more and more politicians talk about energy independence, that does not mean to them, 'use renewable energy rather than foreign oil and gas'; instead it means 'dig for more oil and gas in America or nearby in Canada and Mexico'. And then when you ratchet down to the local level and it all has to do with who controls the local money and economics. That's the bottom line; hence the scope of what you're trying to do.

CS: Yes, exactly. I'm just trying to make sense of this thing from the standpoint of economics. It seems like with grid parity as close as it seems to be in wind and PV, it's unclear why we aren't super-focused on making this happen. For instance, we have people who say 'Well, we need nuclear power as part of our long term energy policy.' But here we are in 2011. If you get the permit for a nuclear reactor this afternoon, you wouldn't have it online for a minimum of eight years. What trajectory for nuclear is there going to be eight years hence when the cost of renewables is coming steadily down? I just don't understand.

WC: Well, we met when I was talking at the Annual Renewable Energy Finance Forum in San Francisco, right?

CS: Yes, but briefly. There would not have been any reason for you to remember me.

WC: No, I do remember you. I am aware of your last book. But in terms of my talk, do you remember my talking about the U.S. Department of Energy resource supply chart? The chart that I showed had uranium as one of those four critical areas for energy resources? That chart which came out in 2001, which I understand they're revising now; they do that every decade. It will be out this year (2011). It was showing the supply of natural gas, oil, coal, and uranium. Now, some colleagues of mine who are essentially nuclear scientists and experts in this area have criticized that data because they're saying it's not the full story. But the fact remains that according to the Department of Energy itself, there's a supply of uranium that will last about 61 years. That was ten years ago. And there are plants being built in China right now. The supply is shrinking; the world is going to run out of uranium soon. Why spend the enormous amounts of money on nuclear power plants? And, since the Fukushima Plant destruction, scientists and leaders need to reconsider the use of nuclear power. Today, however, the building and even continued operation of nuclear power plants needs to end.

But there's the cost of those plants, and we haven't even talked about the waste control issue. So that whole thing to me is a non-starter. People who talk about nuclear as clean energy are just one more group of charlatans, frankly, like those who use "clean" to describe coal.

That's why I developed the field called "qualitative economics" because there is a continued misuse of the word "clean" as it is certainly not green or renewable. Clean tech (such as natural gas and "clean coal" and even nuclear power), for example, is cleaner than oil or coal mining. But it's still a problem, and it's still one of the reasons we're having this horrific weather all over the world. So to start with, uranium and nuclear power as a savior or solution to our global energy needs – let alone national or regional needs – is ridiculous; it's absolutely insane, non-economic and stupid. I haven't even talked about the security issues attached to it, which are horrific. But the fact of the matter is that it's something we shouldn't be doing, period.

I was giving a talk at a conference to utility companies in the northwest recently, where they wanted me to do a talk about one of the major issues that you just asked about. We have energy, and we need to go into renewable energy. I won't get into the problem of intermittency in the sense that the sun is not always shining and the wind is not always blowing – an issue we tackled when I was Governor (Gray) Davis' renewable energy advisor. We solved the economics of it, by the way, and I'll tell you how in a second.

But to look at replacing coal plants with concentrated solar or other systems is not the answer either. We can do some of it, but we still have transmission and other problems. What we have to do is get those renewable technologies installed locally: onsite at buildings, factories, apartment complexes, condos, shopping malls, parking lots, public buildings, outdoor arenas and movie theaters, anything and everything we can think of.

When you leave this country and land in most countries in Europe or Japan or China, you will see solar energy powering airports and other facilities all over the place. The only place I've seen it in America is San Francisco. We don't see solar panels in Los Angeles.

There are a lot of problems and even historical problems in Los Angeles. Strangely, I have often compared LA to a "developing country" like Burkina Faso in west Africa, the poorest country in the world. For example, there is no train to the airport. They do have trains to the airports in San Francisco, and in other major cities in America and around the world, but not Los Angeles. The roads are always being repaired due to the holes and damage caused by nature. No solar panels on top of roofs or other buildings; there are no bike paths, so that people can walk and get safely to and from work. I'm talking about in both areas: Los Angeles and Burkina Faso. Both "countries" – in fact the entire regions – are ruled and dominated by political infighting by people who have been in economic power for generations and continue to control it. Real estate developers rule and continue to set political and other technology trends. It's exactly the same here in Los Angeles.

And finally the thing that's most disturbing to me is the continued use and expansion of fossil fuel powered motorbikes, cars and trucks. It is unbelievable. It's the same thing that I saw there and here in LA, and it's continuing. Neither "country" has much light rail. I did take a train when I was in Burkina Faso from the capital to another city in the south about 2 hours away, but that was about it. I do the same in LA to San Diego, but getting to the train station in LA from the "westside" requires a car and the freeway. And to be able to do that was not easy, but the fact of the matter is that we have the same kind of problems here in LA, as they do in Burkina Faso. When the public realizes this, it's going to be amazing because people will recognize the problems that we have throughout the United States, let alone just in Los Angeles.

CS: Well, I'm trying not to prove what I've already assumed, but to me, when you say we should *not* be doing nuclear and we *should* be doing something else, the first question in my mind is: why is this going so wrong? And the only answer I can possibly derive is corruption in one form or another, i.e., the influence of money and power over rationality and fairness.

It seems to me that the only reason that we're talking about nuclear in 2011 is because of the money behind that industry. If it weren't because of that money, I could talk about raising daffodils as an energy source and that would get as much attention.

WC: That's my point. That's Burkina Faso corruption and Los Angeles corruption and frankly America today; that's what I'm talking about.

CS: So, I'd like to explore why.

WC: Well, let me back up and give some clarity on that. One of the things I mentioned at a talk in San Francisco is a book I have coming out called *Global Energy Innovations* (Preager Press) in the fall of 2011. The concept actually came from a colleague and friend of mine – environmental columnist Jeremy Rifkin. He wrote about a third industrial revolution that started in the EU as part of a book he did called *The European Dream,* which came out in 2004. My co-author (Grant Cooke) and I expanded on that theme as I am very aware of this being a "green third industrial revolution" much like the dot-com era at the end of the 20th Century.

My book talks about part of what you're asking about called "agile energy systems"; global solutions to the energy crisis in California were parallel to many of the things that Jeremy wrote about. The point he made in his book was focusing on what Europe has been doing and what America is not doing. You may remember there was a book a couple of decades before called *The American Dream,* pointing out that America has fallen behind. Now, his argument is that Europe has moved ahead of the United States into the third industrial revolution which is renewable energy – and not fossil fuels, and not nuclear power.

However, as my book explores this concept, it finds that Japan and South Korea have led the world, even Europe in terms of making it a "green" third industrial revolution. China has now leapfrogged into the green third industrial revolution; I saw this coming two decades ago in China when I was working for the U.S. Department of Energy at Lawrence Livermore National Laboratory – but even so more recently when I did a report for Asia Development Bank about Inner Mongolia (2005-2007) just north of Beijing.

This is the second largest coal-producing region in China, and what the sponsor, Asia Development Bank, wanted, was an analysis of five developed countries and their energy infrastructures. Then the report on how Inner Mongolia – and therefore China – can learn from the mistakes in the West due to their impact on the environment, and then leapfrog in to the next era. "Next" was undefined, and that's where I've defined it as the green third industrial revolution. So my point is indeed that is what's happening. Now, who are the culprits? I should add that my follow up book on these issues will be "The Next Economy" which focuses on what China and northern Europe are doing correctly.

CS: Exactly. People ask me all the time and that's the real question. Everybody agrees that we're behind, but the question is why.

WC: Okay. Then I can start naming them. It goes from ExxonMobil to Shell to BP to Chevron, you name them. All those big oil and gas companies along with the smaller ones, suppliers and distributors. But now let's include the auto industry. The auto industry in America now is in deep trouble. But they brought on the problem to themselves. Detroit is trying to get out of it, but it's got some serious problems. And if you want me to name individual people I can certainly do it because I know some of these people, but the fact of the matter is those companies had a vested interest in keeping their income supply coming from oil and gas and they're continuing it. And by the way, now it's natural gas. They're moving quickly away from oil into natural gas. So the net result of natural gas, will be the stranded costs for its drilling, pipelines and shipping and then distribution stations which result in another 50 years or so of America becoming dependent on this fossil fuel while continuing to pollute the environment.

There are a number of documentary films on these topics, but one called *Fuel* which makes a couple of interesting points including how Henry Ford, who was a farmer, began to use biofuels for his first cars. And then he was forced into oil and gas – oil in particular – because of the oil industry in the early 1920s.

That's a very important issue, and the industry acknowledges it. You look here in Southern California and recall what I said about the comparison to a developing country. There used to be light rail systems throughout this entire region. Not now. You know why it's not here now? It's been proven repeatedly: because of the auto industry. They wanted to see highways to get people in their cars and using fossil fuel at the gas stations. That's the point and that's the problem and that's got to be addressed and put a stop to it soon or our children (especially us baby boomers) will inherit an American Dream that is going to kill them and their children.

CS: Let me ask you about solutions to all this. What are the major efforts to fix the mess, and which ones do you favor?

WC: We have to be very careful. The cap and trade program is the equivalent to smoke and mirrors; it goes back to when I first got in state government in the late 1990s and the energy crisis happened in the year 2000 when we had deregulation, which was manipulated by certain companies. Enron of course is a big example, but there are others. We'll see the same thing happen with cap and trade. It's a way in which financial people make money; investors make money. But does it really solve the problem we're facing? Absolutely not. What it really does is just put off the problem for another generation or two before the next scheme comes up. The solution is to have a carbon tax. That's it. No questions asked. Tax it. Get rid of it now.

CS: Interesting. I know you've been heavily involved with the State of California and its quest to be a leader in clean energy.

WC: Yes. The basic thing comes down to the belief that, for example, when Governor Brown was in office initially in the late 1970s and early '80s, he basically reduced the size of government. It got more efficient. Remember the concept, small is beautiful?

CS: Yes.

WC: He believed it, and he's right about that, and I hope that's what he's going to take into Sacramento now. But the basic thing is that because you don't need layer upon layer of bureaucracy in order to keep people employed or using their skills. There's so much overlap it's just unbelievable. When I was in state government, I saw it personally. But the other part of it is that after Brown was out of office, California had two terms of two Republican Governors, one after the other: George Deukmejian and Pete Wilson. In both cases their beliefs are America is a market economy. Former governor Reagan and then President during much of that time believed in that same ideology. Even though California and even the national governments had democratic legislative dominance, California and Federal governments pushed for deregulation, which is the market economy concept that, if you have utilities controlling energy as an infrastructure, let's deregulate them in order to get private companies to generate power and by competition reduce the costs. Guess what? Just the opposite happened, and is still happening. California became the leader again; but in a negative way with its energy crisis in 2000 which Democratic Governor Gray Davis inherited from the two Republican governors before him.

CS: How so?

WC: Well, the reason is the so-called market economy doesn't mean competition in the Adam Smith classic view of economics. Instead, modern economics really means companies compete and do things illegally; you buy people off; you inflate costs and prices. Or as happened during the energy crisis in 2000, companies shut down plants, trade and auction electricity power as Enron did or have the energy generation plants shut down for so-called "repairs", when in fact all they wanted to do was jack up the prices and manipulate the market. You control supply. Or, more importantly, you make an impact on the consumer. There are companies that are still in business today doing the same thing. A very similar scenario is being developed in California now called "cap and trade" as a way to allow companies to "buy" their way out of reducing their environmental emissions through tradable credits.

The issue is very simple. There's no such thing as a market economy. It's in theory only. Underline it. Underscore it. That's it. It doesn't exist anywhere.

CS: Interesting. I've heard other people make that point.

WC: Well it's more than interesting. It's a fact. And the facts are when you look at a market economy you have to be suspicious because when people talk that way you know what they're after; more money. Here's a good example: I was just in New York giving a talk at a conference in December 2010. New York is one of the most thriving cities I've seen anywhere in recent years. When you talk to people in New York who live and work in New

York, you ask them about that and they agree. New York is doing well and growing, while Boston's stores and shops are closed. People are out of work. Here in Los Angeles, I come back and all kinds of places and stores are closed. Not in New York; New York is like a whole new world. Now, ask yourself the question. Where did the Obama stimulus money go? New York? Wall Street? That's one reason why I think President Obama needs some different kind of advisors quite frankly. He's getting bad advice, and as long as it continues he's not going to serve a second term; that's my prediction.

These people grew up on Wall Street. What else do they know? What other knowledge or economic cultural base do they have? Where else do they go for advice or help or consulting? Nowhere but their friends and neighbors there. They don't have any other places from which to learn. And the worst thing is they don't go outside the United States, because when they start going to Europe or China, they'll learn a different lesson. Fast forward to the economic roller coaster ride in the summer of 2011. I'll give you three examples of what is going on around the world and what America needs to learn from other countries:

First of all, I'm intrigued with China; I've been working with people in China for over 20 years – initially with the U.S. Department of Energy. I was one of fewer than 100 people given Q clearance to work in China during the 1990s. By the way, at that time I was working on clean coal technologies, so I learned it wasn't clean. But what's interesting is what the Chinese have done consistently and I saw it start in the 1990s. Number one, they have five-year plans.

CS: As opposed to a 30-day plan or something?

WC: Or in America, no plans. Or a plan based on politics. Or a plan based on who pays off whom. Or a plan based on who influences whom with money and/or resorts or other free trips, etc. Which is what we have in America and we have in California – and there's plenty of evidence. I won't even start to name all the names. But the debt issue in America, being a global economic issue, resulted in Congress and the President agreeing to have a committee that would come up with a Plan – that was a big step forward. However, the S&P lower ranking of America to a double A plus only re-enforces what I have been saying here: America needs to get its house in order, and it will NOT be based on the neo-classical economics of a market-economy which only continues to benefit the rich. As some put it, America has now been divided into a small group of very rich and a much larger percentage of poor and working people with a greatly reduced middle-class. Look at China: just the opposite is happening.

The second thing they're doing in China today is talking about what we mean by the word "sustainability." They're defining it, and frankly, I helped them do that initially in the work I did for the Asia Development Bank, in the report that came out in 2007; that was one of the things I asked about in their current five-year plan. I had four native speaking Chinese do some research, and they could not find the word "sustainability" used except only once – and it was meant in the context of sustaining current business economic activity, not in the context of the environment. So they're redefining that. The current five year plan (the 12th) came out in March 2011 and does just that. There is a focus on sustainability, and the environment for the entire country. But also with large amounts of funds to support that focus and make it happen.

The third thing which I think is the most critical for America is to have a carbon tax. Our corporate and finance companies won't allow the Americans or anyone else to push them aside and say, "Let's do cap and trade; that's all we need." No. Tax it. The EU has done that for decades: tax the use of fossil fuels for transportation. The result is efficient cars and a complex network of light rail and high-speed trains which get people out of their cars and into mass train transportation. That "tax policy" needs to be in any five-year plan. When that happens, America is going to grow up and that's it. Otherwise, we will become a third world nation controlled by the rich and powerful. That's the end of the story.

CS: Okay. Well, I think everybody agrees that America is behind and I think you've shed a lot of light on exactly why. Here's the simplicity of the thing as I see it and tell me where I'm wrong on this. We subsidize oil. Fossil fuels get many times the subsidies that renewables get. We therefore have an entire macroeconomic environment in which we have artificially inexpensive fossil fuels making capital formation for renewables next to impossible. Isn't that essentially the entire crux of the problem?

WC: Yes. What you just asked actually brings up a couple of cases. The first one is the issue of oil and gas and its being taxed. You may remember that we had a proposition (98) here in California about taxing offshore drilling in California. The estimates ranged from $4-6 billion would be raised annually. We're the only state that doesn't do that. Even Texas does it; states all over the country do it. Proposition 98 was defeated 55 to 45 percent. Chevron in particular came out with $40 plus million to fight that proposition. Governor Schwarzenegger also was against that proposition to have off-shore drilling taxed. Do the math. If Proposition 98 passed a few years ago, the state of California would not be near insolvency (we cannot call it bankruptcy due to its being a government; but that was what it really is) as it was until Governor Brown took office. That tax should have been done and I would argue that is one of the first things that Governor Brown needs to do. There are several other things that Schwarzenegger either vetoed or left on his desk which are still possiblities to be signed into law because there's a two-year window of time. For example, Schwarzenegger even vetoed a law that Governor Brown can bring back: tax-shifting which allows current tax laws (many which are outdated) to be shifted to environmental or other issues. Hence the tax-payer does not pay new taxes as the old tax costs are still in place.

When I say a carbon tax some colleagues of mine in state legislature in California heard me use the word "tax" and they got very upset. So I responded and said, "Okay, call it a carbon incentive." We did this with smoking in California. We had a smoking incentive that is really a tax on smoking which actually has reduced dramatically the amount of smoking that goes on in the state and everywhere. It's not just no-smoking in public buildings anymore, but it's all over. The result is a reduction in health problems and costs due to smoking among other things.

But the third part of this is a carbon "incentive" to pay for renewable energy. Some economists refer to this as "tax-shifting" because a tax in one area is reduced or eliminated, but placed into another category or sector. For the consumer, there is no difference or increase in costs. In other words, the revenue from the incentive at the oil pump or home use then goes to pay for renewable energy so that people buying fossil fuels are also immediately assisting and building electric renewable energy. Trains, light rail, and other systems – getting rid of fossil fuel cars by the state investing funds for electric and hydrogen fuel cell cars: the future can be carbon free. That's what has to happen and I say that because if it doesn't happen we're going to be in deep trouble for decades to come, seriously. Not just California, but the entire United States. In other words, tax-shifting, and getting the real cost out in front which is what you were alluding to.

Next is this whole issue with BP (e.g. derived from British Petroleum as they call themselves today). The issue about what happened with BP and the oil spill was very interesting for lots of reasons. I was in Italy giving some lectures at one of the universities in Torino; I gave about three speeches that week. I must have been interviewed by 15 different press and media people, and I said specifically that one thing that President Obama has to do is continue a moratorium to limit or not allow any more offshore drilling anywhere in the United States. Now, when I was there in Italy, Obama appeared publicly and said that it was okay for offshore drilling in America; we have to reduce our dependency on foreign oil and gas and therefore we need it. That was January of 2010. Fast forward to April of the same year and what happened?

CS: BP.

WC: BP. Obama then said we need a moratorium; we have to stop. But within two months he lifted the moratorium again on offshore drilling, under "strict" US EPA restrictions, which the Republicans are now attacking and wanting to reduce... The President is getting very bad advice and he's got to stop it. If he doesn't, as I said, I predict he will not be there as President for a second term, because there are a lot of people who supported him due to his concerns for the environment and related global issues and he's running totally counter to what he had promised. The more recent lifting of controls to allow for tar sands transportation from Canada through the USA as well as more oil permits within the USA are even more concerning. This is NOT being energy independent. It is being environmentally irresponsible. Instead, being energy independent also means not using fossil fuels and nuclear power as they destroy and threaten our environment and climate.

The point I'm trying to make is that BP is only one of many cases throughout the world. When you look at other countries that also drill for oil and gas offshore—be it South America, Africa or in Asia—you find the same kind of incidents, but the public does not have the information and documentation like we had with BP in the Gulf of Mexico, because those regions of the world and also the USA do not have the kind of active media which tracks such breaking stories.

Around the world there are more and more cases now being documented of offshore drilling where the systems are not even legitimate; they're fragile. They're not going to continue working in the future. I first learned about this when I was at Lawrence Livermore National Laboratory (LLNL) in the 1990s. We had a project for Statoil in Norway. They were seriously considering stopping all oil and gas drilling offshore because they knew that there was a high risk of explosions and other issues with their drilling off-shore in the North Sea that was endangering life as well as the environment. That's one reason why Norway in the 1990s chose to move away from oil and gas which are the main source of revenue for the entire country. Everybody in Norway gets a payment from the government each year. Instead of paying taxes, they get paid. But they are moving away from this oil and gas dependency because they realized they were endangering the environment.

That was an important decision and the Norwegians have been very consistent since then. They have had people studying to find out safer ways to drill oil and gas, but they have consistently said it's difficult, if not impossible. So the point I'm trying to make is that President Obama and others advising him are not getting good advice. They're doing things and making decisions that they should not be doing. They're spending money and endangering our environment; it's going to ruin the entire world, not just the United States. Remember the world is "round", not flat.

Today the basic issues with climate change are the costs. Renewable technologies that are becoming more cost effective. Consider Denmark. There is case after case in Denmark where that entire country – let alone cities and communities – are becoming totally powered by renewable energy systems. There is one city featured in one of my books called Frederikshavn, on the eastern side of Denmark – facing Gothenburg, Sweden which is on the west coast of Sweden, home, by the way, of Volvo – that is now generating 45 percent renewable energy for the entire city of 80,000 people. My point in all of this is they're using renewable systems now, primarily from wind and biomass, to eliminate their dependency on any kind of fossil fuel.

Now fast-forward from my last case. Again, I was in New York, this time giving the afternoon keynote speech for the annual NanoTech conference. My talk was for the session waking up everyone after lunch. But the morning session keynote was given by another Clark: General Wesley Clark. He and I have met casually on several occasions. However, this was the first time that we really had a chance to talk at length, which I found very interesting. He made two points in his talk, which are relevant to this discussion and I'm quoting him exactly. One was he said that the history of America for the last 60 or 80 years has been on security and specifically on energy security. He's absolutely correct.

Which means we have to find ways of generating energy in our country, not importing it or getting it from other parts of the world. And I don't even mean shale oil, coming from Alberta Canada, which is pipelined through the northern part of the United States into the US, because that's destroying that entire region of Canada. I talked to people in Canada and they're very upset by that.

CS: So I understand.

WC: But General Clark also talked about the use of renewables to generate power in the United States. His point was that if we keep being dependent on other parts of the world—and I would argue the same with other countries including China—we're going to have even more serious security and economic problems. Nor is he an advocate for nuclear power, so he's clearly talking about renewable energy sources.

And his next topic that he pointed out and repeated several times is this: he doesn't know "what the next thing is." This is my concept of the green third industrial revolution. Wes said, "Woody, it sounds like you've identified the next thing." If we start thinking about this "next thing" as the green third industrial revolution which has started in other parts of the world, we can start to solve our problems here in America. America needs to stop underwriting the fossil fuel industry which we did in the second industrial revolution and start supporting renewable energy at the same level, or more. That's what needs to happen. By the way, I just completed a book on the green third industrial revolution, called Global Energy Innovations (Preager Press, November 2011) because my grown son who is in his mid-thirties, heard me give a talk in Silicon Valley on this topic. I was invited there by the *San Jose Business Journal* and gave a speech about the green third industrial revolution which led to more talks and even an Op Ed piece in their newspaper.

CS: I think I saw that on YouTube in preparation for this talk, by the way.

WC: Did you?

CS: That's the one where you start out by saying, "I'm not selling the San Jose Business Journal, but everybody should get this."

WC: Yes. You saw that. That is the one that my grown son had seen too—and he said, "Dad, you have to write a book about this." And I didn't realize this, but when he heard me talk about it he started texting his friends and other people he went to school with – and what they were saying back is that "yes, this makes sense." And many of these friends are Republican McCain types.

CS: Great. Now when you say you're a qualitative economist I presume you mean over and against "quantitative."

WC: Right. or at least in equal conjunction with them.

CS: Why don't we talk a little bit about this – especially as I want to get into this issue about job creation. I know there are earnest economists who are extremely convinced that you'll get three nice new green jobs for every brown job lost. So let's talk about how qualitative economics applies to our understanding of the macroeconomic conditions associated with the transition to renewables.

WC: Okay. That's a big question. So I'm just going to start off with why and then get into what it means and then get into what I think the information is showing. I tend to disagree with my colleagues who estimate huge job creation. I think it's a transfer of skills into different areas, basically labeled today as "green". In fact, I am the co-editor of a special issue on *"Global Cases in Energy, Environment, and Climate Change: Some Challenges for the Field of Economics"* for Contemporary Economic Policy Journal (Western Economic International Association, due in early 2012) in which I have a paper about the Green Industrial Revolution.

One of the reasons that I was interested in talking about "qualitative economics" resulted from a trip in late 2010 that I took to Northern Italy to participate in conferences that were having people like myself who are distinguished in some way – in my case, the Nobel Peace Prize, but in other ways too. Athletes, sculptors, painters, whoever participated to find out what made them click or get into their areas. This caused me to do a great deal of inner thinking about myself and the field of qualitative economics that I co-founded.

I came up with a couple of thoughts which I just want to mention quickly. One is that I got involved with sustainability issues actually at a fairly young age, specifically through a couple of things I did when I was about 12 or 13 years old. One was my dad wanting my brothers and me as I was the oldest of three boys—to mow our lawn, which was an acre in Hamden, Connecticut. An acre of lawn when you're 13 years old is a lot of land. Well, when I was 12, I started working on a farm; I just thought it would be a neat thing to do in the summers. And my parents loved the fact that I would bring home fresh corn or raspberries or apples or whatever was being grown (not organically then) and I was picking them. I made $.50 an hour – in those days it was okay. Meanwhile, my parents wanted me to mow the lawn. I made a deal with my father that if we got a sit-down rider lawn mower, then my brothers and I would pay for it by mowing the neighbors' lawns and then we could do the lawn. He agreed; it was a handshake. First deal I ever made.

Being an entrepreneur at 13 years old was how I got a sitting lawnmower. We rode around the lawn; I think twice at the most and the rest of the time my dad did it. And then my brothers and I went to other neighbors and mowed their lawns. That turned into a business through high school and years later, even before I could drive a car. We were doing 20 to 25 lawns a week that were mostly outside of our neighborhood, so my mother would drive us around in a 4-wheel Land Rover with a trailer from Wayne-Wood Nurseries that we bought. So by the time I was a junior in high school I was driving our car and our trailer with our equipment on it, which by than was bigger equipment; we had 40 plus customers a week. That business paid our way through college – for both my brothers and me. The other brother dropped out of high school because at that time the Vietnam War was going on and he didn't want anything to do with it.

Ultimately, we were able to sell our business. It was my first business, and it was in sustainability, because we were doing gardening and landscaping, besides mowing the lawns. We were trimming, planting and taking out overgrown lawns, shrubbery and all kinds of waste and overgrown areas to make the homes look better.

When I was 13 or 14, I also won a first prize for developing a solar cooker in a school district science fair that got me an award from the local newspaper for a free trip to Detroit. They fly me there (my first airplane flight) where I got to drive a Ford Falcon.

Again, I was in ninth or tenth grade and it got me into thinking about renewable energy sources and all sorts of technologies. But it was at that age that I said to my parents... I'll never forget saying it... that I wanted to win a Nobel Prize one day.

CS: Wow. That's vision.

WC: Exactly, and that's the point that I was making to these students and young people listening in Italy. Fast-forward and you ask me about qualitative economics. I want to win the Nobel Prize in economics – because the subtitle of my book that I did on Qualitative Economics (Coxmoor Press, 2008) or QE with co-author in Denmark, Professor Michael Fast, is *"Toward the Science of Economics."* The book took us ten years to get published; and when we did it was a small private UK press. But at the same time, we were offered a contract for the USA rights by a major American press. We turned it down because the book represented the "next economics", topic of my next book!

CS: Ah. Economics, as a science, has taken a hit recently, hasn't it?

WC: Economics is not a science. As such, it means a challenge and change – and Michael and I are not the only people now saying this. We now have the field of economics asking itself that question, finally – including "The Economist" journal itself starting in mid-July 2009, nine months after the global economic collapse in October 2008. QE asks about numbers and definitions and terms, and the meaning in the world all these things have. Like "green" – and "clean" – what's that all about? What exactly are the meanings and definitions of these words? So when people say they have a clean-tech conference or that they're developing new clean-tech jobs, I get suspicious that they don't know what they're talking about, or they have another agenda that is not green.

People like Boone Pickens and many others are talking about natural gas, and keep pushing their propositions so that voters, like in California, will support his business by providing requirements to have trucks using natural gas and refueling stations equipped that way. That's absolutely insane; it's only because it makes him more money and his children's children. That's ridiculous. Natural gas is a fossil fuel. And while a bit cleaner than oil and coal, still requires infrastructures and systems that need to be funded and supported for decades in order to recover the initial costs. These "stranded costs" will inhibit and delay the green industrial revolution.

The second problem is: what do we mean then by green technology and green jobs? Well, I do think it's important that we talk about renewable energy, be it wind, solar, or combinations of those, biomass, geothermal, ocean power, or whatever. That's all part of it. But then the question becomes: what are those jobs and skill sets that are required to do that? And what I believe is happening is not just a creation of new jobs, but the transfer of jobs from the second industrial revolution into the green industrial revolution. For example, the fact is that there's been a big change in the field of engineering. The numbers of people trained – at least in the University of California system and the California State University system – that has gone from mechanical now to electrical and chemical engineering are quite large; the quantitative data is there. It's very clear. I saw this happen in the 1990s. UC Davis is one of the major campuses in the state, and it was very clear what was going on. As a qualitative economist, I asked a lot of questions. With that happening, we're going to see more and more courses for new jobs in green technology, but there are going to be people who are in the second industrial revolution now seeing the future and moving in that direction very quickly. And now the data is being kept by groups and the state Workforce Development Board, which has its own Green Committee. Almost daily, I have people contacting me about this new green sector.

But what else do the jobs and career changes mean? Basically, they mean that there is going to be a reduction in jobs in the second industrial revolution sector. That means shifting of jobs from utilities, the transmission of electrons, natural gas production and pipelines, and also nuclear power along with other fossil fuel sources of energy including coal, oil drilling and related sectors to those in the green industrial revolution. With all of this going on around the world, there will be a significant shift. So it doesn't mean a net gain, but a shift. The gain in green jobs will come later as support systems, companies and financing will be massive and require a workforce. We will have a million people who are employed in the second industrial revolution, but probably have the same million people now transfer over to the green third industrial revolution.

What all this means from my perspective is not just a transfer of jobs from utilities or major companies into green ones. It means also new environmental and entrepreneurial firms. Where are they going to come from? They're going to come from people who are studying these areas in the community colleges for support skills, ranging from technologies to accounting and business, to the Cal State and University of California systems, who see this as their future, and are getting into the green revolution. Someday, there will be an MBA degree along these lines or another major, or to get a certificate in LEED buildings, but it's going to create a whole new scope of activity in green jobs.

But the critical factor is public policy in this state has to change, and that again is the challenge for Governor Brown. On the contrary, Governor Schwarzenegger did not do this or focus on the green industrial revolution because Schwarzenegger and his advisors believed in the market economy which grew out of the second industrial revolution. Schwarzenegger accepted the market economy as an ideology, similar to his predecessors Dukmejian and Wilson. They were wrong, because the fact of the matter is that this country and other countries have always seen their governments take the lead and be a partner in doing new companies, infrastructures, finance and education. To leave a revolution just up to the private sector is a big mistake and turns out to be a fiasco financially and otherwise in the end. If you look at the history of how energy and other infrastructures were built – be it the highways, IT systems, water, waste, all of those things – it has been because of government involvement ranging from land grants and contracts to actual funding and tax incentives.

That's the problem. Schwarzenegger did just that by thinking the market forces will take care of everything due to competition and lower costs. Wrong.

CS: And I suppose you could say it goes back to the granddaddy of trickledown economics, Ronald Reagan, though obviously there were pure-market economists and laissez-faire capitalists long before that.

WC: Well, Margaret Thatcher preceded Reagan actually in the UK, but they were all part of that ideological group from the Wharton, Stanford and Chicago Schools of Economics. It was a "religion", because that is the ideology that they believed in and they took verbatim from their own economists. Part of the problem is, and I'm not saying Reagan was stupid, but he didn't know any better. As an actor, like Schwarzenegger, they are good at reading scripts and just had their advisors come in and tell them what to do. Many of those advisors today have admitted that they were wrong. And they knew they were wrong then, because they were working on a theory that worked in some ways, but that was a perfect world a couple hundred years ago with Adam Smith and his neo-classical economic paradigm.

Certainly today, the UK itself has changed dramatically. If you look at what's happening in the UK with the utility industry, including the nuclear power industry, it's totally different from the neo-classical paradigm of Adam Smith. The UK government is back big-time, and that's an amazing change. However, do we hear or talk about that dramatic economic change of government involvement in California, or anywhere in America? No. We're still in the neo-classical ideology of the second industrial revolution.

CS: Right. But even Adam Smith understood there are certain things that markets do not do well. They may build widgets and so forth, but do they do environmental protection well?

WC: Not only that, I don't think Adam Smith even cared about or knew about it when he was writing.

CS: No, certainly not. But he recognized at a qualitative level there are certain things that a market economy will not take care of.

WC: Right. And that goes to what I discovered in state government when I served from 2000 through 2003 in Sacramento. There were very few elected officials who even knew anything about the connection of energy with the environment, let alone the economics involved. They segregated these areas, and that was due to being both naïve and isolated into their own special interests. Now, a decade later that has changed. The leaders and decision-makers need to integrate those systems and infrastructures to make them very compatible with one another – including energy but also water, waste and transportation by segregating those areas. Again, remember "small is beautiful" due to being sustainable and local. And that's where we cut down our costs. The fact is that these systems need to be integrated.

By the way, that is also true for renewable energy. Today they talk about solar on the one hand and wind separately; that's ridiculous. I teach MBA classes in Southern California and various other parts of the world. I had one group of MBA students of mine at UC Riverside who came up with a class project paper combining wind farms with their rows of wind turbines with solar concentrated systems in between the rows.

CS: Yep. That's an excellent point. It makes me sick to go to one of these conferences like Solar Power International, and you've got tens of thousands of people and nobody mentioning wind or geothermal, as if they're competitors, or lepers. It's ridiculous.

I know there are going to be people reading this chapter who are going to say "wait a second. Small is beautiful, but are you talking about government regulation—a carbon tax? Obviously you're also talking about government being a significant part of the solution."

WC: Yeah. I'll tell you that right now. Let's take the meaning and definition of small is beautiful. Small is beautiful means many things to many people. The key is that small does not mean "no government". Instead, small simply means that management and structures are being more efficient, personal and economical. One of the things I believe is that you're going to find utilities, be they the Department of Water and Power here in Los Angeles or Pacific Gas and Electric in Northern California, that are going to need to change their actual organization; it needs to be reorganized and downsized. This is because they're going to find more power being generated in the communities locally on the roofs of homes, offices and clusters of buildings, or generated from the ocean and other sources. That means in effect that "small" means a reorganization issue of downsizing. It's actually something I experienced at LLNL in the 1990s. They were downsized from about 12,000 people to 8,500 people. I was hired in the downsizing effort because I was the only business economist person in the entire organization. They had 1,300 physicists there, as well as 3,500 engineers and chemists among other scientists. LLNL saw a need for a new beginning in doing technology transfer and commercialization.

I think the same thing is going to happen with utilities; this is my prediction. The green industrial revolution will mean a re-organization of companies and groups, including management and unions. Many people will move to private companies, start their own or work for NGOs. That's the green future which is good actually because what it means is the larger companies are going to be more efficient and better at what they do, focused on getting the renewable energy systems up and running; but also focused on the local community (small) is going to have to do its part of the work. Thus downsizing is important.

If you look at the way that organizations and companies are structured by management and labor, there needs to be changes. I think we need to be more proactive in terms of helping people retire, take their pensions, start new companies and open up opportunities for younger people. That's what we did at Lawrence Livermore National Laboratory when I first came there. There was a whole new generation of people; it's now become a new organization and they've got 12,000 people again. But my point is there's going to have to be change in organizations.

So that's one factor, but there are two other cases. First, the city of Berkeley started a program called the PACE program, or Property Assessment Clean Energy. I know some of the major people involved in this program. They and others felt that what needed to happen is get green energy—renewable energy—for people's homes, their shops, their buildings, and the City of Berkeley government buildings. They got a venture capital group to help sponsor getting the project started, and actually putting these systems on people's homes. Small is beautiful. And the money would be paid back; the projects would be financed by the city and repaid to the city through an additional tax on homeowners or office building owners. The problem was that when PACE went to Fannie Mae and Freddie Mac, by the spring of 2010, they nixed it in terms of private homeowners. Companies were fine. Now the program still exists in some capacity for commercial buildings, but for the private individuals' homes, it's not financeable.

The reason, and this makes sense, is that the Fannie Mae and Freddie Mac staff felt that if there were any foreclosure or mortgage payment problems, the first people to get paid back was not the mortgage, but in fact the City of Berkeley. That was a no-no. And I can see that because that means to Fannie May and Freddie Mac – or any other mortgage company – it could go bankrupt if this happened. The city would get control of the property and not the mortgage company. So PACE was stopped for private homes. But I have a better alternative which I think makes far more sense. Are you ready?

CS: Sure.

WC: Do you want to take notes on this one? Are you ready?

CS: Sure. This is an alternative PACE to Berkeley's PACE?

WC: Exactly. In fact, this is a small is beautiful example. Again, Governor Brown needs to read this and do it. He's in a situation where he could put this idea in place. Make renewable energy part of the home mortgage itself. That is to say, we already have in our homes today plumbing, electricity, toilets, air conditioning, and heating systems. Fifty years ago let alone 80 years ago we didn't have those modern devices and technologies.

CS: Yes, I've heard this recently, but it may be your idea originally.

WC: It might have been. I think I mentioned it at the ACORE conference in San Francisco; I've been public about it because I'm advocating that what we need to see is at least one or two banks start the renewable energy program incorporated into the basic home mortgage on a trial basis somewhere in California. Finance the homes through the mortgage when people are doing refinancing, which I think a lot of people are trying to do these days. Thus renewable energy systems and even storage devices are part of their mortgage – which is what they should be in the green industrial revolution. It's like a roof on your home. They're going to last 20 or 30 years. My point being is that's where small is beautiful – in your own home. It's where it makes a difference and that's where it can be done by everybody.

CS: Okay. Let me ask you about this. You know a lot about renewables at the state level, and that's wonderful. But I have two questions about this. The most obvious is what opponents of this say, i.e., that environmental regulations are anti-business – that they tend to drive business out of the state. And this is potentially correct to the degree that we have neighboring states – Arizona and Nevada that don't have anything like our (clean energy mandate) AB32. So, I go back to the issue of state's rights from James Madison and the other framers of the Constitution, coming to a head again in the Civil War. And it's still a big deal. We've got 50 different sets of statutes making confusion at so many different levels. So doesn't this create some kind of imbalance that is really a mess? And if so, what should we do about it?

WC: Well, when I arrived in the Governor's office in December of 2000, the energy crisis had already started that spring and summer. I was a visiting professor in Denmark at that time; I had been a Fulbright Fellow there in 1994 and I went back every year for at least a week or so to give lectures and talks about entrepreneurship. But I was asked to come back to California, in part because I had told senior people in the Governor Davis administration that they were going to have an energy crisis at some point sooner than later; I told them that in January and February of 2000. They remembered that. I was working with them on eGovernment at the time, which is one of the things Governor Davis was trying to do. Given that working relationship across the USA and Atlantic Ocean, we created a bond and communication. The energy crisis happened and they asked me to come back and help. It's not so much predicting, but *knowing* that there was going to be a problem in terms of the state's de-regulation of its energy. Where it was coming from is extremely important, because it means that there's an issue regarding jobs and the economy. The previous administrations argued that energy would come from the "market". Indeed energy did come from the market – when they wanted to supply it – hence driving up costs, causing brown outs and threatening the economy of the entire state.

The issue about jobs leaving the state because they're being taxed in a certain way, meaning there'll be fewer jobs, and people will go someplace else or go to another state, is one of the most ridiculous arguments I've ever heard. There is no evidence to it whatsoever. You can see in Silicon Valley, the evidence counter to that argument. While some aspects of business (manufacturing in particular) left California, a lot of them stayed and even grew, so that Silicon Valley even to this day, is still considered the international leader of innovation. When companies leave, there are only certain ways in which they leave. In terms of their corporate headquarters, business models, the executives and people who are doing quite well thank you, they stay in California.

Now, I have to say I see this much more in Northern California than I do in Southern California. Again, I am new to Southern California; I've been here a decade now, since the recall of Governor Davis. But the point I'm making is that if you look at California and then you look at Oregon and Washington, there's the same pattern. They're doing the same thing and they're also extremely successful. When I was in Seattle it was clear that was going on. In fact, what I've noticed in Oregon and Washington is there are more creative advancements going on in the environment and energy areas than there are in California; we have fallen behind in that area.

However, in general, there has been very clear evidence that the West Coast is clearly stepped out in front of the curve here. And I don't mean California, but the entire West Coast – the Northwest Coast in particular, and I think that's going to continue. Arizona and Nevada are exceptions as they tend to ignore environmental concerns. Now, in terms of job creation, we're also seeing companies of various types including investment companies coming to California from Asia. If you go back 20 years we saw that same series of financial investments happening with Japan. The Japanese, did it with advice and counsel from people that turned out to be problems in the 1990s; the bubble burst, and their economy has lost a lot because of that.

I think that could happen again with China, but what I've noticed working with people in China even as of yesterday, is that they are very aware of these problems. They are very conscious of the past with Japan and other nations coming to the USA; and they are not going to let it happen to them. I give the Chinese a lot of credit for that. It's partly because their government is going to watch this green industrial revolution very closely in the way in which they both govern and create companies; it's very different than what the Japanese did. Chinese companies tend to be started and continued to be owned in part by their government.

CS: Okay. Maybe we could talk about the federal level.

WC: Can I give you an example of another case?

CS: Of course.

WC: You were asking me how small is beautiful, right? This is to me one of the most revolutionary things having to do with renewable energy. Are you ready? Sitting down? Comfortable? Until the last five or six years, Japanese companies were ahead in solar manufacturing and sales, and then the Germans took over because of their feed-in tariff laws. Now, when I was in state government I got in arguments with people in the solar industry, because I had done some work for the UN Framework Convention on Climate Change. I was their first research director in the mid-1990s, and I led an international panel that studied six developed countries for their "environmentally sound" energy companies (e.g., wind, solar, biomass and others) and how technology could be transferred to developing countries.

Solar was one of the technologies – with specific focus on Japan. When I was in the Governor's Office for a meeting in 2001 with people from the solar industry, they were saying. "You got to buy large amounts of gigawatts of solar today; the price will never be better. The state needs renewable energy. There are only limited amounts of solar panels in the world." He represented a German solar company.

I'll never forget this private closed meeting. We had legal counsel for the Governor's office there, and two of us together were chairing the meeting. Then I said—I'll never forget it. "Well, wait a minute. You're talking about solar. Are you just talking about solar panels from Europe? Or are you also including Japan?" The German representative responded: "I'm not talking about Japan. Those people are crooks. They'll steal everything you own." I turned to him and I said, "What the "hell" are you talking about? That is wrong. The Japanese are not like that. And they have the largest amount of solar panels available today." Then he and I got in this verbal battle and our legal person asked me to come outside and calm down.

I said to our legal person, "The guy's lying. The five leading solar companies in the world are Japanese, from Sharp to Kyocera and others." Now, this is in the year 2001. Well, that's since changed, and it's changed even more because of China who have a different program for strategies to create companies through their Five Year Plans. China has said if groups outside of China want to have renewable energy then it will finance 80 percent of the systems over time. Make sure you're sitting down for this. *80 percent* – as long as you use Chinese manufacturers. That's brilliant.

CS: Wow. They're pretty aggressive about that.

WC: It's one of the most significant financing ideas I've heard. In other words, you're a manufacturer and you're a financier in one package. And why don't we do that in America? Now, as a caveat, those systems from China are only available on a large scale. I think the systems need to be over 15 megawatts, meaning these are massive systems, not ones that can be used for homes and factories as well as , universities, government, and school districts. But my point is that concept is extremely important to keep in mind.

CS: I suppose, but I hearken back to Chuck Schumer's wanting to put a spear through the west Texas wind farm because ARPA-E money was going to the Chinese.

WC: Well, you got to remember that wind farms that are developed in China are actually developed by a company called Vestas, which is headquartered in southern Denmark and went to China in the early 1990s. They formed a joint venture in China, which is the way the Chinese form most of their private companies. They still own an interest in that company, and will always own an interest in it. So the Chinese have a joint venture with Vestas. It's not a Chinese company; it's Vestas. And it is by far the largest wind turbine company in the world.

Now, I say that because that Chinese government investment model in company formation is also a good green industrial revolution economic model. It's also what happened in Germany, when it was going to de-regulate their postal service. The German government kept an interest in the postal service, so that it was not all privatized, and market oriented. The results have been solid and incredible as seen in the German economy today.

CS: I see.

I often shake my head at our lack of an energy policy and the subsidiary issue of federal RPS (renewable portfolio standard). If I were king of the world I don't think it would be that difficult to mandate at a federal level – even though I grant we have varying energy resources – sun in the deserts and wind in the plains and so forth. Every region has some level of renewable resource and I don't think it would be impossible to come up with a fair way of saying, "Here's an aggressive schedule that we're going to adopt over the coming 20 to 30 years." Do you agree that we should do that, and if so, what do you see as the impediments?

WC: Well, I got into that again a decade ago just so you know. When I got into the Governor's office, I had proposed an RPS literally right out of the box. Yet I had to define my role because the governor had other energy advisors, so there were about four or five of us in all, including one or two civil servants. However, I only wanted to focus on renewable energy, so I defined my role, and got it approved by the governor's office, to be renewable energy, emerging technology, and finance advisor, because I felt those were the key elements to the state's energy future.

The first policy issue that I came across was that of an RPS that was advocated by groups primarily in San Francisco and some NGOs. They wanted a 20 percent RPS in California. You have to remember that the state at the time was not much better than the country as a whole today; it was maybe two percent or less using renewable energy, not counting hydroelectric power. That one or two percent was nothing. There were other states that had RPS goals that were all going to be 20 percent or more.

I told the governor's office that instead of 20 percent, we should go for at least a third of our energy – 33 or 35 percent as a goal – and make it as a goal not by 2050, but by 2020 at the latest or maybe 2015.

That was rejected by the governor's office, and I probably know why and who was responsible, but the fact is that for internal political reasons it was not accepted. Fast-forward, and Schwarzenegger comes into office. He took two executive orders from me personally that he gave when he first took office; some of his colleagues were also working with me when Davis was in office, who were also taking the information to Schwarzenegger, which I didn't know about until later. But the fact is that Schwarzenegger then comes out with an executive order a couple of years ago that said by 2015 the state should have 33 percent renewable energy.

CS: Right. But it's non-binding. It's an executive order.

WC: Right, an executive order. That's the trouble; they're not binding. And the point I'm trying to make is that this is part of the issue with RPS, because now at the federal level they're talking about an RPS at 17 percent. So does that mean literally California would be required to do half of what it could be doing which is 35 percent or more? Hence the state does not need to double what it wants to do? That's the problem: states and companies, businesses and even homeowners think this 17 percent – or even 35 percent is the ceiling—you don't have to go above it. That is a mistake.

Big mistake, but that's what happens. It should be the base and there should be incentives to go over that base, not to just meet it. And that's exactly what is going on in Scandinavia, China, Japan and South Korea today. They're now looking at this as the lowest hanging fruit, but just a level to meet.

CS: For sure. Moreover, you bring up a good point about the renewable resource and the economic condition of the area, etc. For instance, I was interviewing a guy at Audubon about wind, and he told me that his state, Wyoming, was supposed to contribute X amount. I replied that I would think, with wind coming out its ears, that we'd probably be hoping for an "over-contribution" from the state of Wyoming.

WC: Right. But this is one of the points that I was making before about Governor Brown. Last fall (2010), I believe there was on Schwarzenegger's desk a bill that he either didn't sign or vetoed to have a RPS standard in law – not just an executive order. I think it was 33 percent or it could have been 30 percent – something significantly higher than 20. I believe that again, Jerry Brown, as former attorney general, has the staff and people to look into this. I believe that he has the authority to take it back on his desk and sign it into law, and that's different than an executive order. Brown has certainly come out proposing much higher levels of renewable energy for California.

And if that's the case that's one of the first things he might do in office – now that the budget has been approved. I'm telling you he would rally the "green" troops and companies in this state and around the world, if he were to do that.

CS: The politics on this must be nasty—and getting worse.

WC: In fact, I'll give you another example of a case. One of the things that I was starting with Governor Davis and then Schwarzenegger took over was the concept of having a California hydrogen highway. We had at one point, hundreds of people in organizations doing the planning, diagramming, outlining, and everything else to make it real. Then Schwarzenegger took over and got a group to organize a Hydrogen Highway Plan in 2004/2005. The report is issued. There was a website link to the governor's office, etc. But Schwarzenegger's attitude was let the market decide. You can't do that. There's no state highway, no transportation, no infrastructure of any kind in the world that ever had so-called "market initiative" do it. And so the consequence was the state got behind. And if you want the evidence for that you can see now hydrogen fuel cell cars are being mass produced in Germany, Japan and now in South Korea. Detroit has them too but nowhere to refuel or put them in the mass market, let alone focus on renewable energy as the electrolyzed energy for these vehicles.

CS: I'm with you. One last issue, if I may. I'm very concerned about corporate personhood and the Supreme Court's recently granting the right of free speech to corporations. This means they can simply buy our elections. We so desperately need campaign finance reform, but what we got here was the precise opposite. Can you comment?

WC: Well, we saw that in our election here in California in November of 2010 where the U.S. Chamber of Commerce and the Sacramento State based Chamber of Commerce (not supported, I might add, by many of the local chapters) was putting lots of money into supporting Republican guber-natorial candidate Meg Whitman, and others of a similar perspective. That is wrong and will keep the state and the nation in the second industrial revolution for another few decades. I totally agree with you. That's one of the things I'm hoping that President Obama is able to deal with while he's still in office and why I hope he stays another term, but he has to make some changes. He's got to be consistent. He's got to deliver to his broad base that elected him.

One suggestion in closing I might make to you that might be useful: I don't know if you want to do this or not, but post some bullet points on your website about some of the issues and ideas that we (and others) have been talking about – particularly with Governor Brown in office. If you want to take some of what we said and do that, it might be useful.

CS: Yes, that's a great idea. Thanks very much for every-thing, Woody.

Craig's Interview with Stephan A. Schwartz

For those who may want a perspective on the migration to renewable energy that you're extremely unlikely to find elsewhere, I present to you Stephan. A. Schwartz, whose life has been spent exploring extraordinary human functioning, and how individuals and small groups can affect, and have affected, social change.

His work in parapsychology, archaeology, anthropology, medicine and healing, creativity, and social policy pair nicely with the questions I ask myself a great deal: What's really going on behind the scenes when it comes to social phenomena?

The reader will note that there are two different subjects addressed here, and that the first of the two is of less obvious relevance to the subject at hand. In fact, I was tempted to edit this first section (the first five pages or so) out of the final manuscript. But upon re-reading it, I've decided to include it here. I believe that most readers will find it as interesting as I did, and I am convinced that what Schwartz is saying is correct: a) human consciousness does, in fact, affect the exterior world, and b), that a small group of enlightened people can have a profoundly positive effect on society and on the future that we ultimately experience.

If this sounds "whacky," I urge the reader not to skip the entire interview, but to advance past that point and rejoin the conversation; it would be a shame to miss the second half, regardless of your feelings about the beginning.

CS: Stephan, thanks so much for taking time for me. I sent you a copy of my last book, didn't I?

SS: Let's see… *Renewable Energy: Facts and Fantasies.* I have it right here. It's at the top of my list.

CS: Well, I'm flattered! So the concept that I've embraced over the last couple of years is this issue of sustainability, specifically focusing on renewable energy and electric transportation as an important thread through this. I published that book last year, and the one I'm working on this year explores various additional dimensions: macroeconomics and the other social sciences, to get at this subject from a humanistic viewpoint.

SS: Sure.

CS: I know you're connected to this subject in a number of different ways, and I'd like to begin by asking you about the part of your work for which you're best known, which I'll call the confluence of quantum physics with the philosophy of mind. I can't say that I'm an authority on this by any means, but coincidentally, I took various courses as a much younger man on quantum mechanics, Zen, existentialism, phenomenology and so forth, and it struck me – even back then—that perhaps the observer and the observed are not two distinct things.

SS: Oh, yes. The evidence for this is now quite over-whelming. Only people who are still trapped in the physi-calist model of thought doubt this. I don't know if I sent you the paper that Larry Dossey—I don't know if that name means anything to you—Larry is one of the found-ers of holistic medicine, and he's the editor of the journal *Explore* for which I write a monthly column. Anyway, we just did a paper on observers of facts, making that exact point in the effects of the observer as a participant and the role that those non-local linkages and local linkages play.

And then there's the whole development that's been going on in quantum biology and neuroscience in general, show-ing that cells operate by going down the timeline. They pick the most optimal future of the futures available to them and then bring that information back and then live into that future.

CS: That's amazing.

SS: There's a whole series of papers – probably, I don't know, maybe 25 in the last year, that have supported this information. What's happening is that the neurosciences, the quantum physics research, and what is now becoming known as quantum biology and parapsychology are all con-verging on this same model of how consciousness works.

CS: And what is that model? How would you articulate that in a paragraph or so?

SS: Well, I would say that it is now clear that conscious-ness of the mind is not only local to the brain. That is, parts of its functions are tied to the neurophysiology of the body. And another part is clearly non-local. That is, it's not limited by space-time. This has been experimentally dem-onstrated in a number of different disciplines. One of the most interesting areas of research is the area where studies are showing that prior to having an experience—about three to ten seconds before you have the experience—your body responds to the experience. You don't even know it's coming. It's not like you know it's coming and it's anticipatory.

To give you an example, and there are many of these, you're staring at a television screen or a monitor and periodically—you don't anticipate it—you don't know when it's going to happen—pictures come up on the screen that you're staring at. So it's white noise, white noise, white noise, picture. And unbeknownst to you, a camera is focusing on the iris of your eye. About three seconds before the picture occurs, the iris of your eye dilates. If the picture is highly numinous, that is, it evokes a strong emotional response—it's erotic or it's violent—the dilation is even stronger. So you can look at the dilation of the eye and not only predict when the picture is coming, but you can determine whether the picture will be numinous or just a picture of a house cat or something like that.

CS: Holy mackerel! Well to explain something like this, it would seem to me that we need to either completely redefine what we mean by "mind," or throw in the existence of the human spirit as so many different sects do, for instance, the Scientologists who suggest that we are not essentially minds and bodies, but we're spirits as well.

SS: I would say to you that until about 500 years ago the only—roughly dating it from Galileo, but you could also think of it as dating from Descartes—I'll leave it with those two. Anyway, until about 500 years ago the only way to conceptualize a non-local experience was as a spiritual experience. It was either God speaking to you or the spirits speaking to you or something that was non-space-time. The only way you could really address that was to describe it in either spiritual or religious terms, and that's true to a certain extent even today. I would say to you that what we call spiritual is in fact the non-local aspect of consciousness. It's just that there was no other way to contextualize it. Only in recent years with the development of scientific protocols which could address this aspect, have we been able to discover that that which was previously called "spiritual" is in fact this aspect of consciousness, and that it's now possible to begin to explore how that aspect of consciousness works.

In fact, I'm writing a paper right now with a mathematician; he has the mathematical formalism that I don't. We provide a model of how this works, but we have a wide body of research from many different disciplines showing us that the limits of mind do not reside entirely in the physicality of the organism. Quantum physics would appear to be—I don't say it is; I would simply say that at the moment it would appear to be—the sort of osmotic membrane that lies between the world of space-time and the informational domain of the non-local; what in traditional terms would have been called the collective unconscious. This domain is informational in nature. It contains information architectures which are created by acts of intentioned awareness. This is why if you look at religions, whatever their dogma is, you will note that they have empirically developed an approach to the opening to their concept of the spiritual— and that is universal. That is, if you look at all the world's religions, you will see that they define a specific space, a physical space, which is the place where people come together to have this experience, whether it's a cathedral or a synagogue or a monastery or whatever. They gather, and they make a statement of intention. If you're a Christian it's the Nicene Creed. If you're a Buddhist it's a sutra. There's a statement of intention because the three things we know about the non-local are intention, numinosity, and entropic process.

So we made the statement that there is usually some form of collective chanting, drumming, dancing, music, singing; the idea of which is to lift people together and studies show that brain entrainment occurs. And then there is a statement of intention to open to the non-local experience, and so then you have everything from speaking on tongues to voodoo possession, to deep meditative transcendental experiences. I'm putting together about 30 of the leading researchers in the world to do a book on psychophysical self-regulation, meditation, spirit, and science.

So you see these same steps reoccur across all of the various ways in which people approach the non-local. If you think of the rituals of spiritual traditions or religions as protocols, then you can see that they mimic or they parallel the same protocols that are used in the laboratory to evoke non-local awareness in say remote viewing or therapeutic intention healing or presentment or random number generation perturbation. All of these things, whether they are framed in the context of religion and spiritual tradition or whether they are poised in the context of scientific protocols, they're all doing the same thing. That is to allow the neuroanatomy of the organism to relax and to be focused and to open to this dimension of consciousness which is outside of space-time: the transcendental part.

CS: Okay. I read the intro to a book the other day about what is consciousness. The guy started off by saying we're actually fairly close to understanding the components of the universe, based on our analysis of the big bang. He thinks we're actually reasonably close to having this answered. Now we've got dark matter and dark energy and so forth and so on, but there's a chance we'll get there. But he goes on to say that he doesn't have a warm feeling about answering the question of what is consciousness. Now, you apparently are a little more sanguine.

So you say that spirituality was a pre-scientific attempt to explain some of these phenomena and now we have a full-blown scientific and mathematical analysis of the situation, but at the end of the day somebody has to explain what is consciousness. Can you answer me that?

SS: Well, I would say that we don't yet know what consciousness is. My speculation is that we're going to discover that consciousness is causal and that matter is an expression of consciousness. That consciousness is ultimately informational and that consciousness shapes space-time and is a subset of the informational domain. That is, ultimately the Buddhists are right. What we think of as consciousness is actually our awareness of the informational domain and that, although we don't know what the mechanism is, we can begin to explore this informational domain on its phenomenological manifestations. So that consciousness, as it is traditionally meant, is that aspect of the informational domain that is expressed through the locality of the neuro-anatomy. In fact, space-time is an illusion. It is an informational construct itself.

CS: Right. Well, Kant said that in 1780 or something like that.

SS: Oh, you can go back to the Sutras of Patanjali in the second century BC and read it. You can go back to Plotinus. People have been having these experiences and have been trying to work in a rational, explanatory model their experiences probably as long as there have been people. So no, I don't think of any of this as being particularly new. What is interesting is that with the tools of science, we are now able to objectively measure and explore this aspect of consciousness.

That's the big development. I don't know that our insights are any deeper of those of Patanjali for instance. If you never read the Sutra of Patanjali, it's definitely worth taking a look at. It's on the 'net you can get it for free. Or you can look up Plotinus; he's another one that stands out for me. But this idea of consciousness as being causal is a very ancient one.

CS: Well, that's amazing. I'm fascinated by this. I hope I get the opportunity to come up and just spend a couple of hours with you. But unfortunately I need to get to the next part of this conversation.

SS: I understand. As you know, I live in several worlds quite comfortably. So now, we can talk about sustainability. I'm also doing a project on the social metrics of the resilient community. You've read the *Schwartz Report,* I presume?

CS: I've seen it. In fact, that's how I initially got a hold of you. I was just completely bowled over by what you were saying in terms of sustainability and how we're off here by about a million miles.

By the way, I can see lots of different connections here; they're not two distinct conversations. Certainly that we're much more causative than we think we are. And that not only the things that we *do*, but the things that we *think* have repercussions on everyone and everything.

SS: Absolutely. We are all interlinked. There's an emerging new model that I've written about; I can send you papers. The physicalist model is that all consciousness is contained within the brain. It's a result of physiological processes that there is no contact other than the traditional sense perceptions, that are limited by space-time. But in fact, what we are now seeing experimentally is that all consciousness is interlinked and interdependent, but only a portion of the mind is local to the physiology.

You can see this playing itself out. For instance, Craig, there is research showing that happiness spreads through a population like a virus. That is, if you go into your drycleaner and all you have in the exchange is a smile and he says, "Good morning Mr. Shields. That will be $6.95 for the shirts." And you say, "Oh, thank you Mr. Chow. It's a pleasure. I hope you're having a good day." Just that simple little exchange results in both of you achieving an increase of happiness and this carries out six generations—six iterations I guess is the way to put it. And we know, for instance, that experimentally that hearing good news about a friend will produce a larger physiological response than being told you just got a $5,000 raise.

So you can look at it in that way. You begin to realize that your consciousness and the reaction that you have in your own personal life affects everybody around you as they in turn affect you and that we are in this matrix of information. For instance, take Roger Nelson's global consciousness project, which has been running for about ten years now. Roger has a particular kind of random event generator salted all over the world. I've forgotten how many; there are like 30 of them now. They show that before a highly traumatic event occurs—the death of Princess Diana for instance is a good one—that the random number generators go non-random.

CS: I've heard that.

SS: It shows that even before the event occurs and immediately after the occurrence of the event, that there is some kind of linkage in the non-local because these people are scattered all over the world and who don't know each other.

That they are nonetheless linked in consciousness, and this consciousness is sufficient to produce a perturbation in a random number generator which by definition is supposed to be random. But it goes non-random. You can go to the Global Consciousness Project website and you can see all of this.

This is part of what we need in thinking about regarding sustainable communities, and it happens to be a project that I'm very involved with now because I believe that we are moving into a new era of history. We're seeing the collapse of the American Empire in which you and I have lived all of our lives up until the last ten years. We have lived all of our lives in a bipolar geopolitical reality which is now shifting to a multi-polar reality with the lives of China, India, Brazil, and other countries as power centers. As the breakdown of the American Empire occurs, a great deal of perturbation is going to occur in the financial and in other national realms; it's already happening.

And that increasingly localism/regionalism and a sustainable community are going to become enormously important. I've been looking at what constitutes a sustainable community. It isn't entirely what you might imagine. As it happens, I've been greatly benefited by the fact that I live in a sustainable community; South Whidbey Island off the coast of Seattle is a very good example of a sustainable community. We have, in the country at large, one in eight families on food assistance. On the island here, one in four is. So we are an order of magnitude more perturbed in terms of food than the country as a whole. We have high unemployment because of what's happened in the economy, and that ought to result in a significant increase in alienation, teenage vandalism, graffiti, violence, spousal abuse, all the negative things that you see in communities that are heavily stressed. But in fact, we don't have any of that. I mean, we have some crime, but our crime is there's a drunk urinating on my front lawn.

The question is: why don't we have what we ought to have? The answer is that the community is volitional; they chose to be here; they didn't get born here. The volitional community has set in motion a series of interlocking support mechanisms, which treat people with dignity. We have an extraordinary sophisticated food bank system for instance, and an organic garden. Teenagers, instead of getting sent to prison get sent to work in the garden, which changes their whole perspective.

A group of women, my wife being one of them, make food for all the children on the island; they make about 1200 lunches. They send these kids on the weekend with extra food so that they're getting not just food, but organic food without any of the additives, so they get decent nutrition.

About 10 percent of our teenagers are homeless living in the woods or couch-surfing. So they started a community coffeehouse where the kids come to work and hangout and if you volunteer so many hours, they'll pay for your college education.

We have something called Friends of Friends which is a program to which people contribute so that people who don't have medical insurance or are underinsured can get the money they need to get the treatments they need. We've given out about $800,000 in the last five years.

We have a hospice system. We have a whole gardening thing growing local food; localism. Hearts and Hammers is another one for elderly people or low income people; if your water heater breaks, you can contact Hearts and Hammers and they'll come fix it. Or if your roof collapses, they'll build you a new roof. So you have this volitional network that supports a decent quality of life for everyone without being condescending to those at the bottom so that they don't feel alienated.

CS: That's fantastic.

SS: And it seems to me that this question usually gets argued as one of: we don't have enough money. But in fact, if you look at it, if you do the research and you go to *Huffington Post* and do a search on my name, you will find a series of my essays on this. It's never the money. It's about creating the priority. When you can create the priority and get people to agree that that's the priority that everyone wants to support, the money appears because it comes out in the form of volunteer activity.

So we need to examine all this as we transit into the perfect storm: the collapse of the American Empire, the rise of the multi-polar political reality, the transition from out of the petroleum age to sustainable energy, the green transition. As all of this is occurring, and climate change and sea-rise is occurring, the real question we need to be asking about sustainable communities is not where's the money going to come from, but what are our real priorities. The real question is how can a small community create an environment in which the quality of life of all of the members of that community is sustained.

CS: Well, that's actually why I wanted to speak with you. What I had originally written about you based on what I read of your work was this whole thing about mutual support and compassion. Midway through my little blog post I wrote, "I have no doubt that the world would be a wonderful place in which to live if all of our leaders in both the public and private sector were as enlightened as Schwartz. But the simple truth is that they're not. While many of them may be smart, hard-working people, they are on missions that have nothing whatsoever to do with improving the quality of life for the other seven billion people on the planet."

SS: Yes.

CS: So I guess the question is I don't dispute what you're saying. As a matter of fact, the reason I'm speaking with you is because I'm a big fan of this. I'm just looking for a way of making it happen. Maybe I'm just cynical, but I see people becoming *less* interested in things like this, *more* afraid, angrier, quicker to point fingers of blame, and less able to take responsibility for their own condition.

SS: Right. Yeah, I understand. I got it exactly. Well, there is another force that is going on. It's a yin-yang operation. That is the rise of willful ignorance. I've written an essay called *The Great Schism* because it is my belief that what's happening now... you remember that I told you about the iris dilation?

CS: Yes.

SS: You can let that stand for a whole class of experiments that are different; they're not all irises. Some have to do with your brain's anticipating a sound before it hears it, and all that kind of thing. So that's a whole class of experiments. What those experiments are telling us is that individuals have a presentment response. That is, they anticipate something coming before it happens and that this collectively—all those individuals together—this collectively is producing a huge schism in our culture. On one side of the schism are people who are fearful and therefore angry; who feel the world as they have known it is breaking up, who are religiously conservative and dogmatic, who are essentially being motivated by fear and anger. That's the tea party movement for instance.

On the other side are people who see that yes, we're going through a massive transition, but this offers us a potential to create a better society—one that is more consistent with the natural forces of the Earth itself, and recognizes the interdependence and interconnection of all life. So you and I, and probably most of our friends, fall on one side of this schism, and Sarah Palin, Glenn Beck, Rush Limbaugh, who fall on the other side.

The other thing that's going on that you have to also mention is that America, for the first time in its history, is going to be a majority nonwhite country. In fact, several states are already majority nonwhite and by 2035 the whole country will be. So that's why you see all the racial stuff that's beginning to come up. So the question is: How do you get the willfully ignorant people on the red side of the schism to awaken to the potential that they need not be so fearful?

The answer I think ultimately gets down to local communities again. It is only when you see something work that you can identify with it. So the way we're going to address the people on the red side of the schism is simply to produce local communities which prosper.

Now, we know for instance that on the red side of the equation, which is religiously conservative, that we have more spousal abuse. This isn't a dispute; this isn't anything to argue about. This is just data. There's more spousal abuse, there's more unwed pregnancy, there's a higher incident of sexually transmitted disease, there's lower performance in the educational institutions, lower income: altogether a lower quality of life than on the blue side of the equation, although it's not really political. It's not Democrat/Republican. That's a manifestation of it, but it's much more about where you fall in the schism. On the red side you have this overpowering and suffocating willful ignorance. You can see this, for instance, in the fact that the recently published study which shows that 13 percent of science teachers in the United States don't believe that evolution is real and basically teach creationism. Or that 60 percent of science teachers in the United States feel compelled, because of the pressures that their community exerts, to teach evolution and creationism as equivalents, which of course they're not.

So the only way you're ever going to get through this as far as I can see is by producing communities that are more functional. First of all, that will attract people who are interested in that functionality. Second of all, as things get more and more desperate, base communities which are most dysfunctional will begin to look at those communities which are more functional, and ask them directly or indirectly how they did it. So I am arguing that to get through this transition we need to focus on local and regional activities—partly because the federal government has no money to help. The states are essentially bankrupt, or many of them anyway. The municipalities are bankrupt. It's not going to come from the government, at least not entirely, because the government either doesn't have the money or doesn't have the will.

So then again, the question is: How does a local community maintain the quality of its life through this transition? The answer becomes it has to be done locally—regionally at the largest component, but locally mostly. And how does that happen? I'm actually working on a project to do that. First, we need to define the social metrics that measure the sustainability in a resilient community. And second of all, we develop the educational products and put them online so communities around the country can download them. Not the community, but city managers, city planners, social workers – all the people that are involved with the well-being of a community.

CS: Well, I find this fascinating for a couple of reasons. One, obviously the whole issue of distributed versus centralized energy generation ties into this. Every time I write about some kind of centralized solar thermal farm in the shape of a square 100 miles on a side that would be more than sufficient to power the entire continent of North America (which is true), there are people who rightfully pushback and say, "Yeah, but you keep thinking in terms of the big utility, the big, for-profit corporate paradigm. The sun is "the people's" power. We don't need that old paradigm."

SS: But think about this also, Craig. Science develops from the mechanical to the electromechanical to the electrical and now we're beginning to move to the biological. That's a very important precept because it directly addresses this issue of decentralization. I believe in decentralization of energy not only for all the reasons that you mentioned, but also because, from a national security point of view, we don't want to have another major blackout.

Remember the precept; the mechanical to the electromechanical to the electrical to the biological.

If you look for instance at wind generation, I would not invest in wind turbines because those are electromechanical. The new thing that is coming up are these waving fronds in which the flexion of the frond itself produces electricity. It can be used both on the sea floor and also put up in small groups even in parks and incorporated into the landscaping. They make no noise. They don't threaten any birds and they produce power just by the flexing of the frond.

I think that the energy solution is not going to be one thing. It's going to be a variety of technologies. Just to give an example, MIT and Dow Corning have announced that they are going to market this spring an inexpensive roof shingle which will link together turning the entire roof into a photovoltaic generator, and that there is a film—like a mylar film—that you put on the windows or retrofit or you build in from scratch in new windows, which also turns all the windows into this. And now there's another one that's just coming along: a paint, which will make a house entirely self-supporting in terms of its energy needs.

And all this will happen in the context of a great deal of other change. We're going to see the demise of pharmaceutical medicine as a result of genetic engineering. We're seeing a great deal of change as a result of the information transition that's occurring. For example, the capacity to transmit templates to manufacture things means that we're going to see the end of large-scale factory manufacturers. It will also become local or regional where there will be some sort of regional storage center where they store raw materials, and a digital template will be downloaded and a local mechanism will make whatever that is. So that mass manufacturing will also be ending.

CS: I was going to ask you about this. In a way, this is the opposite of the idea of globalization in Tom Friedman's *The World is Flat.* In other words, the fact that information is transmitted around the world at the speed of light might mean that we don't have the problems we had before about manufacturing something in Timbuktu. You would think that this might lend itself toward globalization as opposed to localization.

SS: Well, no. By localization I mean that the manufacturing facility will be local. If you think about it, in the model that I am describing, an individual or a company develops some kind of prototype, tests it, and gets it up to speed. But then instead of going into production, they sell the informational matrix which gets downloaded— maybe on a royalty basis or however the financial model works out—to some sort of regional manufacturing place. It would probably be in conjunction with a recycling center where you could recycle the materials and you would download the informational matrix for making, say, a stove. The stove would be made locally. It wouldn't be shipped.

So it would become a global thing in the sense that anybody who could create such an informational matrix, and that we'd be able to download the information and manufacture it. We would not have the kind of shipping of physical objects that we now have.

I'm very familiar with Tom Friedman's stuff. Globalization is then ideational, not the physical.

So therefore it becomes very important if you think of that model, then you realize how terribly important it is to have a good educational system and to have the capacity to develop these prototypes that can then be sold as informational constructs. It could be regionalized and localized because once this energy transition completes, it will no longer be necessary for people to live in great conglomerations. They may choose to do that, but they don't have to.

People moved into cities because it allowed for shared effort and distribution and all of that, but you won't need to do that. This is by the way one of the reasons I think Native Americans are going to become a privileged class. They have reservations that are in all these lands that nobody wanted, that are, in fact, very beautiful. It is now going to be possible to live in a place like that just as comfortably as it would be to live in New York City and be just as informationally hooked in. I mean, I live on Whidbey Island and I would not be able to do that were it not for the Internet, because I don't have any access to big libraries, but I have access to all of the research I need. I subscribe to services that give me full text. So that allows me to live in Whidbey and yet I have a global outreach.

Most of the people I communicate with don't live on Whidbey; they live all over the world and I'm doing projects with them. I'm doing a project for instance right now on geomagnetic fields and local sidereal time and it involves people that I've never met physically. I talk to them all the time on Skype and through email, but we've never actually physically met, and yet we're doing a joint research project. So in that sense it's global, but it's also highly local. That's what I mean by localism and regionalism. The center of your life will be much less about traveling to places and much more about your quality of life in your locality; you will be able to reach out all across the world.

It also offers goodness to small communities; I'm interested in small communities because I think there is a natural human sized community. It's about 5,000 or 10,000 people.

CS: I've heard that.

SS: On Whidbey, again, we have 13,000 people spread across the island and we have several little villages of about 1,000 people each, but it's a very human-sized environment. I think that's the natural flow to which people will return, because for most of our history going back to early man, small groups have been the dominant theme; I think we're genetically programmed for that. I think we're going to see people moving out of large anonymous conglomerations and moving into small conglomerations.

We're going to see at least three major migrations within the United States: the migration away from the coast as a result of seawater rise, the migration out of the southwest as a result of a lack of water and high temperature due to climate change, and a migration into the center states of the country to develop the wind generation and also because of natural beauty as people are able to move into communities as a result of increased informational exchange and this energy breakthrough. So by 2050, I think the United States is going to look very, very different.

CS: Wow, that's a bold prediction.

SS: I'm willing to put my stone on the board for that.

CS: Well, good. Now, when I talk about the great schism I've been talking about this in terms of what I refer to as the "bifurcation of resource" which is another name for the increasing gap between the haves and the have-nots. In other words, there are still people whose kids go to Harvard, but it's harder and harder. I went to Trinity in Hartford in the '70s, and I'm looking at the qualifications of the kids who go there now, and I realize that I could no more get into Trinity now than I could fly to the moon on a surfboard. In other words, there are still good things around, but the competition for them is increasingly intense, and the people who *don't* have those good things become more and more numerous as a percentage of the population. Is this true by your wits?

SS: Yes. I think one of the things that is happening in the United States, and part of the reason why I think by 2050 it's going to be a very different country, is the destruction of the middle class and the transfer of the wealth of the middle class to the ueber-rich. I believe that ultimately that's going to produce political instability just as we saw in Egypt. Believe me, I do not have a utopian, everything will be "well—la la la" point of view. I think the next ten years are going to be extremely difficult. This wealth disparity issue and the capture of the government—I mean, we don't really have a democracy anymore; we have a corporatocracy. The increasing disaffection of local people... that's part of this tea party movement is their disaffection with the federal government. The destruction of the middle class—we're going to see social upheaval somewhere about....if I were guessing, I would say to you about 2025, I think there's a very good chance that the United States is going to break apart or restructure itself, unless this disparity is addressed. The vast middle class in the United States was created after the second World War through government programs, the GI Bill, the GI Education Bill, the GI Housing Bill, all of those things combined to create the opportunity which produced the American middle class, which in turn produced the extraordinary technological innovation which was the hallmark of the United States in the last 50 years.

We are now at a place where college education is becoming increasingly unavailable to average-income people. There are now five colleges in the United States which cost more than $50,000 a year to attend. Well, not many people can afford $50,000 a year for their kids to go to school. What that means is that it's not the brightest kids that are going to go; it's going to be the richest kids.

CS: Yes, which is what it was in the beginning of the 20th century.

SS: That's exactly right, and that's why the beginning of the 20th century, the people who were producing all the big breakthroughs; the Wright brothers, Edison, none of them came out of those schools. They came out of individual experience and local colleges, and they created the beginnings of the breakthrough, which was then brought to fruition after the Second World War with the passage of the various bills that I mentioned. So unless we address this huge disparity of wealth, and I don't think we will; I don't actually think the U.S. government is going to do anything. I think it's essentially so locked up by special interest groups that it's almost impossible to get anything done.

The Supreme Court is now completely politicized on the right. That's the first time that's happened in this way in our history. I have a very bleak view of the United States over the next 15 to 25 years.

CS: Right. Well, the thing that scares me most is this Citizens United v. Federal Elections Commission decision, which I think may be the real back-breaker for this country.

SS: Well, I don't know if it's the back-breaker, but certainly the Citizens United decision was so horrific that we already saw the results in the 2010 election. It has already become clear that this increasing corporatocracy, which is also a kleptocracy, is corrupting the government and is breaking down the institutions of government. And that's why I say that the next ten to 15 years is going to be extraordinarily difficult and it would not surprise me if by 2025 we had the outward appurtenances of the Congress and the Court remaining, but the country is going to be very different. I actually have a very bleak view of the short and mid-range. It's only in the longer range that I have a better view.

CS: Well, do you know what's kind of remarkable? I think you mentioned in some of your writings the movie and book *What the Bleep Do We Know*. Well, I spoke with one of the filmmakers. I told him about my viewpoint which sounded almost exactly like yours, i.e., pessimistic, at least in the short-term, and he said the reason why you're so pessimistic about this is that you and I travel in different circles. You're a businessman, where I travel the world meeting with hundreds and hundreds of these super enlightened, passionate, committed humanitarians. And I can tell you that the power of even a small number – even a minute percentage of the population—that's into this has the power to change everything.

SS: Well, that's true, and I live in both of those worlds rather deeply.

CS: Yes, I know you do.

SS: Individuals and small groups can change history. I've written a great deal about it. I believe it. I'm writing a book about it now: *The Eight Laws of Social Transformation.* While he is correct, what he is describing is the schism; it's the blue side of the schism. You and I live closer to the border, so we have a lot of interaction with the red side of the schism.

And while he's not incorrect that a small group of people can cause enormous change, and I do absolutely believe that it is also true that large historical forces are the result of *all* of it, not just a *piece* of it. Paul Hopkins wrote a very good book on that subject. Jeremy Rifkin's latest book on the empathetic civilization is also a good one.

I belong to a collective of individuals who are actively engaged in social transformation and who have literally affected the lives of millions of people. I can tell you dozens of stories of individuals who have changed the nature of society. With that said, it is also true that the red side of the equation has something to say as well, and it is in that struggle that the conflagration of the status quo is going to occur. So while he's right that there are lots and lots of people who are out doing these things, it is also true that there are lots and lots of people who hate it.

CS: Yeah, that's a good point and they're getting some ink on this; they're getting some power behind them.

SS: Well, they have something to say too. So that's why I said when we began, when you think about this, the real question is how you heal the schism. The answer is you cannot argue people into another position. Willful ignorance will not permit that. What you have to do is show by example that it can be done, and others will emulate it. When I look at the 2050s and the description that they give of the world in 2050, they describe smaller communities some of which are very regimented and quasi-militaristic, while others are more like hippie communes. That is, I think, the result of the energy breakthrough, the informational breakthrough, and the impulse people have to hang out with people of their own kind, and so they're going to sort themselves out into communities. Some of these communities are going to be fearful and angry, and some of them are going to be compassionate and life affirming. That's another reason why I think there's going to be massive change in the United States.

CS: I see. Well, this has been incredible, as I knew it would. I've been looking forward to this, and thank you so much for your time.

SS: All right. You take care.

Craig's Interview with Thomas Konrad, Ph.D.

I met Tom Konrad, a financial analyst specializing in the alternative energy sector, in my quest to align 2GreenEnergy with some heavy-duty know-how in this arena. He's a portfolio manager, and freelance writer – best known for the innumerable blog posts he's written on AltEnergyStocks.com, and at the Green Stocks blog on Forbes.com.

Tom's Ph.D. is in mathematics, specifically "complex dynamics," a branch of chaos theory. His study here led to his conviction that knowing the limits of our ability to predict is much more important than predictions themselves, a lesson he applies to both climate science and the financial markets.

I feel I've learned a great deal from him, and I've very much enjoyed the association.

> **CS:** Tom, thanks for your help here. What I want to know is, from a financial perspective, why aren't we getting to renewable energy any faster than we are?

TK: Well, I actually think a lot of the answer is non-financial. I think it's cultural and psychological. I think the biggest barrier to adoption is our ingrained human emotional resistance to change. Moving to clean energy is in large part a paradigm shift of how we do things. Our energy infrastructure was built to service our appliances. The original model was energy—especially electricity—follows load. Wind and solar can't follow load. They're called "unreliable" by some people; they're called "variable" by their supporters. But regardless, they don't follow load and to use them to their potential we need to actually adapt how we use them. We can still get utility out of them, but it requires a paradigm shift. For humans to change—especially to change our underlying assumptions—it requires more than saying, "This is one cent per kilowatt-hour cheaper."

It requires showing that the old way of doing things is no longer viable; that will get people to shift. When something's unsustainable, it will stop. Unfortunately, when something's unsustainable in human culture, it's usually stopped long after it's been damaging.

CS: Right. Especially in this case.

TK: Well, I actually think this is a normal case. I think this is a normal manifestation of one of the sadder aspects of human psychology and societal structure.

CS: Right. But wouldn't you argue that this is the one that could kill us? In other words, unless you're a global warming denier, you have to think that there's profound ecological long-term damage that's going to be done here. And of course global climate change is just one of half a dozen or so issues.

TK: Right. But humanity has shown time and time again that long term planning is our weakness.

CS: Yes. That's true.

TK: I don't want to offend all the creationists reading your book, but if we had been designed, we would not have this character flaw. We are emotionally designed for hunter-gatherer life. And in hunter-gatherer life, you do the same thing every year if it worked last year. Well, that's exactly what we're doing. But we have come to the point where what we do changes our environment. When you are not a prime mover of your environment, doing the same thing, you get caught when the environment changes. But now we are forcing environmental change faster, and human cultures have collapsed every time the environment changed. The ice age destroyed cultures. We didn't have anything to do with that, of course, but now we're forcing a faster change.

It's true that this time could be different because our technology will enable us to cope with the changing environment—but I don't see a psychological possibility of our making significant enough changes before we actually have to based on environmental and economic consequences of changes.

CS: I.e., peak oil in other words – we're running out of this stuff.

TK: And peak oil may not even do it. Peak oil dealt with by mass exploitation of alternative fuels, shifting to alternative transport, smarter city planning, changing the incentive structure for drivers to make more efficient use of our transport infrastructure with innovations like pay as you drive insurance, and more efficient vehicles. And then that would go for another 20 years maybe, and then we'd be confronted with the exact same problem again and maybe we'd find another solution. So when societies haven't collapsed... there have been a lot of Malthusian cycles.

CS: Malthus—the early economist who said what essentially?

TK: He saw that supply of food grew arithmetically and population grew exponentially. So he just said well, as a mathematical fact, as long as these two things continue to happen, we will have too much population. In his particular case, in England in the late 18th Century, we had a technological revolution in agriculture which allowed agricultural production to make a step change. So the arithmetic growth of food changed because of technology. So that was a Malthusian crisis that didn't happen, although it was the one that got the name. On the other hand, if you ever read the book *Collapse* by Jared Diamond, he also lists a bunch of Malthusian crises that *did* happen. The problem is the victors are the ones who write history. So when we look back at history, we see a series of occurrences we have always overcome in the past.

CS: Because the accounts were not written by dead people.

TK: Right. Because we do not include in the 'we' the ones who didn't make it. If you read *Collapse,* you'll learn about the Norse in Greenland, Easter Island, the Maya; in fact, I think Rome is probably another. So, a societal collapse could totally destroy the species, or just send us back to hunter-gatherer, in which case our population would be one percent of what it is now.

CS: Right. Let me ask you this. You mention that renewables doesn't follow load. There are those that would argue that traditional energy doesn't either. If you have a nuclear reactor or a coal-fired power plant, which is 48 or 49 percent of our electricity in the United States, you've got something that runs 24 hours a day and it's very difficult to cycle. Even in coal, the more often and more deeply you cycle the faster it breaks.

TK: Right. Modern coal plants can be cycled maybe 25 percent. Older ones, very little.

However, load is much less variable than even diversified wind resources. The load varies due to weather patterns and industry, but to take one example I'm familiar with, the maximum load in one region of the Great plains, including Denver where I used to live was only about 50% more than the minimum load over the course of a year. In contrast, our current grid prevents us from using geographic diversification to smooth the output of wind farms, so the output of local wind farms is a function of local weather conditions. Without much better geographic diversification than we now have, maximum wind output in a local balancing area will usually be five to ten times the minimum output over the course of a year. If you add solar into the mix, you can reduce the overall variation of the portfolio of renewables, but I doubt we could get the variation down to something similar to load without a worldwide supergrid.

CS: Okay. So in other words, at four o'clock in the morning we're using 75 percent of what we're using at four o'clock in the afternoon?

TK: Right. And there is seasonal variability as well.

CS: I had no idea that was true. Why is that? What are we doing at four o'clock in the morning? That can't be true of places like Phoenix where it's 120 degrees on a summer afternoon.

TK: Well, we have lots of vampire load. You're fridge is still on; that's one of the biggest users. In my house right now, 80 percent of my load is a dehumidifier in my basement. 85 percent of my average is running almost all the time. Well, it's undersized for my basement, but I have some power tools down there that I don't want to rust. But that's most of my load. Now, I think that's an extreme example partly because I've cut what I can cut.

CS: Okay. Let me check a basic assumption of mine and that is the migration to renewables will happen when and only when people can make a buck with it. And it will not happen until then. Is that fair?

TK: Well, I disagree with that. I think this will happen when it is more painful not to change than it is to change. Energy efficiency is proof that the market in energy is not efficient.

CS: In other words, you can invest a dollar and save two—and people still won't do it.

TK: Exactly. You just described an inefficient market. The market in energy is not efficient. I have absolute proof because there are $20 bills lying on the floor in the old parable about the economists.

CS: I don't know that parable.

TK: Oh, there's a joke. The two economists are walking down the street and one says, "Look there's a $20 bill on the ground." And the other one says, "That can't be a $20 bill; someone would have picked it up already." That's what the efficient type market hypothesis is. There is no free money; that's what it says. Well, there's free money in energy. People aren't taking advantage of it, and therefore it's not an efficient market.

CS: Is it ignorance, would you say?

TK: No, they know it's there. There are tons of people yelling at them saying there's money there. Obama said that.

CS: If we spend a third of our energy on commercial and industrial buildings and the stuff inside them, that money is controlled by CFOs who are making investment decisions all day long having to do with how quickly can I get a return on their cash.

TK: A CFO is paid to make better investment decisions than the other CFOs. And if he can make better investment decisions without going outside his comfort zone, and still think that he's a little bit better than the other CFOs, that's all he needs to do to get his salary.

CS: Okay. The fact that there is something that's even better that may be a little outside his comfort zone doesn't mean anything. Is that your point?

TK: It doesn't mean a lot especially when you consider that energy is no more than ten percent of most companies' budgets. So it's marginal. Is he going to step out of his comfort zone for a marginal gain? A few companies have. Wal-Mart has changed its comfort zone. They've changed so that looking at gains in energy is part of their culture. But they didn't have to change as much because Wal-Mart has always had the culture of penny pinching. And I think those of us who are drawn actually to green; are natural penny pinchers. We have that personality type.

CS: I guess that's true.

TK: Yes, it's a common personality type among greens. I think that's actually part of the reason that you are writing this book and asking this question—part of the reason we have trouble understanding why the rest of humanity doesn't get it when it's so obvious to us is because we don't have the normal personality type.

CS: Well, I guess frugality is part of it. But I would have said that it was more—maybe I'm just being kind to myself—but I would have said it was vision or a sense of myself as a citizen of the world. I.e., I perceive a responsibility to the other people around me now and to the people who will live here in the future.

TK: Well, I think some misers are drawn to it as well as some selfless individuals. But again, that's not the dominant personality type by far. We're talking five percent or less of the population.

Again, if I come back to the idea that we evolved in a hunter-gatherer society; we're evolved to think of our group as 20 to 30 people. There are outliers. They are people like you, and like many people around us who see our group as much larger than that. Some people see a large group; others see their group as a group of one.

Non-normal personality types are drawn to this because it fits our personality. This may be a bit unrelated, but it just reinforces my point: If you talk to an athlete and you're a little overweight, they feel scornful about you. But for those people who are overweight, it's a lot harder for them to lose weight than the athlete. Athletes became athletes because it's easy for them, and they excelled.

CS: It's self-selecting. I see.

TK: Yes, it's self-selecting. We humans think that our positive traits are acquired by will. But really almost everybody has a predilection for them. Whatever our strengths are we probably had a predilection for them because we cultivated those things that we were good at. And so I cultivated finance skills, and I have trouble understanding why other people can't keep a budget. But it's simply because it was easy for me. I came to this realization because I was trying to understand the very question you are asking.

CS: Okay. The strength you mentioned, finance, you analyze a couple dozen publicly traded equities. How did you choose those, first of all?

TK: Well, first I chose to be in clean tech because as an investment analyst, my most valuable resource is my time. It takes a couple of days to really get a handle on any one company. So I know it's just going to be a couple dozen because you have to stay up with them too. So there was zero cost to me for concentrating on clean tech, because my universe is 500 stocks if I go in cleantech, as opposed to 50,000 otherwise.

CS: So there's no cost to you, but you could have gone into agriculture or mining or something.

TK: I could have, but there is a benefit because I feel better about myself.

CS: Ha! Well, that's cool. There's got to be some motivation there. I had to guess it wasn't random!

TK: Yeah. And the other reason I chose this was I saw these trends. The way to make money in investing is to see a truth that the market does not yet see, and act on it the year before they do.

CS: Or, ten minutes before they do would be even better.

TK: Right. And global warming and peak oil are truths. As a trained mathematician I know that there aren't any truths in the absolute sense of the word. So they're as true as I can possibly believe and I realize that they were not recognized in 2005 when I came across peak oil. It's clear that they're not well recognized by the marketplace. And so the only question there, for the standard formula for making money is: When will the marketplace recognize them? They will, yet the "when" is a while out —but it's moving in that direction. They're a step backwards along the way and they always are. So that's the reason. I had a truth, and I knew it wasn't recognized by the marketplace—and therefore it's a good place to be.

CS: You mentioned that it takes a couple of days to get a handle on one of these companies. Do you mind divulging the ingredients in your secret sauce? What would you do during those couple of days that I wouldn't?

TK: I read the annual report. The first thing that I do that you wouldn't do.

CS: Ha! That's for sure. I've written a bunch of the content in them throughout my career, but I can't think of too many things I'd less rather do than read them. Yet I would think that the annual report: a) is available to everybody, b) meets SEC guidelines for honesty, and c) tends to be a bit optimistic.

TK: Right, they'll be as optimistic as they legally can. However, actually, one of the legal requirements is if you don't say something that you know is true in your report, you get sued. But, again, all I'm looking for is an edge.

The other thing I do is this: there are things that people don't know and there are things that people refuse to know. And it's a lot easier to find something that people refuse to know than that they don't know.

CS: So you're looking for the ostrich with his head in the sand.

TK: Yeah, and he's everywhere.

CS: Can you give me an example?

TK: Look at what's happened in solar. Everybody knows in the green community the group of people who are interested in investing in solar. Solar is the energy of the future, because the resource is there many times over. Wind couldn't power the entire world. Solar can do it 1000 times over.

CS: Not necessarily PV, but CSP, etc.

TK: Even PV, although I agree there are timing issues. The amount of energy is there. The technology we don't know. I think that's the key. The ostrich in the sand part is that people confuse the industry with the companies that are currently available to invest in.

In some ways this is an entitlement issue. I see the future of solar. I am entitled to make money in the stock market because I see other people do it. Therefore there must be a company in solar that I can invest in that will make me a lot of money. But the ostrich can't ask the question: Could it be that there isn't a company, even though the industry may be poised to take off? Maybe there isn't a company that I can make a ton of money on. The public companies are just a slice, and now we're not entitled to make money in the stock market, but we want to believe it and so we invest.

CS: Obviously this is a fundamental versus a technical analysis. In other words, you're not looking at charts; you're looking at bald facts about macroeconomics.

TK: Well, first it's behavioral finance. Everything I've been talking to you about now, if you notice, sounds like you're talking to a social psychologist. That's behavioral finance. The market is a manifestation of society, and I look at it through a sociological lens. My first cut is that sociological-emotional-psychological blend, and that tells me which industries to look at. I combine that with an understanding of the potential of the various technologies, and that's because I have a math and physics background. So I can understand the technology. And where those don't match, that's where the investment opportunities are.

CS: I see. That makes a great deal of sense. And not to be antagonistic, but for instance, if you go to a horserace, everybody in the stands thinks he's a better-than-average handicapper. At the end of the day, they lose $.19 on every dollar they bet. 90% of us think we're better-than-average drivers, too.

TK: We all think we're better investors than we are. And you know what? I still don't know if I'm fooling myself. I really don't.

CS: But your track record is good.

TK: Not recently.

CS: Okay. But it has *been* good in the past, right? Am I wrong here? Taxiiii! Just kidding…

TK: [laughs] Yeah. I saw the 2000 financial crises coming and I made a ton of money. However, I saw the 2008 financial crises coming. I saw the bubble was there, but I was lulled by how long it took. I predicted it way too early. I'm usually too early and this time I was way too early and I was starting to doubt myself and when it happened I wasn't prepared.

You have to constantly ask yourself the question: "How can I be wrong here?" And if you're good at asking that question, then you are better than everyone else. I think the key to being better than everyone else is to not make the same dumb mistakes. It's very hard not to make dumb mistakes because as I said, you, I and everyone reading this book has been evolved for a different environment than the stock market. The stock market is about as far from the savanna as you can get in terms of the way things work. Also, I'm a contrarian; I don't like being part of the crowd and I think that helps.

So if I look at the thing that makes investors successful, I have a lot of those things; but I'm not perfect. I've made mistakes in the past, but I'm in it because part of me loves doing it. And I haven't lost money; I've survived; I'm still here. And I've had some success, but I think being humble is absolutely necessary. So I admit that I don't know that I will still be doing this ten years from now.

CS: Right. We happen to be sitting here at the 2011 Renewable Energy Finance Forum in New York City. And I think we've seen some pretty good analysis from the speakers; they wouldn't be sitting up there if they weren't right more than they are wrong. Do you agree?

TK: No, I disagree. Most stock market analysts have bad track records. The problem is another part of our psychology is we want experts and so we just keep on asking them anyway and we don't really ask them about their track record. The story I told you about my really mixed track record is not unusual. It really isn't. And even if we did check everyone's track record, we'd still be a long way from knowing who has skill and who doesn't. As you read on every mutual fund prospectus: "Past performance is no guarantee of future results."

CS: Well, let's figure out why you're either probably right or probably wrong as we sit here today in 2011.

Certainly, the reason that I want to funnel some of my own money in this direction is the fundamentals of this sector are so strong overall. We simply cannot continue with our current approach to energy. The reason we call it "unsustainable" is that it literally can't continue.

TK: True, if something is unsustainable it will stop. However, you could lose all your money *long* before it stops. The market can stay irrational longer than you can stay afloat. And yes, that's part of the reason I'm there too. But the problem is you get in too early and stay in—even though it becomes harder and harder as you lose money.

CS: Right. And that's your position generally on some of these cleantech companies. In other words, they need a balance sheet that's strong enough to be able to withstand ten years of a Republican-controlled House, with positively no support for environmentalism.

TK: The ideal company I look for is one that is green in their products—when you look at a very broad lifecycle—reduced energy use, or reduced carbon emissions, or reduced oil use. That's my definition of a green company. I want it to be green—and then I want it to be currently profitable, and I want it to be financially solid even if the tide turns against it. And if oil prices or carbon prices go up, that company will have a little extra gain. Those are the companies I look for. I look for something that will gain if these macro events we are seeing are recognized. They won't go up the way the speculative companies do that aren't profitable now, but they will gain and they'll be able to hold on for the two to 20 years it may take for them to really take off. And they're helping with the transition when a disaster happens. My portfolio and the portfolios of those I manage will have made the disaster a little less bad.

CS: Okay, that makes sense. Whom do you like now and why?

TK: Okay. My top pick is New Flyer Industries. When your book comes out they may be back up, but at the moment I like them because they are a profitable company. They make buses; they're the largest North American bus manufacturer. They are currently at a P:E ratio of about nine. They're a weird stock and they're going through a transition. Because of that, their current price has been totally hammered; however, if you look at the company behind it, it's a sustainable company even though it's going through a tough time; they're still profitable even though things are very bad for them now. So they pass that durability test. They combine a good price, and a very green proposition: if you want to be green then one of the best steps you can take is to get rid of your car and take the bus.

CS: Yes, I guess that's true. Plus they're into alternative fuel. Is that correct?

TK: They're an "any fuel" company; if their customers want it; they provide it. They built the hydrogen buses for the Vancouver Olympics, but they'll also sell you a diesel. But even a diesel bus is green compared to cars.

CS: That's true.

TK: If you can put ten people on it, it will take cars off the road.

CS: Yes, but I'm wondering if sociologically we can "do" buses. We like trains here on the East Coast, but we don't seem to want to take buses.

TK: Well, I don't think financially we can do trains. If we go back to the societal discussion, we are going to make the transition at the last minute and we're going to be desperate. Bus transit is a much cheaper and quicker to install alternative—and we'll be doing it with tight budgets. So when peak oil hits in a way where it is too painful to maintain a "car culture"—and we actually saw this—bus ridership shot up in 2007 and 2008. It fell back a little bit, but actually shot up surprisingly again.

We do see buses growing as a share. In the Northeast there is a company called Megabus, where the basic fare is a dollar between nearby cities. They'll take you from Baltimore to New York (200 miles) for $21 booking only a day or two in advance, $8 if you book a month in advance. That trip would cost $25-$30 just for gas in a car, or $49 purchased a month ahead on Amtrak. Buses may have a social stigma, but they have economics on their side. That makes a big difference when money is tight.

CS: Can you provide us with another tip that readers might find valuable?

TK: OK, In betting against technologies that are bound to fail, instead of shorting, a better way to do it is buying puts and keeping them enough out of the money that when you cycle them over and over you can still emotionally bear the loss. Shorting can get you in a short squeeze which makes it financially hard to bear and you're forced to get out. It's easier to gauge your own ability to bear the emotional pain of losses which is actually harder than most people think.

CS: But if they're far enough out of the money, the cost of buying the put is so small that it doesn't hurt?

TK: Yeah, but it's still hard to do. Again, you have to frame it right in your head. Framing is a very good way to control your emotions around the market—because our emotions aren't designed for the market. The cause of almost all market mistakes can be traced to emotions.

There are some market mistakes where you basically made a miscalculation, but really the reason that most investors are bad is because of emotional mistakes.

CS: Which is fear and greed essentially, right?

TK: Fear, greed, overconfidence, and confirmation bias. There's a list of behavior economic concepts that is a mile long. And it's been proven statistically that people make them over and over again.

CS: Fascinating! Well, let's go back to the thesis of the book. Why has the transition not happened?

TK: Yes, we strayed a lot into investing strategy, but let's bring the two together. Let's ask ourselves why the market has not acknowledged the future potential. And I think the market has not acknowledged the future potential because the market has gotten interested several times and then it's gotten burned.

CS: OK, can you take us through some specifics on this?

TK: Well, what recently happened with solar. All these companies are quite volatile, and a lot of people got in thinking the renewables boom is the next idea, but it turns out renewables is a lot different from IT. IT is inherently a high-margin business, because there is no physical product.

Renewable energy involves putting steel in the ground and there are physical limits to how much energy you're going to get out. You're never going to get out as much energy from the same square foot using wind or solar as you did out of a gas well or oil well. There you're actually raiding a bank account; nature's bank account. So with renewable energy you're living on the interest; using a financial metaphor.

So I think of energy stores as a bank account, and the current sunlight is the interest, and the accumulated interest which is now capital is the stored box of fuels.

Imagine you inherit something from your grandmother. You could live off the interest or you can spend it all in one year. And you know what? Most people who have a big inheritance or win the lottery; it's gone in a year.

CS: Ah yes. Now I completely understand the metaphor.

TK: And that's what our society is doing with energy.

So what was my point? I was trying to tie why it hasn't happened in the financial markets to why it hasn't happened in the economy. People went into renewable energy with a paradigm for making gains that was based on a history of having made gains of dipping into their bank account and grabbing the capital. They were looking for a new inheritance. Renewable energy will not give us a new inheritance because by definition it will only give us an annuity. It will only give us the interest. It's not as much fun.

We went into solar with the preconception that we were tapping into a new inheritance—a new level of capital. When the reality hit and the returns were not there, we were disappointed. Once burned, twice shy.

That's why I don't think it's happened in the market. We tried to make it happen, but we went in with the wrong viewpoint. And until we can change and go in with the right paradigm, then we're going to be burned again and again.

CS: Yes. This whole thing about the level playing field I find very interesting. Do you think we have one? Do you think we need one?

TK: Well, on a moral stance we need a playing field that favors sustainable energy. If you wanted to say, 'Is the transition going to occur without one?' The answer is yes. It will happen later; possibly too late.

In truth, what will happen is in between those two. Our moral imperative is to make the transition happen as soon as possible, so that the transition will be less painful. The transition will happen in time; but the longer we put it off, the more painful it will be. Once you get your inheritance of $1 million, you can spend it all immediately, or you can make the transition when you have $100,000 left. I'm hoping we're going to get there before we're in debt; I think we've squandered the entire inheritance.

CS: Interesting. I like this metaphor. But my point is that most people would say we have an unlevel playing field in the opposite direction. In other words – the oil companies, the coal companies, the nuclear companies—don't these industries have a huge amount of power in terms of political control?

TK: Yeah, but that's a moot point because renewable energy has endurance; it will win because unsustainable can't win. So it's really only a question about when.

CS: When, exactly.

TK: The more level we can make the playing field the better. But we don't need it to win.

CS: Yes, but when this happens means a great deal, I would argue. The trajectory for a reasonable quality of life for my grandchildren hangs in the balance.

TK: Right. So the better we can make the playing field, the better off we should be. I think that's really just a matter of realpolitik. I don't care what the certain level is; I just want it to get better. Why measure it? It's a waste of effort.

CS: I'm not sure on this. I interviewed the Environmental Law Institute who measures the hell out of it. That's what they do for a living.

TK: Well that is a method to persuade people.

CS: Precisely. That's my point. There is a purpose to it.

TK: Okay, I agree. By the way, I believe that the true cost of fossil fuels is infinite because it's a finite resource and therefore it's scarce in a world where the true demand for energy is infinite when we look at ... hopefully our infinite future.

Just use the argument that resonates with your audience.

CS: Well, that's what I do. That's why I seldom bring up global warming any more. Three years ago I could stand up in front of an audience and talk about global warming as being a fairly noncontroversial fact. Now I can't do that. So rather than have an argument, I just say suppose we talk about peak oil or national security or... pick one.

TK: Right. It's incredibly frustrating, but I think national security and the military is a beautiful example of my example of why pain is really what's necessary to make the transition happen. The military is making the transition because they are feeling the pain of moving fuel to hell zones like Afghanistan and Iraq where their people are dying. They have reached the point where conventional energy is too painful to continue to use in the conventional way. And therefore they are gung-ho. People who you would never think are gung-ho for the transition.

And fortunately, they do have persuasive power that greens sadly don't, because there's an emotional resonance with the people who are protecting us.

CS: Yes, exactly right. And ironically, they were the largest single customer of the oil companies.

TK: Right. And the bleeding edge is getting wider, and the transition will happen. It is happening, but it's painful and I wish we wouldn't have lost so many soldiers before they made that transition. And we're going to lose more soldiers in other sectors because that's really what it takes to change people's behavior.

CS: I guess there's a double irony here. Yes, it's dangerous to be there because the oil supply lines are so long and fragmented. But the reason why we're there in the first places is largely because of oil.

TK: Right. And I think that's the flip side of people don't change unless they have to. We thought we saw an easy way to continue the status quo of using unlimited fossil fuels, but let's just go fix that little mess there. It was wishful thinking. The mess was a quagmire. We thought we could go into Afghanistan and Iraq and make them happy countries that wanted to have us there. And we found out that we couldn't. We wouldn't have gone in if we didn't believe that we weren't wrong.

CS: I don't know. I think I'll go to my grave not knowing why we did this in the first place.

TK: I'm not sure what was exactly going through Bush's mind, but I am sure that it wasn't a clear view of what really would happen. I don't think he's the brightest guy. I don't think he's totally rational, but even if you're not bright and you're not rational, if you saw today, no one would make that decision, because it doesn't look good. Everyone wants to appear good to their peers, to their family; and he doesn't. So he didn't accomplish what he wanted.

It was a mistake, but it was a mistake because we thought it would be easy. It's just standard – one of the reasons people make investment mistakes is overconfidence. Overconfidence is also a root cause of the Iraq war. Same mistakes humans make in investing also appear in real life.

Bubbles are another example in the financial markets. They never look exactly the same, so we can always tell ourselves that this time is different. That's one thing that is true with every bubble. It's the human propensity to say this time is different; and therefore, the lessons we learn don't apply.

CS: Well, fantastic stuff, Tom. Thank you very much.

TK: You're welcome. Good to talk to you.

Craig's Interview with the Environmental Law Institute spokespeople Jay Pendergrass and Lisa Goldman

In my quest to unpack the issues of subsidies and incentives, I wanted to ask the Environmental Law Institute to go on record and explain their graphic "Energy Subsidies Black, Not Green" and the accompanying paper, Estimating U.S. Government Subsidies to Energy Sources: 2002-2008." The organization believes that the current energy and climate debate would benefit from a broader understanding of the explicit and hidden government subsidies that affect energy use throughout the economy. In an effort to examine this issue, they conducted a review of fossil fuel and renewable energy subsidies for those years.

I thank ELI spokespeople Jay Pendergrass and Lisa Goldman for this wonderfully insightful interview.

> CS: Thanks very much for this. This is a great opportunity for me because I think of myself as an advocate for readers who, like me, are trying to make sense of the nonsensical. In other words, why is this migration to renewables moving so slowly? We're all very concerned. There are six or eight completely independent reasons to knock off our commitment to foreign oil—and fossil fuels more generally. But we seem to be making disgustingly little progress on this thing. I'm here to take another step on my path to find out why.

Let's begin by talking about your mission and maybe your great wins and losses over the last few years.

> JP: We say we are, in a sense, the lawyers for the planet. We are trying to promote sustainable development and we are a non-advocacy organization, so we do research and education. To the extent that we are doing research on energy then we advocate in favor of the results of our research.

> CS: In other words, regardless of what those results happen to be.

> JP: Right.

> CS: Can you give me an example? Maybe you're alluding to the fact that sometimes they're kind of surprising. You expected to find X, but you actually found Y.

> JP: In the case of the energy subsidies we started off to look at and compare federal government subsidies for different forms of energy, and I think we were surprised to

find that the amount of subsidies for corn ethanol was a lot larger than we realized. Also, we learned how to categorize things. We had initially thought of it as fossil fuels versus renewables, but as we were going through it, we decided it was a little more complex than that because the corn ethanol is a renewable, but it's got significant climate affects and we weren't trying to quantify those. We did realize that it was at least qualitatively different than solar and wind and geothermal and all kinds of renewables.

CS: So this was ground-up research? You assumed nothing; you just went to the Freedom of Information Act or whatever and just pulled stuff together independently?

JP: We initially thought that there were studies out there that had looked at subsidies, and so we initially thought that we would collect the prior studies, validate them, and largely use what had previously been done and spend some time getting a graphical representation of things. But as we looked at the prior studies we found that a lot of them had a much broader definition of "subsidy" than we were comfortable with. You couldn't get down to the level of detail that we were looking for in terms of fuel sources and things. So it led us to actually having to go and do ground-up research—looking at governmental sources primarily. The Energy Information Agency had a lot, and the joint committee on taxation had a lot of things about tax breaks. But, yes, we did end up doing the ground-up research because we didn't find the secondary sources to be what we were initially thinking they would be.

CS: Okay. I see. Well, I guess that's both good and bad. Bad that you had to go through extra work and that it took a lot longer. Good, of course, that you got it right.

Well, let me ask you this. When I've tried to wrap my wits around this in the past, I've come up with a fact that there isn't one number because there isn't one type of subsidy. This is a compilation of 15 different types of things. For instance, if you can lease BLM (the US Department of the Interior's Bureau of Land Management) land at a preferential rate, that's one thing. If you can borrow money at a preferential rate, that's another thing. If you're exempt from certain restrictions, that's a third thing, etc. So how confident are you that you've exhausted the supply of independent subsidies that lie in any of these quadrants?

LG: Well, we define subsidies in a way that was somewhat conservative. There are studies out there and some have a very expansive definition of "subsidy," where some have a much narrower definition. We really wanted to strike a balance and we wanted our numbers to not be attacked for including things that people might question as real subsidies, for example, military defense in the Middle East. I mean, you can make a connection, but we drew kind of a deliberately cautious line and that partly reflects our status as an independent non-partisan think-tank organization.

All those numbers depend on how the individual studies define subsidies, and we defined ours as a federal government expenditure that benefits a particular fuel sector. Not something that benefits producers or a certain group of people or even consumers, but just going to a fuel provider. Sure, at some point there's a certain degree of line-drawing, but we really tried to do it consistently with definitions that we were using.

CS: So when you say it's an expenditure, I would think that an expenditure is one thing, but there are also forbearances.

JP: Yes, there are two things. The federal government outlay of funds and the deliberate policy-based forbearance of either collecting taxes or collecting royalties or some other. So it's things that have a direct fiscal financial effect on the federal budget. So included would be a tax break directed at a particular fuel where the federal government decided not to collect tax, and you can define an amount for that. Again, that was our definition of subsidy, and then we also said it had to be directed at the fuel source, so if there are a number of tax breaks that are available generally to businesses, we didn't include those. So, there are a lot of tax breaks available to oil companies, but they're also available to manufacturing companies and everything else. So we didn't include those.

CS: I'm with you. You seem to be saying that there are some of these expenditures or forbearances wherein you can't define an amount. Can you give me an example of them?

JP: The loan guarantees for various renewable projects are probably the biggest example. Also for some fossil fuel projects in particular the coal carbon capture and sequestration projects. With a loan guarantee there's no expenditure from the federal government unless and until somebody defaults on the loan. There are some costs for administering the program; establishing the program; we included those because they are direct expenditures, but we did not include any kind of a value for the fact that there's a loan guarantee out there because the federal government hasn't spent any money yet on that. It may have set aside funds for those, but they haven't actually been spent, and that's another part of the difference in the definition. Some people who have looked at these things have tried to quantify the value received by the companies or by the fuel source—and you could do that with a loan guarantee because they are avoiding some costs, but we were looking just strictly at how much the federal government is putting out.

CS: Okay. Now, let's go back to your mission as an independent non-partisan think tank. Tell me a little bit about what that means in terms of the things that you can and cannot do, should and should not do, etc.

JP: It doesn't stop us from doing anything in terms of a substantive project. We look at any kind of issue related to the environment, sustainability or whatever. And we certainly have as our intent to follow the facts and the research and then reach conclusions based on what we learned through the research.

LG: But we don't lobby or litigate. So if our study shows that fossil fuels are receiving more federal dollars than renewables, we won't go to the Hill and lobby specific legislatures to phase out this approach. But other people can do that using our report; they can use those numbers. But we won't advocate politically for a change in outcome. But our policy analysis will show the different policy options if you're interested in shifting, spending, or favoring more sustainable energy sources. You can do that based on our report.

CS: I understand. Well, that's very interesting. So unlike for instance the NRDC (Natural Resources Defense Council) which would take it immediately into the court system... they may take your report and use that as evidence.

LG: Correct. We fit in with other organizations that can use our work in exactly that way. We occupy a different place on the spectrum and both approaches are useful in understanding environmental issues and the different policy options for addressing them.

CS: Okay. How are you funded and why are you here?

JP: We're here to try and improve the environment. That's really what we're working on. The slogan is the

Environmental Law Institute (ELI) is working for people, places, and the planet. The organization is directed at improving the environment and improving environmental law and policy is a tool for doing that. We're funded on project-specific things by foundations, by governmental agencies, and by individuals. This subsidies study was something that we proposed to do, and received funding to do it.

LG: And we're also often viewed as an impartial fact-finder of policy analysts, so that's the value added that ELI brings to an issue that people will come to us for. We're considered unbiased, while there's nothing wrong with groups that have a clear agenda. Everyone knows where they're coming from as well and that's fine; so we just occupy a different place. We like to think that our reports are taken seriously by people on all sides in both the private and public sector.

CS: Well, if it's not too much to ask, who funded this?

JP: The Energy Foundation funded the report on energy subsidies.

CS: Tell me about that please.

JP: It's a private foundation. It actually receives its funding from other foundations. So it collects funding from foundations that have an interest in energy issues and primarily in improving energy efficiency, and shifting the types of energy we use. The Energy Foundation focuses the funding and chooses the projects that they work on.

CS: Is this one of the foundations that sponsors NPR? It's funded by the Pew Charitable Trust or Geraldine R. Dodge Foundation ... in other words, is it philanthropic?

JP: Yes. It's a philanthropic. It is funded by at least four or five foundations.

CS: That's neat. It must be monstrously difficult to maintain a position of neutrality and objectivity. Whenever I open my mouth on my blog, people ask, "Well, why are you saying that? Who's paying you to do that?" I would think there must be an incredibly difficult point of credibility to maintain that you honestly don't have an axe to grind.

JP: It's true. This organization is 41 years old, and from the very beginning it has been very zealous about maintaining the credibility of the work we do, and insuring that we maintain independence. In this one, it's hard to remember, but I think at the start we thought that the difference between fossil fuels and renewables would be larger than what we found.

CS: Yes, in fact I say 12 to 1 and it's certainly not 12 to 1 here ...

JP: It's not even quite 3 to 1. It's 2 point something; two and a half or so. We tried to ferret out everything that we could and we came up with that and we then tried to do a good job of making that information available to people.

CS: That's really neat.

LG: We identify a provision as a subsidy to fossil fuels that serves a socially beneficial use. This is just an example, the LIHEAP program gives assistance to low-income consumers for their home heating. Under our methodology it counts as a government expenditure that benefits fossil fuels so we included it. We didn't include it to say that LIHEAP shouldn't be in existence or that it's a bad program. That's another example and there were a few who misread that in the study and sort of tried to paint us as being against low-income heating assistance. It's just an example of where we included it to be consistent with our methodology without having a policy agenda.

CS: Well, before we leave this thing about the slant or lack thereof, let me ask this. When people come through here and they see the Udalls and the Gores and so forth, but they don't see Bush and Cheney. I'm sure there must be people who take you to task on this thing of independence and non-partisan.

JP: Periodically people do, but we have given awards to Bob Stafford, Sherry Boehlert, and John Chafee. The number of Republicans that have received our award is really large, and it is non-partisan definitely, though we get challenged sometimes. In the past there was a conservative organization that would put out a book several years in a row asserting that companies who were supporters of ELI who give us money were doing so contrary to their own interest because ELI was, they would say, a liberal partisan organization. We would then write to them explaining that we are a non-partisan organization and can cite chapter and verse on it and then they would do a retraction, but they had already published the book.

CS: Right. So the only purpose is to publish information that somebody can use to make laws to protect the environment. Thus the word "law" in "Environmental Law Institute" doesn't mean that you're lawyers or that you're litigators; it means that this will ultimately affect law.

JP: And that we use law to promote the goals. We are a law institute, but we also have scientists on staff, and we've had economists on staff in the past.

CS: Now, when you say you use law to do this, can you give me an example just so I can understand this?

JP: Well, this study looked at what the legal authorizations are. We frequently review the existing law and regulations and then make recommendations on how they can be better implemented. There are times when we look at the law and determine that this is not serving the environmental purpose and make recommendations of ways to change the law to better serve environmental purpose.

CS: All right. Now let's get down to brass tacks on this and then the broader issues if we could. This report clearly corrects some misinformation that most people, myself included, have on the subject. But the first question one would ask is why are we subsidizing a 90-year-old industry that's extremely profitable anyway?

JP: That's a question that we ask in our executive summary. We didn't go into it a lot, but one of our questions that we would like policy makers and legislators to consider is what's the purpose of having a subsidy? And one of them that is frequently put forward as a legitimate policy reason for having a subsidy is that there's something you want to promote and a subsidy will promote that.

CS: But what is the policy that anybody would want to promote with here?

JP: Well, with fossil fuels our view is that it is contributing to climate change. The greenhouse gas emissions from it are significant. Policy makers should look at the various subsidies and re-evaluate whether they are valid given that there is significant environmental externality associated with the burning of fossil fuels.

Corn ethanol is a relatively new industry, and new industries often need subsidies to get started. It's something you want to promote. That one we put on the bottom half of the graph because it also has significant greenhouse gas emissions associated with it.

CS: Right. Not to mention other externalities.

JP: So, but it is a renewable so we thought it's another one that maybe the policy makers should re-examine the reasons for having it. Is it needed? Does it need such subsidies to maintain the industry? Is it the kind of thing that we want to be promoting?

And on the renewables side when you look at just what we call the traditional renewables: wind, solar, hydro, and geothermal; the amount of subsidies for those is a lot smaller. It's smaller than the total amount that goes to corn ethanol and that is a relatively young industry.

LG: We looked at one follow-up question we received on this study, which was how many of these subsidies were permanently enacted versus temporary authorizations. On the fossil fuel side many more of those provisions have been written into the tax code, and so one answer to why these things are still being subsidized could be that maybe there was a perceived policy justification for it back when the different provisions were first enacted, but they require affirmative repealing action by Congress. Whereas, on the renewables side, the provisions have to be re-authorized. So that's one factor when you're looking at why are some things still subsidized irrespective of the economic position of the industry.

CS: It's funny. I'll just make a slight digression and tell you a quick story. I was at a conference and I was sitting next to a guy at lunch who was kind of snubbing the renewables industry. He was a consulting physicist, working for energy companies broadly. He told me, "I don't want to work for people who are supported by the government." And I go,

"Well, you realize that fossil fuels get far more subsidies than renewables." And he replies, "Oh. I guess what I'm saying is, I don't want to work for people who are supported by the government whose subsidies might go away."

JP: [laughter]

LG: That's a very critical distinction in his statement.

JP: Yes. And that was something that we saw in terms of renewables. We looked over a seven-year period from 2002 to 2008 and the amount was quite variable for renewables. It varied for fossil fuels as well, but in terms of percentage change it was more variable for renewables, because there were provisions that were not renewed, other ones came in, and a larger percentage of the amount for renewables is actual grants for spending from the federal government as opposed to tax provisions.

CS: So you're loath to make value judgments. In other words, you say here are the facts, go do with them what you will.

JP: We try to stay there. I think we probably can't avoid making some value judgments at some level, but we do not try to do that.

LG: There's an inherent question in this study, which is the one you asked: why are we subsidizing some of these things? Or is there the same policy justification on both sides?

JP: And we make the comment that the fossil fuel industry is largely a mature industry that seems to be able to operate profitably and that the renewables is a newer one. We don't completely avoid that.

CS: Okay. So let me ask you this. Please help my readers understand why the migration to renewables is proceeding so miserably poorly in the United States, why we're not leading, why we're apparently content to bicker across the aisle while Rome burns, while we quickly become the second largest economic power in the world. Why are we not taking a leadership role in this space? Is that a question that you folks answer officially? Unofficially? Not at all?

JP: Not officially. I think that there's a lot of frustration among the people here at ELI that the United States hasn't moved more towards renewables, and hasn't improved its energy efficiency. One of the things that we did as a sort of adjunct to this project was looking at the sources of our energy and how the energy is used, and in doing that the fact that jumped out was just how much energy we waste. Almost 50 percent of the energy used in the United States goes into the environment as heat without producing any useful work as a result of it.

CS: Right. Well, certainly about 80 percent of internal combustion engines... the energy that goes into that is wasted as heat.

JP: Yes. (Shows graphic.) The two orange arrows: one for transportation and the internal combustion engine and the other one for the generation of electricity ... that is pure waste. In the transportation side the amount of waste is larger than the amount of energy that goes towards producing transportation. And electricity generation is just about half. And that's because nuclear is by its way of defining things, efficient.

CS: I see. Let me ask you to comment on something I believe. Please don't think that I'm trying to get you to say something that you don't want to say. If you don't want to talk about this at all, that's fine. If you want to say this is my belief, it's not necessarily ELI's, that's fine too. But my own personal standpoint is that we face corruption. This is a democracy going in the wrong direction. The oil industry has employed 7,000 lobbyists. It's the biggest lobby on Earth, and you have to think they're getting something for their money. They wouldn't be paying 7,000 people to do this if they weren't. I know it's not the level of corruption that you have in some third world country where government is almost completely based on payoffs and bribes and so forth. But when I try to answer a question like why does this stranglehold on the status quo exist, I can't come up with a single other theory.

LG: Personally I think the way the political process works is that interests that have financial backing can lobby; I think that can certainly explain some of what we're seeing as far as the policies that we have.

JP: Yes, we didn't study it specifically. So officially, that's outside the scope, but I think everybody looks at it and, as Lisa said, the politics is set up so the oil companies in their lobbying they're doing it perfectly legally, or apparently so. There's no reason to think that there's what we would consider corruption there, but our political system is set up so that they have enormous influence. Energy efficiency doesn't have much of a lobby behind it, which I think is really unfortunate. The renewables, they have their industry groups and other things; they just aren't as big.

CS: Well, let me ask you this. I'm sure you've studied things like CSP (concentrated solar power) – or other technologies that probably *do* require more subsidies than others. Just to take CSP as an example, you've got all this heat in the southwestern desert; you also have a grid infrastructure that doesn't easily transmit that power to the population centers. You also have a legal system where eminent domain isn't what it used to be and there's a recent Supreme Court decision that narrows it even further. So if you really want energy independence; clean, inexpensive energy, it's going to take some wrangling for sure in terms of making this happen. Can you comment on that?

JP: It's not something that we've focused on in this. What we really did was look at where the federal government funds are going. There's this common discussion or policy goal out there of not picking winners, and I think that at least for traditional renewables the federal government hasn't picked particular types of things. But the difficulties that you point out are very real. I've studied as part of some other things the legal system—legal rules—for transmission, for setting rates for electricity, etc., are very old and are not well designed for bringing our system into the 21st century and encouraging the new forms of energy. Having a series of regional power grids some of which are not even compatible and able to share power across their grids is not at all conducive to becoming more efficient.

CS: Indeed. Here's a question I meant to ask you in the beginning that I'm trying to understand. When you subsidize oil, do you get artificially inexpensive oil? If so, does that mean that people can afford it? Of course subsidies came out of your pocket and my pocket in the first place, but I suppose that you could argue that without these things we'd have $7 a gallon gasoline.

JP: Actually, I don't think that that's true largely because the price of oil is set on a world market. So the subsidy that we're providing to companies in the U.S. doesn't really affect the price of oil. It's really a transfer of wealth from the taxpayer to the shareholders of the companies receiving the subsidy.

CS: That's very clear, thank you. What else can you tell me about your work here? It must be interesting to just do your work, to call 'em like you see 'em and let other people run with it accordingly.

JP: Yes, our stuff has been picked up and used by the magazines related to ethanol, by the wind and solar industry associations, by an organization that promotes energy efficiency and others that promote renewables. The American Petroleum Institute has been the one consistent objector to the study and complaining about it.

CS: On what basis?

JP: They disagree with some of the things we included and they would prefer to talk about the benefits that they say are being received. They would prefer to not compare the total amount of dollars, but the dollar of subsidy per the amount of energy produced, because fossil fuels are such a large part of our economy, it's much smaller than the dollar per unit of energy produced for the others.

We were really interested in how much money the federal government is spending, not trying to assess what that benefit was. I think every economist we've talked to has wanted to do that calculation of dollar per amount of energy, but I at least don't see what the point of that is because the subsidy is not intended to buy energy.

LG: It doesn't change the nature of the subsidy or the amount. The denominator is kind of irrelevant to the issue which is this amount of money is going here and there.

CS: I completely agree. Moreover, if you believe that the philosophy behind a subsidy is to promote a social good. With renewables you do have a social good; with fossil fuels you have a social evil by pretty much anybody's standards.

And to say that we shouldn't put money into clean energy because it's only two percent of the current grid-mix is like saying we shouldn't have built the Internet in the 1990s because there were only a few people online. It's circular. Of course there were only a few people online, because there wasn't an Internet.

LG: Right. That's what people say. It's not even a question of the industry's getting equal amounts of funding. One could look at the study and argue that the industry is in a development phase that actually requires more. So it's not even an across-the-board comparison necessarily that's useful here.

CS: Yes. I completely agree. You told me that you didn't count this in your study, but I'd like to just have a quick discussion on the externalities associated with oil and coal. It's estimated that we spend $250 billion a year cleaning up the lung disease—the asthma and lung cancer and so forth. Somebody is paying for that; it's our grandchildren.

JP: Or we pay for it in terms of our increased medical bills and therefore our increased insurance costs and many other things. Those things have been poorly estimated, although some people have tried. The National Academy of Sciences did a study a couple of years ago that tried to look at the externalities of coal.

In the end they excluded climate change because they said they couldn't quantify it. They basically focused on the health costs associated with the particulate matter and mercury emissions from coal.

CS: When did they do this and what did they come up with?

JP: I think it was 2009. And they quantify it and show that there were real significant dollar amounts in terms of those externalities, though all they were looking at was the sort of limited set of health impacts. I'm pretty sure it was 2009; it's on their website.

CS: Okay. I'll check that out. I interviewed James Woolsey, the ex-CIA director, who referred me to Boydon Gray. I'm just...

JP: Well, Boydon Gray is a respected Republican, conservative person who has definitely been involved in a lot of the policy making; certainly under George H.W. Bush. He would not be one that I would think of as a real tree-hugger.

CS: Right. Let me ask you this. What would you say is the one thing that people don't know; generally, that they should know that is associated with this mess?

LG: Well, the whole reason that we did this study was that we really wanted to produce that graphic and just to put the numbers out there in a way that you could easily digest in a snapshot view. So one thing is certainly just the fact that some of these things are being subsidized in the first place.

JP: I think people still don't understand that renewables—particularly traditional wind and solar and geothermal and hydro—are not receiving very much in the way of federal government subsidies. There has been a tendency to say that they are not competitive and that they only exist because of subsidies; people think that means there's a huge amount of money going to them, and there really isn't. It seems from the reaction we've gotten from putting this information out that a lot of people didn't understand how much the fossil fuels were receiving in terms of subsidies.

CS: And this got fairly wide play?

JP: Yes, we are still seeing it show up in some news articles and blogs. It's been by far the most downloaded report that we've ever done. It's been downloaded somewhere around 18,000 times.

CS: Wonderful. Based on what you've come across regarding the forces that underlie where we're going, are you pessimistic or optimistic about the future?

JP: I'm quite discouraged that things have not changed. It's cause for despair that we aren't increasing our use of renewables anywhere near as quickly as we could. As you pointed out, we're behind China in this movement. I guess in a lot of ways I'm more concerned that we continue to be so inefficient in our generation of electricity, our modes of transportation, and our use of energy. You just see it everywhere. I live close to one of the Metro stations and transit center where there are a lot of buses—and every bus sits there idling the whole time that they're not in use. There's just no point in that.

CS: Yeah. I do find it amazing. I pick up my daughter from school every afternoon and we wait in a line and I immediately turn off my engine, but I notice everybody else has their engine on.

LG: And that's sort of public education. People don't think about it. If it were well broadcasted that you could save copious amounts of fuel; which is to your own benefit as well, by turning off the car. But it seems to be not well known.

JP: And there's a lot of misinformation about everything. It's hard to get people to change and we haven't figured out what the motivators are, but we also haven't figured out how we change the system so that we get smart meters. I live in Maryland which is a very progressive state. The legislature just prohibited the use of smart meters.

CS: By smart, do you mean time of use or something even more sophisticated?

JP: It was a general kind of thing that would have allowed for feedback and would have allowed you to start seeing the amount that you're using at a particular time. They weren't specifying anything but one of the things that happened was a fear that power companies might be able to shut off your power and a fear that other people would get to see how much you were spending. One of the things that people talk about as a motivator is that if you see how much energy your neighbors are using, you change so that you're not being more profligate than they are.

CS: There's a privacy issue there, obviously.

JP: Yes. Some people got very concerned about privacy. It was never going to be your identifiable neighbor. It was going to be a very broad kind of thing. But here's something that a year and a half ago made absolute sense and wouldn't be difficult to do. And Maryland actually changed its laws in terms of pricing electricity so that power companies couldn't take advantage of it to make money by promoting the use of electricity. But the next step didn't work.

CS: Interesting. Well, the privacy issue surrounding that will get even more intense as smart grid gets more sophisticated. For instance, they can figure out that this guy is probably obese because he's in the refrigerator all the time. Let's start marketing Weight Watchers to him or whatever. There is a lot that can be done with that information; there's no question about it.

LG: Something that seems to make so much sense on a daily basis, you just don't think about what radically different views that people have. And I think that's the thing to me is a little bit frightening. There are very different ways of looking at some of these issues and that to me is very sobering. Renewable energy as a policy choice just seems to make sense for so many different reasons. But there's all different interests that play and that's the thing that is really the sticking point.

CS: My own major concern, by the way, is the recent Supreme Court decision on Citizens United versus Federal Election Commission. As of 2010, corporations generally—could be an oil corporation or anything else—can spend as much as they want advertising to make sure Jay is elected and Craig is thrown out.

JP: Yes. We'll see as this election cycle goes what the results of that are. It was a shocking case. I think it's likely to have a large effect, but we'll see.

LG: Time will tell, but it's certainly... it's highly disturbing.

JP: Right. It overturned more than 100 years worth of precedent and understanding of the meaning of the Constitution. Very strange; it's not the vision of the U.S. democracy. We'll see if it changes what people think or what people want.

CS: There's this thing called www.movetoamend.org you might have run across which is the supposition that without a constitutional amendment that essentially overturns that decision, we're screwed. Whether that happens or not, I don't know. It's got a couple hundred thousand signatures, but it needs tens of millions of signatures.

JP: Yeah.

CS: This has been terrific! Thanks very much to you both.

Craig's Interview with Nate Hagens, Ph.D.

My friend Tom Konrad, interviewed above, introduced me to Nate Hagens, a well-known authority on issues related to global resource depletion. Until recently he was lead editor of The Oil Drum, one of the most popular and highly-respected websites for analysis and discussion of global energy supplies and the future implications of energy decline.

Shortly after the introduction, Nate suggested that I attend a small, private conference at the Aspen Institute in Washington D.C., at which he and some colleagues made a two-hour presentation to about 30 representatives of various NGOs. I was honored, and overwhelmed to be in the presence of so many brilliant people. As I told them as I was leaving the lovely reception that followed, "Sorry, I have to catch a train. And besides, I've absorbed as much as I possibly can in one day. My brain hurts."

Nate and I agreed to a phone interview the following week, the transcript of which is below.

CS: Thanks so much for the opportunity, Nate; good to speak with you again.

As we've discussed, the project deals with answering a central question: Why are we failing so miserably in our quest for renewable energy, given the imperative which is based on half-a-dozen independent and compelling reasons? Why are we so slow at making this happen? Now, to be honest with you, this was all headed in one single direction until I ran across you and your presentation at the Aspen Institute the other day. I immediately realized, "Wow, this is a completely different viewpoint. This guy's explaining this in terms of a world economic crisis."

NH: Yes, our entire crisis is based on constraints to energy and natural resources and the human responses to these constraints. We built industrial society by spending five percent every year of our available energy to procure energy and the other 95 percent could go towards other industry/consumption. We built institutions and infrastructure around this premise. Once energy became more expensive at the margin and we had to spend more than five units out of every hundred on energy, we didn't want to face the physical implications of this to our growth-based system. The way we circumvented this was to start creating money from thin air via our central banks and commercial banks – aka debt.

In one sense, debt is a zero-sum game where a creditor offsets every debtor. But in another sense, all money, all claims on the financial system: stocks, bonds, derivatives, bank accounts, mortgages—are claims on future energy and labor. So if the entire aggregate claims in the system got to be two or three or four times more than could ever be paid back based on the future energy flow rates that we could afford, then that system has to unwind, even at the same time when we're developing viable renewable energy technology. Essentially we still have a lot of fossil BTUs in the ground, but the ease and cost of getting them—both in terms of energy and environmental externality—is higher than the assumptions we built the system on.

So we don't really have a shortage of energy, but rather a "longage" of expectations. We **do** have a shortage of energy needed to power this system that everyone is used to with their financial markers and growth going forward. The good news is the average American consumes around 2500 calories a day of energy endosomatically (within the body) via food, but we consume about 230,000 calories of energy if you calculate all the coal and the natural gas and the oil in our average American daily footprint. It's about 100 times more than our body actually needs. So we could cut that in half or even in two-thirds and we would still have a huge surplus relative to 99 percent of our evolutionary ancestors.

So, as you recall in that lecture that we gave, it's really kind of a counter-intuitive situation here; it's not enough to say wind and solar panel technology are feasible. What we need is a combination of remaining fossil fuels and renewables to get us the four to five cent per kilowatt-hour, non-intermittent, always-on power supply that has underpinned this growth/debt based civilization. I think the most likely non-linear break is going to be in the financial system, as opposed to higher energy prices. I would suggest that it's more likely that we'll have $30 oil for a decade than $300 oil.

CS: I see. And that's because we've reached the end of cheap energy and money, so demand must fall?

NH: Right. Because we're basically broke now, in aggregate, at least in the sense of our expectations of what we 'own'. The only reason that things have been chugging along the last two years is because the government has replaced private commercial credit with government credit via deficit spending. Of course, that's coming to a close now too because you've got this super committee in Washington saying we can't increase the debt ceiling unless we reduce spending, etc. We probably will try to create more credit from thin air, the problem is that while the Federal Reserve is adding all these trillions to the system, there is not the multiplier that there used to be. That money doesn't ripple through the system and expand on its own because 70 percent of Americans are basically broke. The middle class is being squeezed out. Sure, it doesn't matter if gas is $3.00 or $10.00 a gallon for the rich, but the average person is maxed out.

CS: Okay. So, in other words, their borrowing capacity is not there? They couldn't borrow it even if the money were available because they just don't have the collateral?

NH: Right. It is available to those with stellar credit. I've written a lot on these topics. I just emailed you something that's not related to what you heard in D.C., but it's about the timing of flows from various energy alternatives. As human individuals get more stressed—in economic and psychology speak—their impulsivity and their discount rates become steeper. In other words, when you're stressed, you start to care about the future less and you care more and more about the present.

CS: So I've heard. Apparently, this is a big part of the issue we face in getting people concerned about global warming.

NH: Right. This manifests in behavior in a lot of areas; what happens in energy is as follows: you don't just pay a million dollars for an energy project and get the BTUs instantly. There are different timing profiles of how energy is procured. Wind, for one example, requires about 90 percent of its entire lifetime investment before it starts producing. Then it will pay that energy back over 20 or 30 years. In that situation, when individuals or societies are stressed, whether they're broke or whether they're sick or any number of reasons that they're stressed, the prospect of a BTU 10 or 20 years from now is much less valuable than one right now. With natural gas and oil, ironically, you get half to two-thirds of your energy return back in the first 18 months. So, in addition to having other cost benefits over some renewables, fossil fuels actually have a timing/human behavior benefit as well.

There's also the handicap of intermittency with renewables. Then, if our economy is truly not subsidized by the government in making things more affordable—like "cash for clunkers" or the government putting out a "mortgage jubilee" where everyone only pays three percent on their mortgages instead of the market rate—without all those little gimmicks, oil and energy prices would get cut in half—or more, due to demand drops. Look at all the solar companies that are going bust right now.

CS: Yes, I see. It's scary stuff.

Well, let me just ask you to put it together in terms of your whole picture and the way you look at the world here. At the presentation, you mentioned that you had gone through something of an epiphany, which caused you to stop preaching sustainability and look at a vastly different big picture. Do you mind talking about that?

NH: Not at all, but it gets into human behavior which is a topic that rubs many the wrong way. I think that our entire system right now is steered by people who have social power and status – people who either have a financial/economic background or are advised by such. The problems with economic theory are rooted in the fact that all rules of economics that brought us to this day were developed under a very straight-lined, high-growth period of human history where we had surpluses of energy and resources and kind of an empty planet. All those people are not going to say, "You know what? The majority of our assumptions about our economic system are wrong. We screwed up." These people are going to dig in their heels and use the strategies that got them to this point without changing anything of significance which is what we need.

I'm of the opinion that we're headed for a bottleneck and it will happen via revolution, not evolution. They're not going to be baby steps around that change. My view was there need to be people working on the supply and demand balance sheet. What are our energy and natural resources? What are the constraints on the supply side? What would we really accomplish and at what cost? Not in dollar terms because dollars and Euros and yen are so ephemeral in terms of what they really are worth, but in natural resource terms themselves. Ie. How much energy or water or soil or land does it take to create this water or energy?

Then, on the demand side, what are the ways that humanity can pursue "Darwinian happiness?" In other words, what is the neurotransmitter cocktail that our ancestors evolved to allow us to feel good? We get that right now by stock trading and buying yachts and conspicuous consumption, and there are ways to get these same brain chemicals from much lower throughput ways.

CS: Wow. [chuckles] I'm just laughing because we're talking about brain chemistry here. There aren't many disciplines of human thought that you or another of these folks in the project have missed. Go on, please.

NH: Sure. So, there need to be people working on that, but I personally think there are very few people working on understanding the danger zones in the bottleneck. After studying this for ten years, I've gone from focusing on environmental externalities, to energy to human behavior to debt. Now I think the largely overlooked area is the benefit that we get and the sheer dependence that we have on trade. If trade were to either cease because of some overnight currency event or get severely truncated through some sort of 2011 version of the (1930) Smoot-Hawley Tariff Act or protectionism or any breakdown in trade, the impact would be catastrophic—for us, anyway; countries like India or Pakistan would be fine.

Again, low energy costs have subsidized the entire move towards globalization, so trade can breakdown due to much higher energy costs. People haven't looked at the shortfall risk of that. They haven't looked at what would a 20, 30, 50 percent reduction in trade imply for our country, because everything has become so complex, so just-in-time. As one example, which we mentioned in D.C., a few weeks after that earthquake in Fukushima, there were no black cars made in Detroit from Ford because that's the only place in the world that provided that pigment for paint. That's one tiny example. Things shut down pretty quickly in unexpected ways if trade doesn't continue. And we've squelched and suppressed import substitution strategies for decades in other countries—in the name of economic profits and efficiency. It's the "trading guns for butter makes everyone better off" type of argument. It's true, but only with stable/declining energy prices and unlimited credit availability. If the credit spigot dries up and energy prices go up, some of these trade connections break down.

So, to get back to your question on sustainability, it's finally dawned on me that teaching people how to be sustainable is like telling teenage girls to dress uglier. It's absolutely not in their nature. To consume less is not in the environmental cues that we're being given by our culture. It's hard to have advertisements on TV to buy a BMW and try to be like this real estate baron who's super successful, and at the same time tell people to live more sustainably. It's just not going to happen. Facts are going to have to change, then what people aspire to will change.

CS: I see. Speaking of sustainability, let's talk about sustainable growth in GDP per capita which you seem to think is impossible at the core. What was the point of inflexion here? What happened? What makes you believe that we can't simply grow our way out of this the way we have in the last half a century or the last century or so?

NH: Well, the last century or so was a continued period of adding more and more mechanical labor to replace human labor, while it was something like a thousand times less expensive than human labor. I can send you some specifics on the numbers, but at some point, the marginal cost of energy increases—as it is now. I mean, even in a recession we've got $100 oil. You cannot continue that trajectory of adding more and more mechanical labor to make higher productivity and things cheaper. And you certainly can't do it based on intermittent renewables, etc.

You know the argument with energy return on investment. Yes, wind turbine and solar panels are net producers of energy, but they're not producers of energy at the scale where we can replace an increasing amount of human labor with them the way we did the last generation with fossil fuels. First of all I think sustainable and growth in the same sentence are an oxymoron. Sustainability implies no growth and growth implies no sustainability. I think that sustainable growth is such a buzzword right now in world policy circles, and I cringe every time I hear it. I think people have to come to terms that growth and decline are both part of natural systems and we are near the end of a period of growth and now there's going to be a period of decline. Decline doesn't have to be horrible or even bad, but it does need to be prepared for.

CS: I understand. There are those who say that we're experiencing the end of the American empire, by which I presume they mean vis-a-vis China.

NH: I don't know that that's what they're saying. I just think that we peaked in oil production 40 years ago and in reaction to that we immediately, within one year, went off the gold standard so our dollar could no longer be convertible into gold, and from there we turned to debt and the seniorage that we've received from having the world's reserve currency and we exported our model to other nations. Globalization afforded Americans generations of over-consumption, but now even that model—the credit model—is coming to an end.

I think the end of the American empire is the end of the global OECD (Organization for Economic Co-operation and Development) growth empire. I don't think that America is going to fall by the wayside and a bunch of other countries are going to replace her. In fact, I think China is in much worse shape than America. They've followed our "build on credit" model over the last two or three years in spades. Their central bank is creating money from nothing in order to pay people to build things, and the end demand for those products just isn't there. So once that unwinds, I'm very worried about China because again, how many of our goods here—our little components for our chainsaws and spark plugs and tools and things like that—come from China? If they implode, what happens here, where in the drive for efficiency and profits we outsourced the production of important parts and goods?

The reason (well one of them) that economists missed this is that our entire economic system is based on the assumption that energy is just like any other input into the production function; like a coffee cup or mittens or a garbage can. The truth is that energy is critical and special and should be treated outside of capital and labor as its own input into the production function, but no mainstream economist thinks of it that way. In other words, they think that at $120 oil we naturally will have some combination of conserving and developing new alternatives. That's just not true. Biophysical economic tenets assert that price does not create its own supply because it takes increasing natural resources to obtain energy as it depletes.

CS: Really? What would make conservation or finding competitive goods and services not happen?

In other words, suppose oil went to $200 a barrel—and the removal of the subsidies would at least contribute to that. Wouldn't that produce an incentive to invest in renewable resources?

NH: No, I don't agree with that. First of all, the amount of subsidies given to the fossil fuel industry sounds large, but relative to how much money our government is printing from thin air, it's like a mosquito bite. Secondly, my point before was that, yes, people will conserve at $140 oil because they're broke. My main point was that new energy sources won't automatically emerge at $140 or at $200 or at $400. In other words, without cheap energy, growth stops. Without growth we could never have $200 oil because there would be social upheaval.

I'm talking about the theory and the reason why people were never worried about the things that you and I are discussing, which is that they always assumed that human ingenuity would overtake depletion. In fact, they never even thought about it in those terms. That's how I look at it: technology is in a race with depletion and depletion is winning. In other words, in the 1930's we invested in one barrel of oil to get out 100. That was like Beverly Hillbilly stuff, where oil was right under the ground. Then we had to drill deeper, and that ratio went to 30 to 1. Then we went offshore, and the ratio went to 10 to 1. So, all this time technology was improving and U.S. oil production was declining, yet no one realized that energy is a biophysical construct that requires energy and water inputs itself. Now the mainstream economists are starting to realize that there's a problem with energy. I mean, academia works much too slowly, but if energy were a special input into the production function, I think there would be a lot more economists recognizing that end of growth is nigh.

CS: Well, do you think there is "willful ignorance?" You must have some theory that explains why you are, if not singular, then certainly rare in terms of looking at this and analyzing this problem. Why do you think this viewpoint isn't more common in our normal discussion?

NH: Well, I have a couple of answers to that. Number one is there are a lot of very smart people out there thinking about these issues—far smarter than I am. But I've had the advantage of taking nine years now to become relatively knowledgeable on a lot of different subjects. If the best energy minds in the world don't also understand human behavior, economics, or trade, and finance, they can't put together a coherent holistic energy story.

For example, look at all the peak oilers out there that were pretty much correct that oil would peak sooner rather than 2030 to 2040 – the CERA story. But they didn't understand the importance of credit to our economic system. They were predicting $200 oil, then $300 oil etc. as depletion took over without understanding that debt has borrowed from future affordability of oil (and other things) and there's just no way that oil is ever going to get to $300. Ever. We couldn't afford it. Maybe on the black market some day, some time, but that's just not going to happen with public markets

So number one, I think there's an absolute scarcity of people thinking in systems and crossing numerous disciplines to explain the world.

Number two is that the implications of some of the things I talk about are threatening, and I'm sure you know enough about psychology and sociology that you've heard about cognitive dissonance. If something is very threatening to someone's job or the future of their kids or whatever, they tend to read things that disprove or ignore that threatening thing. They don't really want to delve into it because it's so scary.

I think there's a lot of that. Then what I said earlier is it's not like the physicists or the nuclear engineers or the chemists are the ones in charge of our society. The ones in charge are Larry Summers and Tim Geithner and Ben Bernanke; those are the people that are making the calls. And to agree with some of the things that I'm telling you now, Ben Bernanke, even if he cognitively thought I was right, he could never emotionally acknowledge such, as he would lose all of his status.

It's a rare person that will get up there and say, "Everything I thought before was wrong." That just makes them look like a fool. I would love for Obama to get up and say, "We thought that this stimulus would help, and it *did* help, but the truth is we live in a biophysical world and our inputs have become more expensive. And you know what I learned? We're not going to be able to grow into the future like the last few generations have. And that could be a good thing for our economy and here's what we have to do." But, you know, I just don't see that happening.

CS: Right. Well, to that degree I suppose it's an extension of what I've been hearing for the last couple of years in writing these books, i.e., we can't expect elected leaders to make statements that are tantamount to career suicide. In other words, they won't make decisions that don't have a tangible effect within that election cycle.

NH: That was my third reason why people aren't connecting these things. And this goes back to the sustainability question. There's something in economics called the discount rate – how much we favor the present over the future in our behaviors, and there are certain demographics of society that have steeper discount rates than others. Men more than women, drug users, high stimulation people, drinkers, adrenaline junkies, etc. Certain people value the present very highly versus the future, and just can't envision what their life might look like 10 years from now. In other words, for most Americans there is no future. That doesn't mean they're not going to be alive and enjoying a meaningful life 10 years from now. It just means that having them care about something ten or 15 years in the future has the weight of one gram in their life, and what they're going to do this weekend is prominent.

CS: Yes. That's certainly true; it's more true of Americans now than it has ever been in the past it seems to me.

NH: Well, we're kind of self-selected. I can't prove this, but I think there is a genetic component of the restless individuals who left Europe and came to America; we have unique alleles on our dopamine receptors. There is some evidence of this in a book called <u>American Mania</u> by neuroscientist Peter Whybrow. I think we are more concerned about the present culturally than Europeans or Japanese. I'm not saying this is a genetic thing, but culturally they do make better decisions about the future sometimes than we do.

CS: This is amazing. So if we elected Nate Hagens, what would we get in the next couple of years?

NH: I would never run for office. I like free time and naps.

What we need to do on the government institutional level is literally buy American – buy products that are made in America. We need to replace our dependence on foreign products—not just oil, but components, medicines, food supply chains, etc.. How many pitchforks and garden tools and spark plugs are made within a two-state radius of where you are? Or tools to get food moved in our own country? There needs to be huge research done on our supply chains.

CS: In other words, protectionism?

NH: It's not protectionism per se because I think trade is still going to be very important. Once you reduce trade, you reduce our standard of living dramatically, but we need to look at it. Basic goods: food, water, medicine, sanitation; need to be completely regionalized and localized so that there's no large systemic risk. Government needs to be working on that.

On the individual level, we need to prepare psychologically for a world with less, where we don't think 5, 10, 20 years from now we're going to be making more money than we are today, and have more toys and more stuff. This is something that you can't tell someone: "Hey, be happier with less." In my experience, you have to either lead by example, or walk them into trying it for themselves and seeing that, for selfish reasons, they're better off biking to work because it's healthier for them, it's cheaper for them, and they're just happier. It's not because we need to save a few gallons of oil that China will probably use anyway. We need to ground these behavioral changes ultimately with selfish reasoning I think.

You and I are similar ages. When we were kids we used between a third and a half of what we use now, and we had great childhoods.

CS: Yes, that's true.

NH: So the problem is we can't magically wish our way back to the '50s or '60s or '70s because this system does not work well in reverse. So there needs to be a bridge and that's what my colleagues and I are working on. How do we provide time for these alternative energy and alternative economic system gurus to come up with things while the financial system bottleneck kind of blows up in our face? How do we on the supply side use less, and on the behavioral side not blame people and go postal in the meantime?

CS: Right. Wow, this is fascinating stuff Nate. I knew this would be good.

NH: It is kind of a complex web. I understand that you're surprised at how few people are connecting these dots, but I've been fortunate in my life—both on Wall Street and then beyond—to be surrounded by super-smart people. I have a curiosity about the world that borders on addiction so I'm friends with evolutionary biologists and energy experts and human behavior economists. I just glean a little bit from each of them and then eventually I came up with some sort of a coherent picture. I'm sure I'm missing something still, but I think the things that I'm missing—not to be arrogant—are becoming fewer. I think this is a reasonably good extrapolation of what we face.

But, again, it's really not all that gloomy. The frustrating thing is we don't have to do that much with what we have now to make things, maybe not better, but certainly very good. The really sad and frustrating thing is how little is actually being done. Most people are just saying, "Okay. We need growth; we need energy, so let's create more energy using some combination of corn, soil, natural gas, and water." In other words, ethanol, and that's our answer to our crisis. It's just so myopic.

CS: All right. I thank you very much. I certainly hope to run into you again in the near future. This has been fantastic.

NH: Glad to help.

Short Essays on the Subject

Electric Vehicle Adoption — What Do We Really Know?

I concluded a recent talk at the Electric Vehicle Summit with a reminder that, in terms of the EV adoption curve, we don't really know as much as we think we do.

"Let's put this in perspective," I told the audience near the end of my 45-minute presentation. "You folks are listening to me, and, I'd like to think, trusting what I'm telling you. But I got my information from various sources, that, in turn, got their information from other sources. At the end of the day, it's possible that, pardon the pun, we're all just breathing one another's exhaust. When there are so many variables, and so much of our world changes month to month, I look askance at projections that go out 40 years. I think you should too."

I read a poem (Allan Ahlberg's "Please Mrs. Butler") that makes this point, i.e., maybe I've raised more questions than I've provided answers. I acknowledged the chuckles I received, took a few questions, and sat down.

But the idea that we think we know more than we do is an extremely important one, and it certainly applies far more broadly than the EV adoption curve. This subject, called "epistemic arrogance" lies at the root of so much of human folly. I'm reminded of an eminent business leader I've met a few times who takes every opportunity to offer his position on global warming. "It's a hoax. Mankind does not possess the power to alter the incredible power of nature. The concept is absolutely idiotic," he re-asserted at a recent meeting.

"Are you **sure**?" I asked the first time I heard this, my jaw on the floor. "I mean no offense—and I know there are 'climate change deniers' out there—but you seem quite certain about a proposition that flies in the teeth of the peer-reviewed findings that the vast majority of climate scientists have published over the last 30 years." But I couldn't get him to back off even a micron.

I'm wondering where we're going to see the most dramatic and lethal evidence of our epistemic arrogance. It certainly could be global warming, though there's no reason to rule out nutrition. The last hundred years has seen agricultural science develop hundreds of pesticides, herbicides, and fungicides, as well as farming methods that many say have ruined the soil. Others believe that our GMOs represent a terrible biohazard. Almost no one thinks that commercially raised tomatoes have any flavor, but, more importantly, anyone who's studied the subject knows that the nutritional value of the food in our grocery stores is a small fraction of what it was a century ago.

We also have skyrocketing rates of diseases that simply didn't exist in the early 1900s. Is there a connection?

And what's the solution? Should we feel comfortable with the approach that ADM, Monsanto, and the other agri-giants are taking, i.e., more unnatural processes and higher doses of more powerful chemicals—aimed at undoing the damage caused by the last round?

While it doesn't seem likely to me that this will fix the problem, and it's certainly not the direction I'd be taking if I were directing this effort, I have to say what I wish other people would admit: "I don't know."

I'm reminded of an important idea in law called the Precautionary Principle, that requires the developer of an action or policy to prove that what he is advocating will cause no harm to the public or the environment. I.e., if a concept could potentially contain a risk to public health and safety, the burden is placed on the concept's proponents to prove that such risk does **not** exist, rather than on the public to prove that it **does**.

But in cases like the food supply as discussed here, it's obvious that we as a civilization are light-years away from any meaningful implementation of this principle. Agribusiness makes decisions that affect the health of everyone living on this planet. We eat what they feed us, and we suffer the consequences.

Occasionally it would be nice to hear, "Look, we clearly have no idea of the unintended consequences of what we're doing here, so let's err on the side of caution." Wouldn't that be refreshing?

Civilization Faces Many Crises, So Let's Abandon Science

Wednesday, I was lucky enough to attend a conference presented by the Institute for Integrated Economic Research, a non-profit research organization focused on developing an unbiased view of global economic processes. In fact, it was here that I first met Nate Hagens, who was a presenter at the conference; Nate wanted me to come up to speed on his thinking before we spoke, so that I could ask better questions when the time came for the interview whose transcription appears above.

I'm very glad I didn't miss this opportunity, as there were a couple of important take-aways. First: there is no such thing as a "natural environment" left on Earth; there are PCBs in the arctic, and the blood streams of every one of us carry between 140 and 150 different synthetic chemicals. There is not a square centimeter of the planet, nor a single animal or plant species that has not been affected by human activity of some kind. We need to become active in restoring our environment, just as we are in restoring our man-made infrastructure so that it does not crumble and fall apart.

The second major theme was exploring the global economic scenario in which continued growth in GDP simply doesn't happen. What happens to a civilization of seven billion, which is in the process of expanding to nine billion by 2050, if the meltdown that began in 2008 marks the beginning of an extended period of negative growth? I'll skip the details, and simply say that grappling with these issues successfully will require our best minds in the humanities and the sciences. Even if we can bring such thinking to bear, the prospects are scary.

And here's something even scarier. It is quite possible that this country may soon be led by a person who wields an utter contempt for science. Each of the Republican front-runners expresses this somewhat differently, but the dismissal of science as elitist, corrupt, or "just one way of looking at the world" is an important theme in the discourse of Michele Bachmann, Mitt Romney, Rick Perry, and of course, Sarah Palin.

Rick Perry dismisses evolution as "just a theory," one that has "got some gaps in it." Isn't that a remarkable thing for a man to say who wishes to be taken seriously in the 21st Century? In the circle of biologists, the theory of evolution has the same status as Newton's universal gravitation and Einstein's relativity have among physicists.

On climate change, Governor Perry tells us: "I think there are a substantial number of scientists who have manipulated data so that they will have dollars rolling into their projects. And I think we are seeing almost weekly, or even daily, scientists are coming forward and questioning the original idea that man-made global warming is what is causing the climate to change."

The idea that thousands of scientists are conspiring in secret to perpetrate a hoax is preposterous, and the second part of Perry's statement is patently false: the scientific consensus about man-made global warming includes 97 percent to 98 percent of researchers in the field, according to the National Academy of Sciences. Moreover, the evidence is becoming stronger, not weaker.

If we as a civilization truly are facing existential threats in terms of global financial crises and environmental catastrophe, I'm not sure that this a good time to disregard science and create important policies based on "gut instinct" or whatever drives these people's thinking.

Electric Vehicles: If You're Looking for Harmony and Consensus, Seek Elsewhere

There are some highly respected thinkers who completely and vocally reject the idea of electric vehicles. I spoke recently with John Petersen of SeekingAlpha.com fame, whose recent article: "It's Time To Kill The Electric Car, Drive A Stake Through Its Heart And Burn The Corpse" has stirred a great deal of conversation on the subject. He points out that electric cars are uneconomic at several levels. They are energy intensive to manufacture, require scarce metals, and you have to drive them many, many miles to get any economic value out of them, which means they have to be charged more, reducing the life of the battery and requiring even earlier replacement.

It goes without saying that Bill Moore, editor of EVWorld. com, sees the subject quite differently. To summarize his very thoughtful rebuttal, abandoning the pursuit of EVs is tantamount to "perpetuating the cycle of waste epitomized by the internal combustion engine and our fossil fuel run thermal power plants, both of which throw away 50-85% of the energy they consume." We need a solution, not a devil's advocate. Moore concludes by acknowledging that Petersen is a fan of reducing energy waste, and noting:

"So, John, isn't what we need to be doing is driving that oaken stake through the heart of the status quo instead of through a promising, albeit still immature technology that is seeking to achieve— imperfectly, no doubt—what you yourself are espousing?"

I would point out three things that I see missing or requiring amplification here:

1) "Perpetuating the cycle of waste epitomized by the internal combustion engine and our fossil fuel run thermal power plants"

isn't a good thing, to be sure, but it's not the worst, either. The true costs of fossil fuels to our society are far higher than most of us imagine. The externalities in terms of war, illness, national security, long-term environmental damage are generally under-counted or ignored altogether—and they're huge. It's only a matter of time before we realize the catastrophe we have on our hands, and it's quite possible that we'll be too late. Think I'm exaggerating? Go ask the families of the 13,200 Americans who died last year from inhaling the aromatics of coal, or the families whose kids have been killed or dismembered in wars in the Middle East; it's certainly too late for them.

2) Peak oil is a reality that will cause incredible social chaos and suffering, and the longer we wait the more severe will be the consequences.

3) EVs are imperfect in many different ways, but there are dozens of improvements currently in the R&D phase that have the potential to change all of this. Check out Eos Energy Storage, soon to offer a zinc-air battery solution at $165/kWh. I'm reminded of a conversation I had with lithium-ion battery manufacturer Ener1's CEO Charles Gassenheimer, in which I asked him about the potential for a lithium shortage. "We didn't think there was much oil in the ground either – until we started looking for it in the early 20th Century," he told me. "Unfortunately, we found all the easy stuff—and then we burned it."

Are we right around the corner from electric Class 8 trucks and aircraft? Of course not. Will we ever get there? Who knows? But it's clear to me that Nissan-Renault CEO Carlos Ghosn is 100% correct in the assessment he gave the crowd at the Los Angeles Auto Show a couple of years ago: "Electric transportation is the #1 priority in the automotive world right now."

Of course there are challenges: technological, economic, and political. But this is a game we can't afford to lose. If I told you that there was a safe that contained the cure for cancer, you could say, "Oh, the combination might be too tough to figure out. Let's give up." Or you could say, "Let's do whatever it takes to get in that safe." I'd be the latter of the two. How about you?

Should Government Pick Winners and Losers in Energy Technology?

Solyndra is an unfortunate debacle that's thrown a cold swimming pool of water on the already foundering US renewable energy industry.

I'd love to know how this happened in the first place. I talk to people in the private sector all the time who swear they saw this train-wreck coming far in advance. At a meeting I had with Kleiner Perkins managing partner Ray Lane earlier this year, he told me, "We knew that technology wouldn't scale. We had been telling the DoE that for over a year, but no one would listen."

So what are we to believe? That the public sector knew this too but made it happen for "political purposes?" Sorry, I think there's more to the story than that. Yet God help me if I can add more clarity. I feel rather like those trying to figure out the JFK assassination; I know what **didn't** happen, but not exactly what **did**.

I thought the DoE spokespeople did a good job in handling the question that was being asked so often: Shouldn't the market, rather than government, pick the winners and losers in technology? Or the parallel question: Ought our government to support the development of technologies?

The spokesperson pointed out that it's not a matter of "should" or "ought." It's a matter of "is." This is precisely what the governments of the large countries in Asia and Europe **are**, in fact, doing. The question is: Do we Americans want to do the same, or sit on the sidelines while we become irrelevant in the 21st Century global energy industry? Personally, I think he's nailed this one.

But making this happen will be exceptionally difficult given the political climate, and voter expectation. Let's examine those expectations for a second.

Except for the dwindling few of Americans who lived through the Great Depression, most of us have been exceptionally privileged with an outrageously high standard of living. And in the process, we've demonstrated a near-complete lack of attention to sustainability and an utter disregard for the consequences of over-consumption and under-preparation. So now we expect our elected leaders to bring us back from the precipice? We think someone's going to win an election on an "austerity" platform, and force us to reduce the ridiculous levels of gluttony that all of us take for granted? Even if there were such a person, he couldn't get elected dogcatcher.

Recall that cold swimming pool of water I mentioned? Get ready to be thrown into it.

Biden's Clean Energy Speech: US Will Lead the Global Clean-Energy Revolution. Great! Can We Get Started Soon?

Joe Biden believes that the US, armed as it is with its "entrepreneurial spirit and innovative national labs," will "lead the global clean energy revolution and reap the economic and environmental benefits that go with it." At least, this is what he told an audience that packed an auditorium at the National Renewable Energy Laboratory (NREL).

Damn! I'm **so** sorry I missed that speech, as I'm sure it was grounded in solid fact, as most political speeches are. Hey, he didn't happen to mention **when** all this was supposed to get started, did he?

Democrats make empty speeches about US leadership in clean energy. But I suppose that's marginally better than Republicans, who have relatively little to say on the subject other than convincing voters that environmentalism is bad for the economy, that the imperative to move away from fossil fuels is over-hyped, and that the super-profitable oil companies still need huge subsidies from taxpayers.

However, while we here in the US are busy talking about renewables (or remaining silent about it, as the case may be), the Chinese and others are actually making it happen. China has a large and ever-widening lead in global clean energy investment; according to Bloomberg, they'll spend 5 trillion yuan (nearly $740 billion) over the next 10 years on renewable energy projects.

America lives with constant uncertainty and the vigorous flip-flops that immediately follow every two-year election cycle. While all this makes for lively debate, which I suppose is good for voter turnout, it understandably renders investors quite nervous. In fact, it means death to any hope for the solid stream of capital formation that will be necessary to make clean energy a reality.

We're good at rancor; we've proven that, year after year. Now we need something that we've not yet been able to demonstrate: a commitment to go beyond the name-calling and gross over-simplifications—the strength to build a consensus that will move us forward in an effective and practical manner.

But does there really seem to be any change on the horizon? If there is, I sure don't see it. I liken this to the alcoholic who, until he hits rock bottom, refuses to cart himself off to rehab and clean up his life. I see the same situation for clean energy in the US; we haven't sunk low enough to create the necessary motivation.

Unless there is a dramatic shift in our approach, in about a decade Americans will wake up one day to realize that the country they love is now number three or four in clean energy – an industry that will have come to dominate the world economy. We will have lost the most important economic battle in the 21st Century. Maybe better said: we will have sat on the sidelines and watched the rest of the world fight the most important economic battle in the 21st Century.

I predict that this tragic event will spawn some real change in leadership, albeit too late, as we're a nation that really doesn't like to lose. I'm reminded of the words of George C. Scott as General George Patton: "Americans love a winner, and they will not tolerate a loser."

Yes, Americans will eventually place a limit on their tolerance for failure and humiliation. But wouldn't it be easier to fight hard and win now?

Can Someone Explain Toyota's Lethargy in the Electric Vehicle Space?

I often wonder what caused Toyota to invest $50 million in Tesla. Obviously they deemed it important in expediting their introduction of electric vehicles. But doesn't a company the size of Toyota have a considerable gaggle of engineers who know their way around EVs, after a decade of tinkering with the Prius?

Perhaps Toyota is so wrapped up in engineering and PR problems that it wanted to get some of the R&D workload in electric vehicles off its plate. Or maybe they figured that Tesla's nimble management style might be able to make faster progress. And note that currently, Toyota is not only a stockholder, but a customer as well; it placed an order for 35 electric conversions of the RAV4 EV, the competitor to the Ford Escape, Honda CRV, and Chevy Equinox, all small sport utility vehicles.

I know others also struggle to make sense of some of the auto behemoths' decisions, but I find Toyota's behavior in the EV space to be especially mysterious. After the homerun they hit with the Prius, it seems otherworldly that they haven't done a better job in advancing electric transportation. They claim to have no fewer than 10 EV models "under development," and I suppose that could be true. But why on Earth would you wait while other folks take the lead and render you an afterthought in a strategic part of the industry?

Here's a theory: it's obvious that the car companies have gone into the EV age kicking and screaming. But resisting this change, while it was certainly in their interest, was not within their power—and now their hand has been forced. My guess is that Toyota misread the timing of the pressure they would receive from Nissan and the others. Now, they're playing catch-up—and under horribly adverse circumstances – part of which is the damage they sustained recently to their supply chain, with numerous vendors wiped out by the tsunami.

Nothing else can explain their lethargy in this space, and announcements of totally lame products, like the Prius V. Here we are in late 2011 and the new Prius still has no plug?

Sorry. No plug? No deal.

Government Subsidies to the Oil Companies

All Americans should be aware of what's happening in Washington in this critically important area that affects every one of us. Earlier in 2011, 48 senators, including three Democrats and all but two senate Republicans voted to defeat a bill that would have ended tax breaks for the five biggest oil companies.

What could cause such outrageous behavior? How about the $39.5 million that the oil and gas companies spent lobbying Congress in the first quarter of this year alone? Or might it be the fact that the industry donated nearly $18 million directly to the political campaigns of senators who voted against ending these subsidies— five times more than to senators who supported ending them?

Yet the measure to end these handouts to the oil industry came fairly close to passing (we needed 60 votes, and got 52). The message: if you care about things like this, I urge you to exercise your rights as a citizen and let your elected leaders know where you stand.

Subsidies for Oil Companies — Hot Debate in Washington DC

The discussions in Washington DC in which lawmakers quizzed the CEOs of the five largest oil companies concerning the subsidies they receive from US taxpayers sure were interesting. Several senators asked the industry to defend this transfer of wealth from taxpayer to shareholder, given that we live in a time of massive profits – and record gasoline prices.

But the oil company execs were armed for bear, vigorously attacking the hearings themselves. Here's John Watson, CEO of Chevron, criticizing the Senate:

Singling out five companies because of their size is even more troubling. Such measures are anti-competitive and discriminatory. After all, our five companies are providing the technical, operating and managerial expertise that is allowing the global energy industry to operate at the forefront of energy development.

ConocoPhillips responded similarly, pointing out that it would be "Un-American" to end billions of dollars in subsidies to the oil industry.

I want to take lessons in salesmanship from anyone who can convince us that we as a country should continue to deny basic human services in favor of boosting oil company profits to new heights.

How Soon Will the Auto OEMs Offer Us Electric Vehicles in Production Quantities?

I was speaking earlier today with a friend whose current business life revolves around making sense of the auto OEMs' embrace of electric vehicles. "If I were a cynic," he began, "I wouldn't see too much sincerity in what these folks are doing. I read what you wrote recently in the 2GreenEnergy blog about the BMW's stalled electric vehicle plans, and it seems to echo what I see with the Mitsubishi i-MiEV, and the dozens of other players who claim that they're running as fast as they can in this direction."

My friend went on to make a couple of points:

1) There is nothing in it for the OEMs to rush into the EV space. From the standpoint of making and selling a profitable car, they all win from dragging this out as long as possible. The lifetime profit associated with a customer who purchases an EV is a small fraction compared to that of one who buys a gas-powered vehicle, since EVs last a relative eternity, and require virtually no maintenance and replacement parts.

2) From the standpoint of overall risk-management, the idea of the OEMs rushing to offer EVs is even more idiotic. Suppose you're Mitsubishi, with the super-cool i-MiEV whose introduction into the U.S., for some reason (wink, wink) you keep postponing. Why not put it off as long as possible? If Nissan wants to lead the way with its LEAF, fine. But what's the incentive for you (or Ford, or anyone else) to be a leader here? Surely, you have no obligations to anyone but your shareholders; you're not in the business for any other reason than immediate profits—and that means one word: delays. Why not let the government, at the peril of those in charge, bring down the costs of batteries and charging infrastructure, and enter the market at your leisure?

I see my friend's point here, and thus advise this spring's graduates: If you think you may want a job with the top auto OEMs so you can make the world a better place, you may want to look for work elsewhere.

Reason to Consider Renewable Energy: The US Dependence on Foreign Oil Empowers Our Enemies

One of the central problems with our dependence on oil (of which we have very little domestically) is that our borrowing $1 billion per day to buy it from foreign governments empowers our enemies. In response, frequent commenter MarcoPolo writes:

Craig, I'm curious, what are those 'enemy' regimes you speak of?

I mean Chavez is a bit of a buffoon, and has no love for the US, but an active enemy? I am unaware that North Korea is oil rich. And since the US imports no oil from Iran, that leaves the four biggest US oil imports from Canada, Saudi Arabia, Mexico, and Nigeria.

Yes, well I can see your point with Canada!

Allies, Craig, the US imports from allies!

In response, I would just tell you what (ex-CIA Director) James Woolsey told me when I spoke with him last year:

Craig, read Larry Diamond's book if you haven't already. If you look at the 22 countries that count on two-thirds or more of their national income from oil—it's fair to say all 22 of those countries are autocratic kingdoms or dictatorships.

And I haven't compared that list with Freedom House's list of the forty, basically – those that Freedom House calls "Not Free." There are about 120 democracies in the world, I mean not perfect, but nonetheless regular elections and another 20 countries like Bahrain that are reasonably well and decently governed, even though not democratically so. And then you've got 40 really bad guys. And I'm pretty sure that list of 22 in Larry Diamond's book is virtually all from the list of 40 bad guys—or "Not Free," in Freedom House's terms.

So it's really a pretty decisive set of statistics, I think, and then if you look at other numbers, set out in places like Mort Halprin's book The Democracy Advantage, it's pretty clear that basically democracies don't fight each other. They occasionally get really pissed off, but they mainly choose up sides and argue about trade sanctions and stuff. It's not impossible but it's really hard, even going back into the 19th century, but certainly since 1945, finding democracies fighting each other. They just don't.

So you've got oil locking some states that depend so heavily on it into autocracy and dictatorship and worse. And those are the folks who also fund the terrorists, who invade neighboring countries, etc. So there's a large national security point here.

I guess what I'm saying is that a thriving oil market empowers the enemies of democracy, whether they are active and avowed enemies of the US or not.

Chevron's Situation in Ecuador Won't Be Easily Dismissed

It looks like Chevron's situation in Ecuador is coming to a head. In a couple of weeks, the oil giant will face a watershed event in the court case in which it's been ordered to pay $9.5 billion to repair the damage it did (operating as Texaco) to the people and environment of this formerly pristine part of the Amazon jungle. AmazonWatch.org is a small but fierce non-profit that's been working hard to focus world attention—and bring justice—to this horrific matter.

In my mind, what makes this all the more disgusting is where it happened, and why it happened there. We're talking about a company whose leaders premeditated to commit an atrocity in a part of the world populated with men, women and children in whom "civilization" simply has no interest. The people of the entire region are invisible; they hold no currency; they do not matter. If the executives responsible had perpetrated the same thing in the US, they would have been making license plates for the next 15 – 20 years—and they knew it. We have clear laws in place —and a judicial system that *does* manage to lock up an occasional CEO or two for gross violations. So the folks in charge thought they would make some money by destroying a remote part of the world, and its forgotten people—all with total impunity.

And even though decades of jurisprudence finally produced a crystal-clear guilty verdict, they just might pull it off. Chevron has deployed many hundreds of the world's finest and best-paid litigators to the case, and have vowed to fight this to the bitter end. Besides, they must be heartened by the success that ExxonMobil enjoyed in dragging out its payments on the Valdez oil spill in Alaska for more than 25 years before agreeing to pay a small portion—over a *quarter of a century later*. No fewer than 8,000 beneficiaries of the ExxonMobil restitution *died* while they were waiting for their money to come in. I have to imagine that Chevron finds this travesty most encouraging.

Sorry to have to bring you news like this. And it's not all that good for me either, as I routinely take considerable flack when I present stuff of this kind. But I do it anyway.

Chevron Ordered to Pay Ecuador $8.6 Billion for Environmental Damages

Those of us who have seen the film documentary "Crude"—as well as millions of others following the story—were heartened as a court in Ecuador has ordered the oil giant Chevron to pay $8.6 billion for dumping millions of gallons of toxic oil waste into Ecuador's rain forest. The judgement is one of the largest ever imposed for environmental contamination in any court.

However, we were not at all surprised to hear that Chevron said it would appeal the ruling. Hell, ExxonMobil robo-appealed the Valdez judgement, consistently postponing the payment of damages.

The Exxon Valdez tanker spilled more than 11 million gallons of crude oil into Alaska's Prince William Sound, and eventually contaminated approximately 1,300 miles of shoreline. Yet, according to Climate Change, the group Time Magazine hails as "Internet's most influential climate-change blogger," Exxon fought paying damages and appealed court decisions multiple times, and they have still not paid in full.

"Years of fighting and court appeals on Exxon's part finally concluded with a U.S. Supreme Court decision in 2008 that found that Exxon only had to pay $507.5 million of the original 1994 court decree for $5 billion in punitive damages. And as of 2009, Exxon had paid only $383 million of this $507.5 million to those who sued, stalling on the rest and fighting the $500 million in interest owed to fishermen and other small businesses from more than 12 years of litigation.

"Twenty years later, some of the original plaintiffs are no longer alive to receive, or continue fighting for, their damages. An estimated

8,000 of the original Exxon Valdez plaintiffs have died since the spill while waiting for their compensation as Exxon fought them in court."

Is there any reason to expect that Chevron will behave any differently? Sure, the cases have some radically different features. In particular, Chevron's acts were not simple accidents stemming from negligence on its part; they were willful acts of criminality, deliberately and brazenly perpetrated against a people whom Chevron (then Texaco) erroneously presumed to be too weak and poorly represented to defend themselves. One could argue that Chevron would be well advised to get this atrocity out of the news and safely behind them so that they can immediately hire some high-priced public relations firm and get to work rebuilding some sort of credibility as a decent corporate citizen. It's going to be a very long road—why not start now?

But that won't happen; I would have found it astonishing to hear that Chevron had taken a different tack here. They made a cool $5.3 billion last quarter, and they employ the very best lawyers on Earth. Why pay up—and clean up—when you can put that legal team to good use?

And it will be equally amazing if they don't ultimately enjoy a similar experience to Exxon's thrill of victory in abusing the legal system until this judgment is overturned or reduced to a tiny sliver of the $8.6 billion.

It's shameful stuff. But sadly, it's the new standard.

Btw, in addition to comments supporting what I've written here, I'm fully expecting the normal barrage of hate mail that I receive every time I publish something like this, suggesting that I'm a "lefty" or somehow "unAmerican." I couldn't be less concerned;

please feel free to express your true feelings. But *please* don't try to tell me that behavior like this is what America stands for in the world; this garbage most positively *does not* represent the country for which our forefathers fought and died.

John Hofmeister's "Why We Hate The Oil Companies"

A reader writes in about my blog post on John Hofmeister's "Why We Hate The Oil Companies" in which I point out that the author, the ex-CEO of Shell Oil, though hardly a radical, calls upon the oil industry to act in better conformity with the needs of "grass-roots Americans." The inquiry reads:

He (Hofmeister) questions why oil companies act only with self-interest. Isn't it because their role is to make money? Does he think that selfishness is going to be eliminated? It seems to me that selfishness is the driving force in everything I can think of (unfortunately). Please enlighten me.

I respond:

You bring up an interesting point. It seems to me that the history of our society is really about finding a balance between selfishness and its ultimate catastrophic effects. At any time until the signing of the Magna Carta in 1215, the king/pharaoh/you-name-it could imprison, torture, and kill anyone he wanted, for any reason. Before the Emancipation Proclamation in 1863, Americans could legally own slaves. Until the US Civil Rights Act of 1964, there were laws that cut across the rights of US citizens to vote and take part in many other activities that we all take for granted today. Clearly, the last few thousand years have taught us that selfishness needs the moderation that is brought along by the forces of reason and decency, and that this moderation cannot be an option taken only by the enlightened; it needs to be made a part of our laws.

Now there is no doubt that the self-interest that lies at the base of free-market capitalism does certain things very well. It sets prices and supply/demand curves and, in most cases, rewards people who work hard. All of these are good. But we need to recognize that there are things that capitalism doesn't do at all well — some of which we've seen emphasized in the recent financial meltdowns. Witness Enron, Bernie Madoff, and the devastation wreaked by the present-day Wall Street bandits, which has ruined the lives of countless millions of Americans and turned our financial markets upside down. Perhaps most horrifying in all this is the realization that it's only a matter of time until this exact same stream of events recurs.

As much as we love the efficiency with which capitalism creates the markets that set our prices and determine the range of products and services we offer, we need to accept that it fails to deal well with at least two main issues:

1) Sustainable Wealth Distribution. As we observe every day, unbridled capitalism ensures that the rich get richer while the poor get poorer. And, as much as some people may think this is just fine, this eventual dissolution of the middle class will ultimately lead to collapse. We actually had this a few centuries ago; it's called "feudalism," and it really wasn't all that good.

2) Environmental Protection. The economic self-interest of our day has led us to a point where our planet is in real danger. It is a sad truth that leaving each of us more or less on our own to self-regulate the level of toxins we dump into our environment has brought us to the brink of disaster. Not everyone agrees with me here, but it is, according to my research, alarmingly true.

There is more at stake now than an inequitable distribution of wealth that causes miserable lives for the impoverished majority of Earth's seven billion current inhabitants. We've reached the point at which we're sentencing huge levels of suffering on even more of us to come.

It is for this reason that I believe we need enlightened government— one that will force compliance with critical environmental issues—an important one of which is our renewable energy portfolio. But goodness knows from where this government may derive; we certainly seem to be a million miles from it in what we have in Washington DC today.

I hope that you'll support us in our search for solutions. Thanks so much for writing.

Subsidies for Oil, Energy Policy, and Climate Change

I would like to reply to the three very thoughtful comments of 2GreenEnergy reader James Gover, who writes:

1) We can talk about the oil subsidies and toss numbers around, but I have yet to see defensible, detailed comparisons of the magnitude of subsidies to various energy sources. If someone in this group has defensible data, please send me a reference. I do not consider special interest groups that start with the answer to be credible.

Without a doubt, this is a problem – and for several reasons. First, as you suggest, anyone trying to ascertain that number has a reason for doing so which normally carries with it a financial or political interest in the matter and taints the legitimacy of the findings. And we need also to understand that there are over a dozen different kinds of subsidies, some extremely nebulous and debatable by their very nature. As you look down this list, you'll see what I mean:

- Construction bonds at low interest rates or tax-free
- Research-and-development programs at low or no cost
- Assuming the legal risks of exploration and development in a company's stead
- Below-cost loans with lenient repayment conditions
- Income tax breaks, especially featuring obscure provisions in tax laws designed to receive little congressional oversight when they expire
- Sales tax breaks – taxes on petroleum products are lower than average sales tax rates for other goods
- Giving money to international financial institutions (the U.S. has given tens of billions of dollars to the World Bank and U.S. Export-Import Bank to encourage oil production internationally, according to Friends of the Earth)
- The U.S. Strategic Petroleum Reserve

- Construction and protection of the nation's highway system
- Relaxing the amount of royalties to be paid—apparently, we get about 40% of revenues from oil on public land vs. 60% – 65% in most other countries
- Not forcing the industry to deal with the "externalities" — healthcare costs, long-term environmental damage, etc.— costs that are becoming increasingly clear and subject to quantification

2) We can talk about what the US government should do regarding energy, but what the government will do is decided by their constituents, the American public, not the government. Until the general public is educated on the costs, sustainability and risks of various energy alternatives, the inclination is to maintain the status quo. The simple fact is that all sources of energy have a downside. What matters is how this compares to the upside.

This is exactly right—and it happens to be the basic reason I write this stuff every day. Until people understand the issues, and put pressure on their elected leaders to move us in the right direction, our energy policy will continue to languish as the rest of the world leaves us in the dust while we choke ourselves slowly to death. We get the government we deserve, which is why I join you in refraining from placing too much blame on Congress itself.

Having said that, the recent US Supreme Court decision Citizen's United vs. the Federal Election Commission has removed much of the power formerly held by "We The People" to effect the changes we desire. See MoveToAmend.org.

3) A majority of the public, many seemingly well educated, at least formally, do not believe that mankind's contribution to global warming is significant. People are no longer willing to accept that because climate experts believe this or that, they should follow suit and accept the expert claims to be factual. Scientific bodies have little credibility in the eyes of the general public and are seen as just another special interest seeking to get their hands in the pockets of taxpayers.

It is true that the Climate Change Deniers have done a fantastic job in turning huge masses of people against the vast majority of climate scientists; this is a PR coup the likes of which we've rarely seen in human history. The idea that research scientists have a greater motive to bend their figures to raise more grant money than the oil companies have in selling trillions of gallons of gasoline and diesel is laughable, to me at least, but clearly many people don't see it that way.

Yet I don't know why I'm surprised. We should never underestimate the power of effective public relations; it was only 75 years ago that the German people, swayed by demagoguery and PR, supported the Nazis in their attempts at genocide. We must never forget that people will believe anything.

Thanks again for writing in with this terrific perspective, James.

Late-Night Radio Show Caller Rants Over Subsidies for Renewables

I got a call shortly after dinner one night from a radio host in Denver, explaining that due to a last-minute cancellation, he had an hour-long opening on his show. He asked if he could call me for the interview – at 1 AM!

I agreed, stayed up late, reading, checking out Jay Leno, and fighting off the yawns.

The highlight of the show for me was a caller attacking clean energy based on the fact that the government subsidizes it. When I pointed out that fossil fuels get 12 times the amount of subsidies as clean energy, he responded that since clean energy is only 2% of the total grid-mix, the subsidies it receives represent four times those of fossil fuels per installed megawatt. In other words, because clean energy *hasn't* happened, there is no reason to *make* it happen.

I asked the caller if he happened to be a hard-line libertarian who believes government has no business effecting changes in the public landscape. When he said no, I indicated that his position strikes me as considerably shortsighted, in that it employs a kind of circular logic. It's like saying that we shouldn't have built the Internet in the 1990s because there were a only few people online; his argument is really no better than that.

And in the case of renewable energy, I pointed out, we're talking about a subject that really doesn't compare well to the Internet; the imperative to move to clean energy goes well beyond the convenience and niceties of our modern age. Whether your concern is long-term environmental damage, national security, lung disease, the ballooning national debt (just take your choice), we are dealing with real dangers here that government, I believe, is duty-bound to address.

I also note that the subsidies for oil have been in place for 80 – 90 years—long past the point that the industry became incredibly profitable. Yet Washington is so completely bought off by the oil companies and the 7000 lobbyists they employ that it simply doesn't have the integrity to bring this disgusting state of affairs to a close; this is rank corruption in its purest and most obvious form. By contrast, you'll have a hell of a hard time finding an advocate of clean energy who thinks renewables should be subsidized through the year 2190—and on indefinitely.

Did I change his—or anyone's—mind on this subject? Who knows; I was too tired to think about it.

On The Fukushima Nuclear Situation

A reader suggests that we should have a post about the current Fukushima nuclear power plant situation, calling for me to bring this whole thing into perspective.

I reply...

Thanks so much for the note. I deeply appreciate the trust and respect you have placed in me. But the truth is that I don't have any greater insight into the extent and ramifications of this disaster than anyone else, and thus I feel that I have no value to add here.

Of course, I could point out that the millions of people (of whom I'm only one) who have been warning the world about the dangers of nuclear power were right—as if that makes anyone feel better. It goes without saying that I'm not into that. In the last few days, I've had people from all over the world emailing me about this, a few of them obviously in tears as they wrote. The world is in a state of shock and mourning, as well it should be.

I'm reminded of the BP oil spill, where some of my friends simply couldn't understand why I wasn't "capitalizing" on it. In truth, there's nothing to capitalize on. It's a disaster, period, and I think that more or less everyone understands this.

Like Chernobyl, the radius of the circle we draw around Fukushima will be hotly debated. And like the BP oil spill, industry spokespeople will attempt to minimize their culpability and the damage to the credibility of the nuclear program as a whole.

But, to the point: Does the disaster bring us all closer to an understanding of the imperative to migrate to clean energy? I hope so. Can I explicate it any further or better than what you're seeing and reading? No, sorry.

In the last year, we've had the BP situation, the $8.6 billion judgment against Chevron in Ecuador, the bloodshed in Northern Africa in reaction to the exploitation that was enabled by oil money, and now, the nuclear catastrophe in Japan. If this succession of events fails to make the case for renewable energy, I hate to imagine what will.

Again, I appreciate your trust and friendship. But, outside of offering my most sincere sympathies, I'm out of words. I'm afraid the facts speak for themselves.

Externalities of the Oil Industry — Great Comments

There have been some fantastic comments to the pieces I have written on the externalities of fossil fuels, including that of frequent blogger Cameron Atwood, to whom I reply:

Unfortunately, this corporatocracy has gotten so strong that it's really tough to refocus people on what's happening at a high level, which you've nailed with 100% accuracy in your excellent remarks. There's a great deal of mainstream coverage of the perils of Lindsay Lohan, but very little insight into the true cost of oil and gas. So when you write:

The next time you talk with a child, apologize to them for bankrupting their future, because that's when the bulk of these costs will come due... but our parents' children – we who sit here today – will also surely suffer personally, far more than we do presently. Do we possess the collective wisdom and will to stem that tide of pain and change the course of our nation?

... I'm afraid that I have to say that the answer at this point appears to be No.

I have a post in which I discuss and provide some excerpts from my interview the other day with Ray Lane, Managing Partner at Kleiner Perkins. When you think about it, he's actually one of the most powerful people on Earth, as the decisions he makes shape the future of the disruptive technologies that are brought forward into our lives.

He's a fantastic, committed, and passionate guy. I happened to ask him about the huge subsidies for oil, and he replied, "I'm a Republican. And even I don't understand why we as a nation are still doing this."

Well, sadly, I do. It's called corruption. Pick a euphemism for it if it makes you feel better, but that's what it is.

Global Warming — A Quick Overview

When people ask me to explain my position on global warming, I normally tell them what I've learned from the interviews I've conducted, while politely acknowledging that I'm not an expert on the subject. I also point out that the specifics of the subject that are yet to be—and probably never will be—fully understood. When I encounter adamant climate change deniers, I calmly suggest that they find one of any number of other reasons to urge a rapid migration away from fossil fuels: national security, public health, etc.

However, when pressed for my true beliefs, I have to admit that I get really stern. What remaining hair I have on the back of my arms stands up and blood vessels swell in my forehead as I forcibly suggest that they read Jeremy Grantham's piece on the subject: Everything You Need To Know About Global Warming in Five Minutes. It's a short essay that, in my estimation, sums up the world's best thinking on the subject.

His analysis of the science and the logic of the subject is excellent. But his analysis of the idea of climate scientists' motive to cheat on their findings is even better. He writes:

"... They formed a conspiracy to pull off a massive hoax because they...?"

There really is no good answer to that question—and who but Grantham could have made that point in such a casual, unadorned style? Everyone reading this knows a few scientists, but I don't think anybody knows one who likes limelight, drama, testifying in front of Congress, or loud, embarrassing arguments with ultra-rightwing radio talkshow buffoons.

If you told me that the moguls of Hollywood, or Madison Avenue, or Wall Street were trying to pull off such a conspiracy, you might have earned my attention. But the overwhelming majority of university professors? Sorry.

Grantham's hardly a bleeding-heart liberal; he's an icon of modern-day unapologetic super-capitalism, managing $107 billion in assets. I hope you'll enjoy his level-headed common sense thinking on the topic.

Ah, good. Having written this has calmed me down. Those pulsating blood vessels have subsided. But don't get me started again, or I swear by God I'll . . . . refer you to another article.

World Energy — Where Are We Going?

I think we're all a bit curious about the ultimate disposition of the energy industry – both here in the US and around the globe. In the States, 49% of our electricity comes from coal, and the penetration of renewables is under 2%. Worldwide, about 80% of energy for all purposes comes from burning hydrocarbons. So if that's where we are, where are we going?

In the US, we have a complicated array of vectors in this space. We have constantly falling prices for PV and wind, and promising new technologies coming along right behind them, yet we have a Republican majority in the Senate that has aggressively begun to block all actions that would mitigate global climate change.

So, again, what are the most likely scenarios for change, if any, through the coming decades? I was lucky enough to have received a crystal ball for Christmas that comes in handy on occasions like this; let me pull it out, and I'll tell you. But first, maybe we should look at a few high-level questions that frame the discussion:

From the standpoint of pure engineering, how much longer will fossil fuels last? It's clear that unconventional technologies (e.g., shale oil, tar sands, fracking, etc.) will become increasingly important. But will there be a natural limit to the success of these technologies – especially in light of the fact that they too come along with their own environmental consequences? I've listened to the reassurances of the oil industry spokespeople—and even *they* don't claim the supply will last forever.

On the legal and political front, will society continue to allow the energy industry to pass along the costs of the externalities to its customers now and in future generations? There are many scenarios that could play out here. I know people who predict that, in the long-term, we'll relive the experience we had with the tobacco industry: a century of business as usual, followed by a few "smoking gun" pieces of evidence (pardon the pun), followed by decades of lawsuits. Under this vision of the future, we'll come to terms (albeit too late) with the damage to human health and ecosystems that oil, gas and coal have had—both issues that they openly acknowledged at the time, and those they successfully covered up. Everyone will suffer but the lawyers, who will enjoy another enormous payday. Interesting to be sure—but will history prove this right or wrong?

We all assume that the fossil fuel industry will not simply dry up and blow away. In tens of thousands of years of modern human history, there is not a single precedent for big money willingly conceding its power. But what exactly will happen when solar and wind reach and pass "grid parity" in a few years, meaning that the incremental cost of a megawatt of solar electricity costs *less* than the equivalent from coal? Won't that change the decision-making process? I want to take lessons in salesmanship from the guy who can get a utility to buy another coal-fired power plant when that decision both damages the world *and* costs more.

Will the public sector in the US continue to have essentially zero forward thrust behind renewables? Right now, despite the rhetoric, our government's position in granting subsidies to create artificially inexpensive oil constitutes a de facto attack on clean energy. Will some to-be-named phenomenon cause voters to wake up and make a course correction?

Will there be world events (famines, storms, desertification, extinctions, island submersions, seismic changes in temperature) that will shock the world and convince even the global warming deniers about the nature of the crisis confronting our civilization?

Who will be the big financial winners ultimately? I've often written that the world is *most definitely* going in the direction of renewable energy, despite the catfights of the early 21st Century.

As I mentioned, even the oil people have a tough time speculating that we'll be extracting, refining and burning crude in 100 years—especially that world energy consumption will have grown many times past where it is today. At that time, we will have further developed several ways to harness the small percentage of the sun's energy (currently 1/6000th) that we need to provide clean energy to everyone on Earth. But who will have done this – and made a fortune in the process?

OK—enough questions. Now for some answers.

Hold on just a second, folks, sorry for the delay. Damn! What did I do with that crystal ball? I know I had it here someplace...

Our Leaders Should Understand Basic Science

John Boehner, Speaker of the House, told a crowd recently:

The idea that carbon dioxide is a carcinogen that is harmful to our environment is almost comical. Every time we exhale, we exhale carbon dioxide. Every cow in the world, when they do what they do, we've got more carbon dioxide.

I know there are people who don't know the difference between carbon dioxide and methane, or what a carcinogen is, and I'm completely fine with that; ignorance in the general population, the result of a failing school system, "is what it is." But when stuff like this comes out of the mouth of one of the most powerful lawmakers on Earth, *I'm not at all OK with that.* We need to do a better job in electing people who have a basic command of the core issues that affect our survival.

Science Is Under Violent Attack on Global Climate Change

As a civilization, we're in trouble whenever politics trumps science—and we've seen plenty of that lately. That's why the world is so frustrated with the inaction of the COP meeting in Cancun, as we listen to diplomats drone on in vague, glib language while scientists beg for resolutions to save us from what virtually all of them believe to be impending disaster. Clearly, mankind is never well served to put its scientists in a position of subservience to big money/power, where they feel they must toe the line on **any** issue, whether it's global warming, cold fusion, "clean coal," etc.

Yet I would argue that we face an even bigger problem when religion and science cross paths. For example, last year, Illinois Congressman John Shimkus, who aspires to be chairman of the super-powerful House Committee on Energy and Commerce, quoted the bible (the books of Genesis and Matthew) as reason not to act on climate change, reading:

And He will send his angels with a loud trumpet call and they will gather his elect from the four winds from one end of the heavens to the other. The Earth will end only when God declares it is time for it to be over. Man will not destroy this Earth.

Shimkus continued, asserting, "There is a theological debate that this is in fact a carbon-starved planet, not that we have too much carbon."

I hesitate to challenge anyone's faith, but I don't hesitate for a second in recommending against electing lawmakers whose policy decision-making process so clearly and aggressively flies in the teeth of critically relevant scientific discoveries. I'm sorry if I'm coming off as disrespectful here, but I urge our civilization to come up with a better way in dealing with the lethally important challenges we face.

Plug-In Hybrid Electric Vehicles and Their Enemies

I note a certain level of confusion surrounding plug-in hybrid electric vehicles. And I can certainly understand some level of bewilderment, as there are numerous variations on the plug-hybrid theme – as well as jargon that, in my opinion, serves to make the matter even worse—BEVs, ZEVs, PHEVs, REEVs, etc. But it's clear that the enemies of electric transportation, whose motives remain unclear to me, are capitalizing on this moment of confusion to seize the day and turn people away from an important advancement in clean transportation.

In particular, I noted the recent fracas that resulted when GM announced the specifics behind the Chevy Volt's drivetrain. Conservative columnist George Will loudly accused GM of deceit. "It's just a hybrid!" he and his fellow cynics screamed last week, somehow overlooking the fact that many Volt drivers will never need to put a drop of gasoline in their cars.

I have to say I was stunned. Isn't George Will an intellectual? But here he was, sounding like one of the AM talk radio entertainer-buffoons, noisily lambasting GM and the Obama Administration for dumping public funds into a "hybrid"—as if that term somehow clarified something – or as if anyone cared exactly how the guts of the Volt operate.

We can ask ourselves: Has GM finally gotten something right? Will the Obama Administration ultimately be vindicated for keeping GM from going down? To be honest, I don't know. But I'm pretty damn sure of this, George: deliberately confusing American car-buyers about an important new trend in automotive engineering—simply so you can throw rocks at the president of the United States—isn't helping anyone—especially yourself.

I urge car-buyers to ignore the jargon and ultra-rightwing partisan diatribes and keep one core fact in mind: the degree to which your car's energy comes through your wall sockets is the degree to which it offers the potential for low-cost, clean transportation. It's that simple.

Free-Market Capitalism and Energy Policy: What's the Proper Role of Government?

The proper role of government in our lives is the biggest single issue confronting politically involved Americans today. Want to rile up an audience about healthcare, for instance? Just tell them either:

a) The government with its bloated bureaucracies, inefficiencies, and corrupt catering to special interests is taking over healthcare and doling it out, at your expense, to people who haven't earned it, or

b) Healthcare should continue to be run by profit-motivated corporations whose goal is to minimize costs by denying medical coverage (especially to those who need it most)—and government has no business interfering in this cruel and inhuman process.

The same polar arguments could be made for financial regulation, labor and unemployment, economic stimulus, and almost every other major area of debate we face as a society.

I bring this up because it arose in the interview (transcript above) I conducted with Dr. Robert Pollin, of the University of Massachusetts—Amherst's Department of Economics and Political Economy Research Institute.

One of the many great concepts I took away from these talks is insight into the spirit of American free-market capitalism, and the notion of the role of government within that framework.

"What do free markets do well, and what do they do poorly?" Bob asked rhetorically. "(Scottish economist and moral philosopher) Adam Smith himself, writing the capitalism 'bible,' first published in 1776 (The Wealth of Nations) understood that government was necessary to perform tasks that markets simply could not be rationally expected to achieve. For instance, it would be foolish to think that free markets are likely to do a good job in environmental protection. Thus, we need subsidies, incentives, and regulation that push the private sector in a direction that it might not otherwise go."

But as I see it, the problem isn't that we need more subsidies; in fact, we have them in *spades*. "It seems to me that the subsidies we have in place—and have had for the last 80 years—provide incentives for the precise opposite private sector investments versus where we need to go. Don't the fossil fuel industries receive several dollars in subsidies for ever $1 given to renewables?" I asked. "And doesn't this artificially inexpensive oil directly block investment in clean energy?"

Bob disputes the accuracy of these numbers, though he acknowledges that the precise number is impossible to pin down, as it's an amalgam of many different components—some of them hidden. Having said that, he agrees that there is no question that I've pointed to a problem that needs a solution. In particular, he concurs that we as an electorate have a great deal of work to do in this space, i.e., bringing our leaders to the point where they put the proper policies into place, rather than acting at the behest of the traditional energy industry.

Clean Energy, Job Creation, and the US Supreme Court

At this early point in the development of my new book on clean energy job creation, I'm still just trying to find my feet. As the creation of new jobs for Americans is largely a subject of politics and macroeconomics, and as I'm an expert in neither, my choice of interview subjects and understanding exactly what I'm attempting to glean from folks in these areas is going to be of paramount importance. Thus, I'm treading very slowly and carefully at this point.

Having said that, I'm starting to make some rough guesses as to what direction this project will ultimately take. And here's an early front-runner: an exploration of the effects of the January 2010 US Supreme Court decision (Citizens United v. Federal Election Commission) to grant corporations (fictitious persons) the same rights under the Constitution as real persons. The implications to our precious democracy are staggering, the tip of the iceberg of which we are just now starting to feel. Within a few years at the outside, we can expect the transnational corporate entities to extend their powers over every aspect of public policy, owning and controlling the actions of everyone from the President of the United States down to your local assemblyman.

Think this is some sort of nutty exaggeration? Let me ask you a few quick questions:

- Is most of the food you eat genetically modified? Yes. Is that a good thing? To be honest, I'm not sure. But I'm sure of this: Neither you nor your elected representative had anything whatsoever to do with making that decision; it was made by Monsanto and ADM.
- Who made our national policies in healthcare? Although the vast majority of Americans (and their doctors) favor

universal healthcare, the big pharmaceutical and insurance companies create the policies that determine who get healthcare and how they get it.

• What about energy and transportation? Ask yourself: who created the terrain of the playing field on which oil and coal receive several times the subsidies that are given to renewable energy? The answer is as clear as it is sickening: *the energy industry itself*, with its 7000 lobbyists who control every thought and every breath of the Congress you think is working for your best interests.

I'm going to go out a limb here and make my guess. I have to think that the decision to grant corporations the right to affect our democracy, with no limit to the money they can spend to buy your votes and corrupt the process, is going to be central to the book. How can it not be?

For what it's worth, corporations themselves are not to blame; in fact, fictitious entities with limited liability serve an important, time-honored purpose. Corporations played a critical role in the development of ancient Rome (universities, aqueducts, roads, the Coliseum), the exploration of the New World, and the colonization of what is now the US. Corporations are not evil; they're just a tool, like a hammer or a knife, that can be used for good or evil—a tool that is now grossly misused by a legal system that has provided them with rights and powers that were never even intended.

Once I understood the impact of the Supreme Court ruling, I saw that the migration to clean energy will be excruciatingly slow until that decision is overturned. If we fail to install a Constitutional amendment that reinstates the crystal clear intent of the founding fathers, i.e., that government exist of, by, and for the people, we're all spinning our wheels, watching our fledgling industry flounder and our democracy implode.

I hope you'll want to learn more. Check out MoveToAmend.Org—the move to amend our Constitution so as to restore our government to the people.

What Will It Take to Achieve a US Renewable Portfolio Standard?

I was keeping a tally sheet at a recent conference called the "Renewable Energy Finance Forum," so I could let readers know the issue that was brought up most often and granted the most overall prominence. The clear winner: *China is eating our lunch in the migration to renewables.* Inexplicably and tragically, the US is content to drop further and further behind in the development of energy technology with each passing week. While China is hiring, researching, developing, importing, exporting—and dominating the world of 21st Century energy, we seem to be content to argue and point fingers at each other.

As Winston Churchill observed, "America will always do the right thing—after it has exhausted all other options." But can anyone see this moving anytime soon—for any reason—least of all because it's "the right thing?" None of the promises of renewable energy: jobs, national security, addressing concerns about peak oil and the climate issue—seem to motivate action on our part.

Perhaps the most visible proof of our nation's abdication of technology leadership is the absence of a federal renewable energy portfolio standard (RPS). What are we to make of the fact that we seem to be a million miles from such a piece of legislation? Clearly, it's the result of leaders' pandering for votes, while scrupulously avoiding areas of controversy that might be used against them.

And now, with the recent Supreme Court decision enabling corporations to provide unlimited funding to anonymous entities that can, in turn, spend millions of campaign advertising dollars to defeat perceived enemies, our leaders need to be even more careful than they were when their enemies had to identify themselves and use their own money to slander opponents. This, of course, is another true disaster for those of us who care about free and fair elections and continue (foolishly?) to hold out hope for the effectiveness of the democratic process.

But enough about that. What about the federal RPS? Is there any hope that we can re-establish ourselves as the leader in energy technology? Here's another tidbit from the conference: Adding nuclear power into the mix of renewables might provide the political muscle to pass a federal RPS. After all, it IS carbon-free. Proponents claim, "Nuclear energy presents a safe, clean, and inexpensive alternative to other methods of producing electricity. Nuclear waste can either be reprocessed or disposed of safely."

But is any of this true? No. Do most renewable energy supporters believe that nuclear should be included in the list of clean energy technologies? Of course not. But who cares? In the 10-or-so years it takes to plan and permit the next nuclear reactor, the cost/benefit of photovoltaics, wind, concentrating solar power, geothermal, and biomass will have improved to such a point that nuclear will be completely irrelevant.

Go on; invite them to the party. Give them all the political support they've worked so long and hard to purchase. In the end, it won't matter. Despite the rhetoric, you'll never see another nuke deployed in the US.

Predicting Our Energy Future

I'm one of those people who constantly tries to see into the future – not that I have any eerie talent for things like that. The future of energy and transportation, for example, is clear as a bell. Does anyone think we're going to be driving Hummers in 40 years? Could a reasonable person believe there'll be plenty of cheap oil in 2050 when the world population has increased 22% from today and the number of cars on the world's roads has doubled?

Alternative energy *will* become a reality; that's not in question. The question is: who's going to get rich in the process?

Here's a fact: the people who made the last fortune in energy (1910 – 2010) want to make *damn sure* they'll be the ones to do it again.

And here's my prediction: Unless something unforeseen and incredibly dramatic happens, that's *precisely* what's going to happen. Here are some details, lest you think I'm one of these tawdry fortune-tellers who speaks in fortune-cookie generalities:

Alternative energy will take an eternity to get here. We (in the US) will find a way to delay the establishment of an energy policy for an inconceivably long period of time, while the biosphere continues its path of slow but rapidly accelerating degradation.

Those of us who have worked to make clean energy happen in a timely fashion will eventually be crushed like grapes financially, caused by 10-or-so different types of government subsidies that make oil artificially cheap and renewable energy uncompetitive with fossil fuels. Eventually, most of us will be gone; they will have made it rain longer than we could tread water. In posterity, we'll come to be regarded as pathetic "do-gooders" or quaint, historic relics, "regrettably ahead of their time."

But finally (presuming we still have a planet that supports life, with a bit of clean water to drink, etc.) when the energy giants have determined how they can dominate this new landscape, we'll have abundant clean energy, generated and delivered profitably and without undue competition—and the traditional energy people will have succeeded in their quest to make their next great fortune.

Oh, but what's this I see? Is there, in fact, something unforeseen and incredibly dramatic that might happen? A grassroots uprising? People as furious with our lame approach to energy as they were to the Vietnam War 40 years ago? Henry Kissinger said recently, "If it weren't for the loathing that the common American had for the war, *we'd still be there*." I suppose public outcry actually *could* make a difference ....

But .... oh, rats. The crystal has gone dark. That's all for now.

Sorry to be a bit indecisive, but The Great Shieldsini sees a future that could go either way. Perhaps what the crystal is telling me is that our energy future is not a matter of fate. Rather, it lies in our own hands.

Moore's Law and the Trajectory for Renewable Energy

Each year, we come across a new set of discussions on the subject of Moore's Law – the idea that the potency of technology doubles every two years. Intel co-founder Gordon Moore observed that the number of transistors that could be put onto an integrated circuit doubled with that regularity—and that this exponential growth persisted for an astonishingly long period of time.

Of course, we look upon this "law" figuratively. There is no secret force that makes it apply to every technology – or that requires the period of time in question to be exactly two years. But we've all seen adequate proof of the "spirit of the law," i.e., that many technologies do, in fact, experience some sort of geometric expansion.

As we should have expected, it was only a matter of time until pundits began to debate the relation of Moore's law to the energy industry. Recently we've seen numerous conversations regarding its application to the development of renewable energy technologies.

However, many people say that it simply doesn't apply in this case, as such projected growth ignores the basic realities of energy: the long-term maturation of technologies, and the hard limits in efficiency that are put on us by more senior laws – namely those of physics itself. But here are a few points to consider:

1) The most exciting part of the energy industry is not about exploration for increasingly scarce fossil fuels; it's about technology in areas that have nothing to do with oil and gas—and that are in the same nascent state today as IT was in the second half of the 20th Century when Moore was making his now-famous observation. In fact, clean energy is about dozens of different technologies: nano, bio, semiconductor, quantum mechanical, materials science, and nuclear—to name a few. Simultaneous to mankind's pumping its

oil fields dry, today we have frequent breakthroughs in dozens of different areas affecting renewable energy. Why shouldn't we think that Moore's Law is at least as applicable to this myriad of technologies as it is to silicon chips?

2) There remain many possibilities for "Black Swan" events in energy. Nassim Taleb's theory of Black Swan events looks at the impact of one-off occurrences that are uncomputable and unforeseeable; the disaster of 9/11 and the development of the Internet are two examples that he and other scholars commonly offer. I'm sure you've heard people ask, for instance, "What's the next Google?" I.e., what's the next paradigm shift? That's a legitimate question, don't you think? I personally am quite convinced that the energy industry will experience quite a number of Googles in the coming 50 years or so.

3) Keep in mind the nature and scope of the problem we're trying to solve. The Earth receives 6000 times more energy from the sun each day than all 7 billion of us consume. All we need is a solution that results in our capturing $1/6000^{th}$ of this energy as useful work. For the entire continent of North America, we need a distributed solar thermal array totaling about 1/12 the size of New Mexico.

Would this be a challenge? Sure. So was gearing up to win World War II – but we did it. And once this is done, we can all turn our attention to something else—you name it – how about the eradication of poverty, illiteracy, and disease? Does that do anything for you? How about space exploration? My point here is that there *is* an "end game" – and that I believe we're actually fairly close to seeing it.

Now, the idea that we're just around the corner from this end game is good news for most people. But is it good for the traditional energy industry? No. And perhaps that's why getting there will be so monstrously difficult. But we mustn't dismiss the idea merely because it perturbs a few wealthy and powerful people who are hell-bent on becoming even wealthier and more powerful – even at the expense of the health and well-being of the rest of us. What we must do, on the contrary, is to know that the migration to renewables is a clear and immediate threat to the traditional energy industry – and that this creates political challenges that are 10 times tougher than the technology issues.

It's going to take some real work getting there. But the prize is— shall we say— *considerable.*

Pay It NOW — In Energy Policy, Or Anywhere Else, It's Wrong To Pass Burdens On

More people each day are disgusted with the course our civilization is taking. Whether your main concern is social injustice, proliferation of nuclear weapons, environmental ruination, white-collar criminality, the decay of morality, growing rates of addiction to recreational and psychiatric drugs, the decline in educational standards, or the ravages of corporatocracy, one thing's for sure: you're one of very few if you believe the human race is on the right track.

I don't have a lot of answers. But I think I can say this without fear of contradiction: It's up to all of us to raise our voices when we see things we don't like.

Here's something else I suggest we do with issues: analyze them honestly. Is there any commonality among all these social ills? I believe there is: the concept that someone else – another person living now somewhere on Earth – or someone who will be born in the future – should pay for the benefit you're taking here and now.

When Ford famously made the decision to build and sell the Pinto in the early 1970s – a car they knew very well a certain percentage of which would explode on impact due to an engineering defect, they opted to take the gain (the profit unencumbered by the cost of fixing the mistake) and passed those costs (pain, death, trauma, and loss) onto its customers, and the healthcare costs (healing the burns, fixing the broken bones, etc.) onto the healthcare system. Each year we learn of dozens of examples of this very phenomenon, and wonder how many lie beneath the tip of the iceberg. And while these examples of criminality are the extreme, think of all the industries that are legal whose products knowingly and invariably damage their users: fast food, tobacco, degraded entertainment, cheap products designed to fall apart 10 minutes after their warranty expires – to name a few.

I don't approve of the high rates of litigation we suffer here in the US, but it can certainly be justified as an attempt to right a wrong, i.e., to force the party that rightfully caused the damage to pay for it.

I often write about the need to internalize the externalities of energy. I point out that if we as a society would identify and pay the true and complete costs of the energy produced by oil and coal – including the long-term environmental damage, healthcare costs, etc. – and wrote the check as they were being incurred, clean energy solutions – all of them – would be hailed as the bargain of the century, and businesses based on fossil fuels would close more or less instantly.

Now some of these calculations are more straightforward than others. It's well documented that:

- The estimated health cost of human exposure to outdoor air pollutants is $250 billion a year.
- An estimated 50,000 to 120,000 premature deaths are associated with exposure to air pollutants.
- People with asthma experience more than 100 million days of restrictive activity annually, costing $4 billion a year.
- Death rates from asthma are up over 40 percent in the past few years.

But what are the costs of global climate change, of the acidification of our oceans, and of the other horrors we're inflicting upon our planet and all its life forms? People make a stab at this all the time, but it's hard to put much credence in the figures that are produced.

We've all seen the bumpersticker that reads: "If you think education is expensive, try ignorance" – a clever and pithy way of making my exact point. Again, however, while it's easy to add up what we're spending on public and private education, it's quite a task even to list all the consequences of ignorance, let alone the costs associated with them. In addition to the obvious costs of unemployment and loss to the tax base, you'd have to include the incremental burden to the systems involved in criminal justice, healthcare, supporting unwanted children, and dozens of other items.

I'm completely convinced that if there is a civilization here at all in 100 years, it will regard us generally as most of now regard litterbugs – essentially as inconsiderate slobs who would coldly disregard the idea they share the planet with 7 billions others. Or perhaps we'll be remembered as thieves, with our deeply defective sense of ownership – appropriating things for our own use that clearly do not belong to us.

In any case, difficult though it is, this is the challenge that we face: to refuse to engage in practices in any arena – at any level—that are simply unsustainable. If there is any good in any of this, maybe it's that we're starting to remember how profoundly brilliant Thomas Jefferson was, with his ideas like: "It is incumbent on every generation to pay its own debts as it goes." Imagine: cleaning up after yourself. Not burdening your grandchildren with the costs of your wars, entitlements, and ecological recklessness. All we have to do is to find a way to live that does the accounting and enforces prompt payment.

Sustainability Means More Than Merely Cleantech

As we scour our civilization in an effort to identify and rid ourselves of all things unsustainable, perhaps we should look past cleantech for a moment and examine wider circles of our lives – perhaps including our involvement with medicine. Rightfully, we're all very grateful for the advancements in medical technology that are enabling us to live longer and healthier lives. But don't we have an inkling that, just as we look back on the standards of medical practice 100 years ago with a mixture of pity and horror, the world even a few decades hence will regard what we're doing here and now in the same way?

In particular, posterity will remember our generation for its fanaticism with the diagnosis of "disease" and the over-prescription of drugs for an enormous and ever-growing set of physical and mental conditions. This morning, 8 million school children in the U.S. alone received a dose of Ritalin, an extremely powerful psycho-active drug given to quiet the child's mind – and thus his body, creating greater docility in an effort to address the effects of an ostensible disease, ADHD. Elsewhere today, tens of millions of adults will pop pills to deal with a wider range of other "diseases"— from restless leg syndrome to sexual dysfunction. For more on this, Google "pharmaceutical companies invent diseases" and check out some of the 1,120,000 sites that offer additional detail.

All this has a connection, albeit an unlikely one, to the fact that today is the 200th birthday of Hungarian composer and piano virtuoso Franz Liszt. Here's a quote from The Writer's Almanac:

> *Liszt was also charismatic, and his onstage presence inspired what may have been the first example of widespread fan frenzy. It began in Berlin in 1842 and came to be known as "Lisztomania." His admirers would follow him around, snatching up his discarded*

cigar butts, coffee dregs, and broken piano strings. They fought over his handkerchiefs and gloves, and would scream and faint at his performances. Rather than being considered a harmless and amusing fad, Lisztomania was viewed as a serious, and contagious, medical condition.

From our vantage point today, we're easily able to see that "Lisztomania" was really not a medical condition at all, and that labeling it so was only really saying that the medical community at the time had not sufficiently advanced to a point that it could see the proper limit of its dominion. But aren't we in the same boat today? Somehow we (most of us, anyway) can't see this same phenomenon at play with ADHD; we're perfectly happy to pump drugs into 8 million school kids, most of whom only need a better diet, smaller school-class sizes, better teachers, more exercise, more rest, and less television.

Food for thought as we discuss sustainability in the larger sense.

In any case, happy birthday Franz! To celebrate, please go to YouTube, and listen to Evgeny Kissin (in my opinion the world's greatest living pianist) performing Listz's La Campanella (The Little Bell). If you will make this investment of four minutes of your life and checking this out, you'll see how people could have been deeply moved by the fabulously tall, handsome, and dynamic Listz as he belted this one out to an adoring audience.

Fox News: Four Dirty Secrets about Clean Energy

Apparently, the Fox News article "Four Dirty Secrets about Clean Energy" went viral, as I got it from a friend who is normally not too closely connected to the subject. I have to hand it to these guys; they're sure good at getting their word out.

In addition to admiring the sheer aggression with which Fox promotes its beliefs, one has to like their cleverness as well. Even the ploy of referring to their enemies' concepts as "Dirty Secrets," implying as it does the existence of some clandestine group with a malicious, hidden agenda is really a very bright idea from a public relations perspective.

In any case, I promised my friend that I would take a few minutes and respond to each of these damnable "dirty tricks," so here goes:

Dirty Secret #1: If "clean energy" were actually cheaper than fossil fuels, it wouldn't need a policy.

The cost of renewable energy is anything but a secret. No one disputes that, in each of its many forms as they currently exist, clean energy is more expensive than coal – especially when it's burned in the absence of scrubbers on the plants to remove the most damaging components of its emissions. And, though the prices of renewables are falling constantly, this inequality will remain in place for at least the next few years. The larger issue that the author elected not to discuss, of course, is that fossil fuels come with huge but generally unseen costs in terms of the health of our people, our society and our environment.

Dirty Secret #2: Clean energy advocates want to force us to use solar, wind, and biofuels, even though there is no evidence these can power modern civilization.

This ties into #1 above. No one who has seriously looked at the matter doubts that clean energy can power the civilization, but the issue is cost. As Dr. Peter Lilienthal, world energy expert whose software is used by power utilities in more than 80 countries says, "There's plenty of clean energy, if you don't care what you pay for it." Most clean energy advocates suggest weaning ourselves off fossil fuels using the market forces that would be created by establishing a level playing field in which the true costs of all forms of energy are taken into consideration and "internalized." We also hope for a bit of help from government; it would be good (as well as fair and wise) to remove the enormous subsidies bestowed upon the fossil fuel companies – and perhaps send the funds thus freed up in the direction of renewables, as the latter clearly represents a public good (as opposed to a public hazard).

Dirty Secret #3: There are promising carbon-free energy sources– hydroelectric and nuclear–but "clean energy" policies oppose them as not "green" enough.

Most clean energy advocates see obvious and serious dangers in nuclear power. I'm not sure what planet someone would have to be living on not to share these concerns.

Dirty Secret #4: The environmentalists behind clean energy policy are anti-energy.

It is true that there are environmental extremists who are unwilling to make any compromises, and thus become *de facto* advocates for the end of economic prosperity, a return to an agrarian society, etc. Pointing to a few people with fringe views may stir up the passions of a largely uninformed audience, but it's hardly to the point. I'm sure you could find a few who believe in astrology as well, though I can't see the relevance of that either.

The vast majority of clean energy advocates are honestly looking for trade-offs that make sense. In fact, we don't see this issue as "us vs. them," as all seven billion of us live on the same sick planet. Our main agenda is doing what's right for this sorry world; I'm not sure Fox News can say the same.

Again, I congratulate Fox on its cleverness, though its command of the facts and the intellectual honesty it displays in dealing with them are dubious at best.

William Penn's Legacy of Peace and Environmental Stewardship

I spent my K–12 years at a Quaker school in Philadelphia, William Penn Charter. And as one would imagine, an education based on Quaker values is rife with reminders of brotherly love and peaceful resolution of conflict. In fact, the Greek motto in the school's seal translates into English as the command: "Love one another."

I smiled as I read the school's quarterly magazine when it came in the mail recently. My chest swelled with pride as I learned that the new Center for the Performing Arts was granted a coveted LEED certification (Leadership in Energy and Environmental Design) for its use of wind energy, recycled materials and natural insulation. How effortlessly Quaker philosophy and environmentalism go hand-in-hand; the imperative to make the world a better place lies at the very core of this warm and contemplative way of life.

William Penn and his values had a profound influence on his time (late 17th / early 18th Century—the school was chartered in 1689; Penn died in 1718) though, sadly, that influence has diminished greatly over the years. In particular, the Quaker belief that all people are equal under God served as a beacon of reason and civility in dealings with the native Americans in the entire Delaware region, until its flame was all but extinguished by the barbarism of the other settlers from England and Europe. Eventually, it became clear that Penn's teachings and leadership by example were no match for the ceaseless violence and exploitation that have come to dominate the Western world since that time. To take an example of the day, when the English set fire to a Pequot village and massacred men, women and children, the Puritan theologian Cotton Mather (still extremely well regarded by history) said in celebration: "It was supposed that no less than 600 Pequot souls were brought down to hell that day."

But Penn refused to succumb to the utter stupidity and brutality of the time. Undeterred by the constant stream of atrocities around him, he continued to dedicate himself and his brothers to kindness, decency, and the commonality of all humankind. In fact, he politely but firmly rejected any aspect of human relations that wasn't based on this notion of equality and fraternity. When, late in life, he sailed back to England to meet King William III, he was urged to kneel and use supplicating language as he entered. Penn replied calmly, "I don't think that will be necessary, since the king and I are both men."

Members of the royal court held their collective breath as they looked on at this act of defiance, fearing a horrible outcome. Yet Penn walked in confidently with his chin up, smiled warmly, extended his hand to the king in friendship, and said in the purest of simplicity for which the Quakers will always be known, "Hello, I'm William Penn. It's a pleasure to meet you."

I'm proud to be among three centuries of Penn Charter graduates who echo the same gratitude towards Penn, and share an abiding respect for his principles and legacy. It was indeed a pleasure – as well as a profound honor—to have met you, sir.

Conclusion

There is no way to get anywhere near this subject and not feel a tremendous, broadspread imperative to reduce our dependence on fossil fuels; the half dozen or so independent reasons for this are all quite compelling. So why is it that we're doing such a poor job in heading in this direction – especially in the US? It's clear: This simply won't happen without some sort of stimulation from the public sector, but business interests that are threatened by renewable energy exert near-complete control over our elected leaders.

So should I "put a period" on this, walk away, and go enjoy the days I have left on this planet as it chokes, starves, and bombs itself to death? Even if I found that tempting, it's not an option, since, now that I know the truth, I've fallen into the grasp of Emerson's great adage: "You can have truth or repose, but you cannot have both." Of course, I could have chosen Einstein's famous: "Those who have the privilege to know have the duty to act."

And to whatever degree, you have become subject to this phenomenon as well. Like it or not, we both find ourselves in a position where we are bound by a sort of duty to get involved – to tell others, write emails, join groups, and generally be as noisy as possible in our quest to turn this horrible situation around while (we hope) there is still time. If you think this is hyperbole, I suggest you ask the families of the 13,200 who died of respiratory disease last year as a result of inhalation of the aromatics from burning coal; it's most certainly too late for them.

What can be done, specifically? If I were making only one suggestion, it would be to get behind MoveToAmend.Org. As long as corporate business interests can exert as much power as they wish to influence our political processes, it is quite incorrect to say that we live in a democratic republic. If there is a place to start, it is restoring some meaningful form of democracy, and ensuring, in the words of Lincoln, "that government of the people, by the people, for the people, shall not perish from the Earth."

Thanks for reading my book.

—Craig Shields

FREE!
Subscribe to the
2GreenEnergy Alert
eNewsletter

Through an ever-expanding network of industry contacts, 2GreenEnergy reports on the renewable energy industry without the distortions of "Big Corporate Energy."

Subscribe to the free 2GreenEnergy Alert and get the latest on Clean Energy:

- News
- Interviews
- Technology Analysis
- Investment Tips

FIND OUT FOR YOURSELF
by visiting the following link:

http://2greenenergy.com/truth/

www.ingramcontent.com/pod-product-compliance
Lightning Source LLC
Chambersburg PA
CBHW060321200326

41519CB00011BA/1800